THE STYLE OF SLEAZE

edinburghuniversitypress.com/series/tiac

THE STYLE OF SLEAZE
The American Exploitation Film, 1959–1977

Calum Waddell

EDINBURGH
University Press

Edinburgh University Press is one of the leading university presses in the UK. We publish academic books and journals in our selected subject areas across the humanities and social sciences, combining cutting-edge scholarship with high editorial and production values to produce academic works of lasting importance. For more information visit our website: edinburghuniversitypress.com

Edinburgh University Press Ltd
The Tun – Holyrood Road
12 (2f) Jackson's Entry
Edinburgh EH8 8PJ

Typeset in 10/12.5pt Sabon by
Servis Filmsetting Ltd, Stockport, Cheshire,
and printed and bound in Great Britain.

A CIP record for this book is available from the British Library

ISBN 978 1 4744 0925 4 (hardback)
ISBN 978 1 4744 0926 1 (webready PDF)
ISBN 978 1 4744 0927 8 (epub)

CONTENTS

FIGURES

ACKNOWLEDGEMENTS

In developing this book, I wish to give my thanks, first and foremost, to Professor Alan Marcus and Doctor Leigh Clayton at the University of Aberdeen and Doctor Mikel Koven at the University of Worcester. I am also grateful to my good friend Doctor Iain Robert Smith, who was there at the genesis of this project, and Gillian Leslie at the Edinburgh University Press (EUP) who has been a delight to work with. In the time of writing *The Style of Sleaze* four of the directors focused upon have sadly passed away: Wes Craven, Tobe Hooper, Radley Metzger and George Romero. While I would meet Metzger and Romero only in passing, I had the privilege and honour of interviewing Mr Craven several times, from my start as a budding young film critic in 2003 to my final encounter with him in Los Angeles in 2012. Always a gentleman, a fiercely intelligent and independently minded director and the creator of many of my favourite nightmares, it saddens me that he will never be able to read a copy of this book.

I dedicate *The Style of Sleaze* to his iconic memory.

INTRODUCTION

What is an exploitation film?

This may seem like an obvious question with an equally obvious answer. The term itself perhaps conjures up the carny marketing of old, low-budget movies – typically generic – offering gory or sexy thrills. A beautiful bound woman having her tongue pulled out in the West German production *Mark of the Devil* (Michael Armstrong, Adrian Hoven, 1970), which also offered 'barf bags' to those who dared to attend a screening. The infamous shot of a young, blonde lady, hung up by hooks through her breasts after falling afoul of a jungle tribe in the Amazon, in the Italian 'video nasty' *Cannibal Ferox* (Umberto Lenzi, 1981) – a film that sold itself on 'being banned in thirty-one countries'. Or a notorious horror such as *SS Experiment Camp* (Sergio Garrone, 1976). Or perhaps the term 'exploitation' raises images of the seventies porno chic period – such as the unforgettably named *Debbie Does Dallas* (Jim Buckley, 1978) – and Richard Roundtree as Shaft (Gordon Parks, 1971), with some Hong Kong kung fu and Spanish werewolf films – all rolled into a twenty-four-hour grindhouse cinema on 42nd Street in New York circa the era of *Taxi Driver* (Martin Scorsese, 1976). In other words, it is films that are wild, garish, explicit, *free* . . . It just *is* exploitation. We know it, perhaps, when we see it.

And yet nothing, it seems, is quite this straightforward. In fact, as one scours through writing on 'exploitation' cinema it soon becomes apparent that no two (usually vague) definitions are the same. A simple web search for the term, for instance, offers one list of '10 Noteworthy Exploitation Films' that features the Hong Kong Bruce Lee kung fu classic *The Big Boss* (Wei Lo, 1971) at number one. This ground-breaking film is placed behind an Italian splatter movie, shot in Colombia, *Cannibal Holocaust* (Ruggero Deodato, 1980) and a major Hollywood studio production, *Vanishing Point* (Richard C. Sarafian, 1971). None of these texts appear to have much, if anything, in common with one another, including their nationality – although the author of the article claims that the exploitation film genre 'is actually made up of many more specific subgenres that are commonly bound by characteristic over-the-top action, violence and sex'.[1] If this were the case then *Vanishing Point*, a slickly produced road drama, would surely struggle to qualify for inclusion – and even these facets – '*over-the-top action, violence and sex*' – would make exploitation a large and almost limitless 'genre'. Indeed, it would also, surely, indicate that such recent Hollywood blockbusters as *Jurassic World* (Colin Trevorrow, 2015), *Jason Bourne* (Paul Greengrass, 2016) and *Transformers: The Last Knight* (Michael Bay, 2017) may make the cut, despite a general acceptance that exploitation films are a thing of cinema's past.[2] On the other hand, Wikipedia defines exploitation as 'any film which tries to succeed financially by "exploiting" a current trend, a niche genre, or a lurid subject matter'.[3] If judged by these elements, *The Big Boss*, which invented and defined the contemporary kung fu film, and cemented Bruce Lee as an international icon, would hardly qualify either.

For at least one author, it is noted that exploitation films are better defined by 'a discourse of systemisation'.[4] Arguing that 'exploitation defies generic definitions',[5] the form is discussed as a historical trend that emerged from the censorship era of American filmmaking to tease and show illicit 'forbidden' images. This system of address – the promotion of the spectacle is as important as the film itself – can, it is said, now be found in the 'capital-intensive patterns of film production' around the world.[6] For the author, this method of sensational 'hype' is now the mainstream: '*all* cinema is, to a greater or lesser extent, exploitation cinema'.[7] However, a term broad enough to mean anything effectively means nothing.

In the academic field, recent and more astute writing from Church regards the exploitation film 'as more of a broad mode or sensibility than a distinct genre in its own right'.[8] Church maintains that exploitation, which has become increasingly interchangeable with the blanket term 'grindhouse' in magazines and modern DVD copy, is probably linked to an imagined sense of pastness – an idea of urban inner-city theatres that deliberately played the most excessively sexy and violent films from around the world. This point returns me to the idea of exploitation as a marketing gimmick – inner-city cinemas that housed unexplainably bizarre films that have frequently escaped fixed categorisation and even canonisation.

Meanwhile, Fisher notes, 'Not all of the exploitation films from the 1960s,

1970s and 1980s were made "beyond" the mainstream.'[9] Indeed, the success of almost every hit independent genre film – regardless of whether or not one may claim it to be 'exploitation' – resulted in a capital-driven flood of sound-alike and even look-alike productions (think of the zombie movies that flooded the market after *Night of the Living Dead* (George Romero, 1968)). In addition, the mainstream American studios were not opposed to greenlighting exploitation-alike films even if, as in the famous example of the sort-of sexploitationer *Last Tango in Paris* (Bernardo Bertolucci, 1972), the visual depiction of intercourse was less gratuitous and the leading man (Marlon Brando) was opposed to showing his appendage. While I will go on to discuss this phenomenon, which was especially prevalent during the product-extensive period of the 1970s, the *idea* of exploitation should be separated from what this book proposes may be viewed as a stylistic movement in film history. This approach is unique to *The Style of Sleaze* and while my argument may not alter the ingrained concept of exploitation as a blanket term for a subjectively 'trashy' cinema, I do hope that it will encourage future writing to pursue such umbrella labels with far more consideration.

Indeed, my own interest in defining exploitation cinema as something more than 'just' a vague referent to films that highlighted graphic sex and violence began in 2008 when I became involved in writing and producing the documentary that would become *American Grindhouse* (Elijah Drenner, 2010). The end result was not what I hoped for, and my suggestions were largely discarded – including the fact that any study of so-called 'grindhouse' cinema could not possibly avoid the adult film boom of the 1970s or the impact of Asian and European genre cinema, which swamped urban cinemas and greatly influenced later American genre filmmaking. I began to understand, during the gestation of the production, that the American exploitation film was increasingly becoming confused with the American B-movie and a romanticised sense of 42nd Street and 'cult' anti-Hollywood thinking. The idea that exploitation cinema deliberately attempted to trail a counterculture path to 'protest' the safety of studio films is a romantic theory but incorrect: these were capital-intensive projects, made for a fast profit. The narrative of *American Grindhouse* avoided this fact – instead presenting a free-for-all celebration of a hodgepodge of genre cinema with only passing lip service to time, place and identity. In his essay 'Grinding out the Grind House: Exploitation, Myth and Memory', Ward correctly mentions how in the documentary 'grindhouse and exploitation are used interchangeably'.[10] He also acknowledges that 'despite trumpeting the transgressive and graphic qualities of exploitation fare, many fan and academic cult film texts keep hardcore at arm's length'.[11] Both observations are precise – and *The Style of Sleaze* acts as an apology, of sorts, for the slapdash nature of *American Grindhouse*, a deeply flawed endeavour that, nonetheless, points to how subjective terms such as 'exploitation', 'grindhouse', 'cult' and even 'paracinema' are to the individual academic or cineaste (we may even say 'it's all in the eye of the beholder'). If these terms currently act as referents to the same thing (generally an imagined homogenous clump of cinema that is defined only by a loose sense of generic outlandishness), then, it is hoped, this book will offer an alternative approach to understanding and identifying exploitation cinema.

Church has also claimed that exploitation 'seems closer to a style or sensibility that can be recognised in a broad range of genres and subgenres'.[12] The author continues, 'the reductive descriptor "grindhouse style" has appeared in countless popular press sources as widespread cultural shorthand for the particular look and feel associated with archaic exploitation trailers'.[13] However, rather than any identifiable movement of filmmaking, Church is referring to the way in which, in particular, *Grindhouse* (Quentin Tarantino/Robert Rodriguez, 2007) paid homage to the worn-out prints, grainy film stock (often the result of shooting on short ends) and violent subject matter of the halcyon days of independent American horror cinema in the 1960s and 1970s. The *style* on show in this film, however, and Church also acknowledges this, has more to do with a fan-made narrative: the concept of sitting in a rundown 42nd Street movie theatre in old New York. Certainly, the actual aesthetic and thematic connection between the productions that Tarantino and Rodriguez take their inspiration from and their Hollywood counterpart is remarkably thin. The idea that exploitation films launched themselves on 42nd Street, as some kind of esteemed premiere, or were solely associated with outrageous displays of gore and psycho-sexual brutality is also incorrect. I examined this confusion, in detail, in my own self-directed, later documentary *42nd Street Memories* (2015). With this said, the word 'style' is revealing because what Church is indicating is that – decades after these films made their debut in urban theatres – there is still a distinct signifier within the exploitation pantheon that may let us know that this is not, let's say, a glossy mainstream product. I sense that, however clumsy this signifier may be (a sense of heightened taboo from another era?) it has inspired the current nostalgia for paying homage to an exploitation past that never really existed.

Hence, the Tarantino/Rodriguez *Grindhouse* – its own title indicating a pastiche of the past – played on the idea that, as a studio release, it also had to portray the *look* of something else – a signifier to audiences that it belonged to another time entirely. Of course, even if we were to accept that 'exploitation' may refer to the *appearance* of a grimy, old, worn-out film – ideally, as defined by Tarantino and Rodriguez, one that delivers more outrage than the audience may anticipate – we would still encounter problems. Most notably, how does the word 'exploitation' seek to give us a clear indication about a film's identity – generic or otherwise – or even its relationship to a specific time and place? For example, mention film noir and certain images surely come to mind – a shadowy monochrome aesthetic, a sexy femme fatale, a prying detective, smoke, whiskey, maybe even the 1940s – but if exploitation is, in effect, just another term for some kind of vaguely 'excessive' low-budget cinema, presented in the here and now to a cine-literate, self-conscious audience, then what *do* we think of? What function does the term provide if not to suggest a concise type of cinema? Does a studio film, such as *Vanishing Point*, qualify as exploitation simply because it features lengthy breakneck car chases? Is a supposed 'grindhouse style' indicating anything other than a homage to revival house showings of battered old movie prints?

There is also a danger of any appreciation of exploitation films becoming tangled up in a sense of ironic distance per *Grindhouse* and its wink-wink, nudge-nudge pastiche of the past. Jeffrey Sconce, whose 'paracinema' label, for instance, is used to signify an appreciation of cult and exploitation cinema frequently uses the term 'trash' to refer to these films. Unfortunately, his use of the word 'trash' carries a negative attachment: the term has not been cultivated for any broader political point and there is little sense that the author is 'reclaiming' the word, or finding a space of resistance against orthodox/ entrenched perspectives (as has been evident with – for example – 'queer theory'). This factor further troubles the author's agenda – that is, to 'valorise' hitherto disregarded or undefined cinema. Instead, Sconce initiates a more postmodern approach to cinema's marginal past – resulting in a highbrow/ lowbrow split within the film studies spectrum among academics and students: 'the paracinematic community defines itself in opposition not only to mainstream Hollywood cinema, but to the (perceived) counter-cinema of aesthetes and the cinematic academy'.[14] Exploitation films were not so much in opposition to Hollywood cinema, however, as they were dependent on its inability to provoke the same salacious images in order to turn a profit. The key texts of this study astutely recognised what audiences may pay to see – and, free from the studio system, deliberately pushed a spectacle, on austerity budgets, that caused controversy and, in some cases, censorship. But the bottom line was to make money based on showing things that Hollywood simply could not provide.

Therefore, in *The Style of Sleaze* I argue that exploitation can and should be seen as a style of filmmaking, specifically linked with a number of trailblazing independently made American productions that occurred in the 1960s and 1970s. Why American? Mainly because the scope of this book alone could not possibly begin to also entertain the concept of an identifiable exploitation style in Italian or Spanish films of the same era. Mathijs and Mendik, discussing European examples of the form, explain exploitation as relating to 'a series of texts that do not belong to the recognised repertoire, mostly because they are not deemed worthy enough'.[15] Despite ignoring the enthusiastic critical reception that some exploitation films gained, this statement indicates that exploitation could also refer to a substantial amount of texts with nationality being neither here nor there. The authors, while assembling a fascinating look at marginal European cinema, choose not to discriminate between the economic, production and industrial differences (as well as the aesthetic and thematic influences) that would, for instance, disaffiliate a French director working on low budgets in Paris during the 1970s from an American filmmaker shooting multi-million-dollar projects in contemporary Barcelona. Both of these examples are presented by the authors alongside a German art student struggling to make his first no-budget horror feature on 8 mm in the late 1980s, a British *King Kong* spin-off from the mid-1970s and an article spawning the history of Russian horror cinema (from 1917 to the present day).[16] If each of these examples of diverse world cinema, indicative of different languages, nationalities, cultures and eras, can be considered 'exploitation' then it is questionable that the label actually tells us anything valuable, or at least immediately identifiable, about the films that it perceives to 'contain'.

At a *push*, we may conclude that exploitation could be seen to identify a glut of taboo-breaking international genre films – whether prolifically distributed or otherwise. However, it is still questionable that we should accept *any* sort of cinema, marginal or otherwise, by such transnational disparity. Indeed, is the famous Italian horror master Dario Argento, for instance, an exploitation filmmaker? Some, doubtlessly, would argue that he is because of the general sexual and violent nature of his best-known work – symbolic of the sort of 'excess' that some commentators have viewed as indicative of *all* exploitation cinema. On the other hand, the director's best-known productions were a mainstream phenomenon in his native Italy, inspiring copycat films that aimed to repeat the domestic box office of, for instance, *Profondo Rosso* (1975) or *Suspiria* (1977). According to Sconce, who brackets exploitation as a 'subculture' beloved by 'bad' cinema aficionados,[17] this factor may well eliminate a filmmaker such as Argento from the canon. In addition, as Italian and other global genre films began to play in American theatres the move from low-budget genre productions that directly address (or rather exploit) domestic taboo and concerns begins to fade. Most notably, we start to see productions that are clearly inspired by a more international style. John Carpenter's *Halloween* (1978), and its many imitators, mimic the giallo style of Dario Argento while *Dawn of the Dead* (1978), itself financed by the Argento family, trades in the Italian director's garishly bloody and operatic set pieces. Even sexploitation, as hardcore begins to fade as a legitimate cinematic attraction, veers towards the soft-focus erotica of the French blockbuster *Emmanuelle* (Just Jaeckin, 1974) as seen with *Young Lady Chatterley* (Alan Roberts, 1977), which steals the former film's leading lady, or the later *9 1/2 Weeks* (Adrian Lyne, 1986) – both major theatrical attractions. While I acknowledge that American exploitation could be seen to have moved into other avenues – be it Troma Entertainment, straight-to-video horror, VHS pornography or even sleazy late-night made-for-cable thrillers (which briefly made Shannon Tweed a minor star) – the idea of the form as a film movement, with an interrelated style between the three main demarcations, has long ceased to exist. As I hope this book will explain, when the 1970s came to a conclusion so did American exploitation – at least insofar as it could be easily identified as a movement of filmmaking. Part of the reason why exploitation has become an umbrella term for a vaguely identified 'excess' within low-budget cinema is perhaps because during its boom-time the biggest hits spawned so many copycats. By the arrival of the 1980s there *was* an identifiable excess – but it was an excess of studio and independent horror productions that, by and large, were doing the same thing – confusing the boundaries between 'mainstream' and 'indie' – while blaxploitation and adult cinema had run their course as popular commercial entities.

Certainly, although foreign countries have doubtlessly had their own trend in making similar genre cinema, given the vague definition of 'exploitation' in general – and the huge variety of low-budget horror and sex films produced in countries such as Italy or even Indonesia or South Africa – it would probably take a book on each nation to really conclude on what constitutes each territory's relationship with the form. As such, identifying and discussing American exploitation cinema as a movement is an imposing task in its own right. Consequently, *The Style of Sleaze* is the first study to single out three key exploitation demarcations and to argue that, based on the evolution of aesthetic and thematic elements within each genre – represented by their most trend-setting texts – we may see this form of cinema as a legitimate film movement. Inevitably, this movement is associated with a specific era: the relaxation of cinema censorship in America. Once these battles were fought and won, however, the exploitation movement had nowhere to go – as witnessed by the rapid decline of low-budget genre cinema to videotape (with few exceptions).

I have also intended for *The Style of Sleaze* to be viewed as a follow-up, of sorts, to the excellent Eric Schaefer tome *'Bold! Daring! Shocking! True!'* A *History of Exploitation Films, 1919–1959*.[18] Schaefer closes his own study in 1959, arguing that this represents 'the end of the classical exploitation film'. The author further states: 'For audiences, critics, and the film industry itself, it was becoming more difficult to make the distinction between exploitation and mainstream product that had been so clear as little as a decade earlier.'[19] However, I believe that exploitation cinema, especially in its stylistic approach, continued to be distinct from the Hollywood mainstream for long after 1959. This factor is especially obvious when one takes into account the brief popularity of hardcore sex acts, which resulted in films such as *The Devil in Miss Jones* (Gerard Damiano, 1973) becoming legitimate box-office blockbusters. Furthermore, unlike Schaefer, I believe that the post-classical form also bears a clear stylistic lineage to the earlier films of the classical exploitation era – a close analysis of hardcore and softcore sex pictures, for instance, indicates that both probably belong within the same genre and movement. *The Style of Sleaze*, unlike other studies on exploitation cinema, argues that softcore and hardcore films are not stylistically dissimilar, and that the latter was an inevitable evolution from the former – not just in terms of pushing commercial boundaries but because the aesthetic was compromised by the simulation of the sex act. In other words, exploitation evolved in the years after 1959 and, in doing so, eventually began to influence and change some of the approaches, both aesthetic and thematic, to taboo material in the studio mainstream.

In their famous study on classical Hollywood cinema, Bordwell, Staiger and Thompson determined that film has evolved through various advances in technological sophistication: colour, camera space, widescreen and so forth.[20] I would also argue that equally essential to the progression of cinema is the believable depiction of sex, violence, race and gender roles. American exploitation filmmakers capitalised on social anxieties of the 1960s and 1970s by relying on spectacles that could not be offered by their mainstream counterpart. Audiences were frequently faced with imagery and stories that appropriated recognisable facets of contemporary socio-political 'taboo': interracial sex, the insatiable female, a vérité approach to torture and murder, African-American hypersexuality and revolt. That such spectacle was unhidden was not just a stylistic concern but one of financial interest: exploitation cinema would frequently market itself as providing an oppositional 'thrill' to that that was available from the major studios. That the major studios then took such imagery and made it more visually proficient perhaps attests to why so many exploitation films, watched today, seem like cinema beamed from another planet. Perhaps this is why Sconce has imagined these films as 'outsider art' – however, the exploitation style was mimicked across a number of low-budget productions and even minor independent studios such as Sam Arkoff's American International Pictures. Ironically, by attempting to expand the exploitation approach into a glossier format, Arkoff – and those with similar intent (perhaps best described as '*I Can't Believe it's Not Exploitation*') – stripped the style of its 'edge'. The films, while thematically similar to what came before, looked a little too 'Hollywood' and it is this factor that, arguably, began to signal the fall of the main exploitation demarcations as blockbuster commercial genres. While VHS played a part, I think looking at the evolving style of the exploitation movement indicates that a marriage of both spectacle and production values, caused by commercial ambition, exhausted transgression.

Of course, 'exploitation' has been used as a wider blanket term to appeal to ideas of 'sensational' or 'forbidden' cinema for quite some time and it would be wrong to ignore this fact. In the late 1980s, the British fanzine *Shock Xpress* claimed to be 'the essential guide to exploitation cinema'.[21] Advertising itself as 'essential reading for fans of wild, weird, wonderful and downright sleazy films' – the publication promised coverage of everything from major studio filmmakers such as David Cronenberg and Joe Dante to Philippine monster movies and 1970s British horror. The legacy of 'exploitation' as an umbrella term for 'sleaze' or 'wild' movies is extensive and possibly even ingrained: Brottman states that 'the term has broadened dramatically in its implication and is now used to refer to almost any low budget genre movie'.[22] In defining exploitation filmmaking as a style I will differentiate between the productions that grounded the movement and those other 'low-budget genre movies' that may be thought of as representative of the same trend. The large amount of films that were released to capitalise on the major commercial successes of the exploitation trend make it understandable why other scholars have bracketed this activity under makeshift indications of worth such as 'sleaze' or 'trash'. My own argument is that each film needs to be treated as an individual entity: stylistic consistency is more evident if closer scrutiny is given to a small number of productions, in identifiable demarcations, which transcend the accepted presentation of generic tropes. Each of the key films selected for closer study in this publication evidences a linkage of style and also historical importance in inspiring the release of various 'copycat' productions. For instance, the popularity of *Sweet Sweetback's Baadasssss Song* (Melvin Van Peebles, 1971) not only opened the door for what became identified as 'blaxploitation' but defined a *style* of cinema that was only built upon by a small number of successive titles. By being tagged as part of a larger 'blaxploitation' revolution, alongside, for instance, the aesthetically and thematically different Hollywood production *Shaft* (Gordon Parks, 1971), the film's stylistic connection to other exploitation cinema is lost. This is not to say that later films with similar tropes, such as *The Mack* (Michael Campus, 1973), are not exploitation but rather that they run with a style of filmmaking that has already proven to be commercially proficient. In other words: those films that defined the exploitation style amount to only a small number – that other producers pilfered this approach, and even subject matter, is an inevitability of any successful box-office production. These are the films that *exploit* exploitation, if you will.

In Chapter One, 'Not Quite Hollywood', I distinguish exploitation cinema from Hollywood filmmaking, discuss the difference between the movement and the B-movie and conclude on the three major demarcations studied in this book. In Chapter Two, 'Emerging from Another Era, Narrative and Style in Modern Exploitation Cinema' I discuss the similarities between the classical exploitation film and how the form evolved, especially in regard to its storytelling, after 1959. Chapter Three, 'Can We Call It Sexploitation?' introduces the sexploitation genre and the five key texts of this demarcation, while in Chapter Four, 'Sex Morality Plays: Character in Adult Cinema', I look at the thematic evolution of the female personalities in the central X-rated films. In

Chapter Five, 'The Body is Everything: Sexploitation Spectacle', I discuss how the sexploitation style presents the female body and evolves from simulations to the 'reality' of intercourse. Chapter Six, 'Exploitation-Horror Cinema', introduces the second demarcation explored by this study and Chapter Seven, 'Cannibalising Tradition: Romero's Zombies and a Blood Feast', continues this discussion with a close focus on the early trendsetters in this trend. In Chapter Eight, 'Slash and Burn: The Exploitation-Horror Film in Transition', I conclude my study of this genre and its role in the wider exploitation movement. In Chapter Nine, 'Blaxploitation Cinema: Race and Rebellion', I introduce and discuss the blaxploitation genre of the 1970s while in the follow-up chapters 'Sex, Violence and Urban Escape: Blaxploitation Tropes and Tales' and 'The Blaxploitation Female' I trace how the form evolves its style concurrent with the other exploitation demarcations. Finally, in Chapter Twelve, 'Exploitation as a Movement' I conclude on the benefits of approaching American exploitation cinema from this perspective.

Many of the key films of this study continue to appeal to contemporaneous viewers, critics and academics and will doubtlessly continue to be analysed for years and decades to come. In writing *The Style of Sleaze* I understand that, in working towards a more fixed terminology for the exploitation term, and providing a definition grounded within a historical movement, further debate is likely to evolve. While I welcome this discourse, what *is* most problematic at present is the blanketing together of various filmic texts without any concern for nationality, release and reception or even a basic understanding of the difference between mainstream and non-mainstream production processes. As such, in my first chapter I will begin to approach this contentious issue in more detail – first by defining exploitation cinema outwith the Hollywood studio system.

NOTES

1. Clark, J, '10 Noteworthy Exploitation Films' (n.d.), http://entertainment.howstuff-works.com/10-noteworthy-exploitation-films.htm#page=0https://en.wikipedia.org/wiki/Exploitation_film
2. Church, D, *Grindhouse Nostalgia: Memory, Home Video and Exploitation Film Fandom* (Edinburgh University Press, Edinburgh, 2016).
3. https://en.wikipedia.org/wiki/Exploitation_film
4. Watson, P, 'There's No Accounting for Taste'. In Cartmell, D, Hunter, I Q, Kaye, H and Whelehan, I (eds), *Trash Aesthetics: Popular Culture and its Audience* (Pluto Press, London and Chicago, 1997), p. 78.
5. Ibid.
6. Ibid., p. 80.
7. Ibid., p. 82; emphasis in the original.
8. Church, D, *Grindhouse Nostalgia: Memory, Home Video and Exploitation Film Fandom* (Edinburgh University Press, Edinburgh, 2016), p. 3.
9. In Fisher, A and Walker, J (eds), *Grindhouse (Global Exploitation Cinemas)* (Bloomsbury Academic, London, 2016), p. 4.

10. Ward, G, 'Grinding out the Grind House: Exploitation, Myth and Memory'. In Fisher, A and Walker, J (eds), *Grindhouse (Global Exploitation Cinemas)* (Bloomsbury Academic, London, 2016), p. 16.
11. Ibid., p. 18.
12. Church, D, *Grindhouse Nostalgia: Memory, Home Video and Exploitation Film Fandom* (Edinburgh University Press, Edinburgh, 2016), p. 10.
13. Ibid., p. 128.
14. Sconce, J, '"Trashing" the Academy: Taste, Excess and an Emerging Politics of Cinematic Style'. In Mathijs, E and Mendik, X (eds), *The Cult Film Reader* (Open University Press, London, 2007), p. 109.
15. Mathijs, E and Mendik, X (eds), *Alternative Europe: Eurotrash and Exploitation Cinema since 1945* (Wallflower Press, London, 2004), p. 3.
16. Odell and Blanc, 'Jean Rollin: Le Sang D'un Poete Du Cinema' (pp. 160–71), Mendik, 'Trans-European Excess: An Interview with Brian Yuzna' (pp. 181–90), Blake, 'Jörg Buttgereit's *Nekromantiks*: Things to do in Germany with the Dead' (pp. 191–202), Hunter, I Q, 'Deep Inside *Queen Kong*: Anatomy of an Extremely Bad Film' (pp. 32–8) and Stojanova, C, 'Mise-En-Scenes of the Impossible: Soviet and Russian Horror Films' (pp. 90–105). In Mathijs, E and Mendik, X (eds) *Alternative Europe: Eurotrash and Exploitation Cinema since 1945* (Wallflower Press, London, 2004).
17. Sconce, J, '"Trashing" the Academy: Taste, Excess and an Emerging Politics of Cinematic Style'. In Mathijs, E and Mendik, X (eds) *The Cult Film Reader* (Open University Press, London, 2007), p. 105.
18. Duke University Press, Durham, NC and London., 1999.
19. Schaefer, E. *'Bold! Daring! Shocking! True!' A History of Exploitation Films, 1919–1959* (Duke University Press, Durham, NC and London, 1999), p. 326.
20. Bordwell, D, Staiger, J and Thompson, K, *The Classical Hollywood Cinema* (Routledge, London, 1991 [1985]).
21. Jaworzyn, S (ed.), *Shock Xpress: The Essential Guide to Exploitation Cinema, Vol. 1* (Titan Books, London, 1991).
22. Brottman, M, *Offensive Films* (Vaderbilt University Press, Nashville, 2005 [1997]), p. 9.

1. NOT QUITE HOLLYWOOD

Exploitation films are not and never were Hollywood movies. The *term* 'Hollywood' may relate to a geographic area but its usage in the popular lexicon frequently pertains to the film industry that enshrines its economic and cultural values.[1] As such, I use Hollywood in this book less as an umbrella term and more as a metonymic one: as a reference to the more conventional style of filmmaking – most famously distinguished and discussed by Bordwell, Staiger and Thompson.[2] Labelled 'an excessively obvious cinema'[3] by the authors, due to a 'conservatism of style'[4] – that is, an orderly beginning, middle and end as well as the narrative use of repeated plot points – I want to further distinguish the exploitation film by, foremost, indicating its more visceral approach. For instance, take a famous film such as *Last Tango in Paris*, which was distributed by a major Hollywood studio and features an A-list American actor (Marlon Brando) but was made and produced in France by an Italian director (Bernardo Bertolucci). Stylistically, *Last Tango in Paris* warrants more comparison to what this book deems to be a 'Hollywood' film than an exploitation film because it *conceals* the sex acts that are nevertheless integral to its plot and story. In an exploitation film of the same era, both the nudity and the sex would be *unhidden*. While Schaefer also indicates the differences between the classical exploitation film and Hollywood cinema, the separation of studio filmmaking and independent filmmaking is a facet that continues to confuse academic discourse on exploitation films. For instance, in his essay 'Blaxploitation and the Misrepresentation of Liberation', Robinson, for instance, fails to distinguish between the studio-produced *Shaft* (Gordon

Parks, 1971) and the non-studio (exploitation) film *Coffy* (Jack Hill, 1973). He sees both films as belonging to a wider spectrum of black exploitation cinema.[5] Yet the two are very different: *Shaft* begins with its hero walking down New York's 42nd Street to the famous Isaac Hayes' soul number on the soundtrack, establishing his 'coolness' and masculinity. *Coffy*, on the other hand, opens with an African-American femme fatale blowing apart a drug dealer's head with a shotgun blast to the face. As the gruesome spectacle unfolds we are neither here nor there as to whether she is someone to be cheered or feared – and this moral ambiguity continues throughout the film. These may be 'black action films' but even from the start they tread a very different path – *Shaft* is for a Hollywood audience; *Coffy* is for an exploitation audience that expects (or demands) some sort of taboo aesthetic.

To show how exploitation and Hollywood continue to be confused, let me turn to Sconce, who describes his paracinema label as a byword for 'just about every other manifestation of exploitation cinema'. The author indicates that the term would include:

> such seemingly disparate subgenres as 'badfilm', splatter-punk, 'mondo' films, sword and sandal epics, Elvis flicks, government hygiene films, Japanese monster movies, beach-party musicals, and just about every other historical manifestation of exploitation cinema from juvenile delinquency documentaries to soft-core pornography.[6]

However, Japanese monster movies, such as *Godzilla* (Ishirô Honda, 1954), bear little comparison, stylistically or otherwise, to the lavish Elvis Presley musicals that were made, and distributed, by the major American studios such as MGM, Paramount and Warner Bros. and frequently rated among the top grossing American releases of their respective years.[7] It is also difficult to accept that either the popular *Godzilla* series (which were produced by a major Japanese studio in Toho) or Elvis Presley musicals were made under the 'impoverished and clandestine' conditions that Sconce indicates distinguishes 'paracinema' productions. Can we really believe that Elvis starred in 'exploitation' movies? Probably not – *but* this is part of the problem with the exploitation label: any sense of irony that can be placed unto the excess of the dated fashions and dances of Elvis films can be redeemed as some sort of garish paracinematic aplomb. This failure to distinguish between studio and non-studio filmmaking is important because Hollywood releases, financed during the timescale of this study, contain elements, both within and outwith their production, which exploitation films lacked: comparatively high budgets, lavish back-lot/set locations, nationwide distribution and, commonly, the attraction of recognisable, bankable performers. A 'beach party musical', for instance, such as *Beach Blanket Bingo* (William Asher, 1965), may have been made by an independent studio in American International Pictures but it had the star power of Frankie Avalon and even Buster Keaton. Exploitation films, in comparison, are remarkably threadbare or, at the very least, lean on stars familiar to their own marginal genres.

To give a further example: in my introduction I mentioned that exploitation is often considered synonymous with marketing – hence the romanticism of the carny advertising tricks of such famous hucksters as Terry Levene.[8] While looking at such promotional tactics in order to define a film as 'exploitation' is unwise (for instance, many low-budget productions were re-released under different titles or re-edited during the heyday of drive-in and urban cinemas) at least one thing that can be concluded is that Hollywood cinema never needed to sell a similar sense of taboo. Take, for instance, the marketing campaign for a mainstream horror film such as *The Exorcist* (William Friedkin, 1973) that did not need to 'hype' its gruesome special effects to achieve audience curiosity. The commodity was the adaptation of a best-selling novel, the presence of an Oscar winning director and a national release, complete with television advertising, from Warner Bros. The need for a lurid slogan such as '*To avoid fainting, keep repeating it's only a movie, only a movie*' – seen on the marketing for the exploitation-horror film *The Last House on the Left* – was not necessary. In place of such commodity is a more 'taboo' or risqué element – the 'exploitable' area, in other words, which a big studio film could not or would not provide to its audience: hence '*blax*ploitation' (exploitation of race) or '*sex*ploitation' (exploitation of sex). This exploitable element consequents and defines the style of these films. Hence, *The Exorcist* could be a legitimate contender for the Best Picture Academy Award, something that *The Last House on the Left* could never be considered for on account of its clear genericism (this *is* a gory horror film) and its unashamed willingness to push boundaries of visual spectacle (including graphic rape).

Exploitation dealt in transgressing the limits of 'acceptable' Hollywood cinema. In doing so, Hollywood, in turn, began to feature elements that had been commercially 'tested' by their exploitation counterparts. Exploitation films courted taboo. This element is apparent from the reception given to pivotal exploitation films and in some cases the censorship/legal battles that were fought.[9] The reviews allude to this transgression: 'best discussed alongside so-called snuff movies',[10] 'sort of like a Jew paying to get into Auschwitz',[11] 'a feast of carrion and squalor'.[12] Douglas claims, 'If taboo is to be treated simply and only as a reaction to the abnormal, the non-natural, the holy as opposed to ordinary "rational" categories, we are no nearer to understanding it.'[13] Thus, it is worth discussing how exploitation cinema cultivates its sense of taboo.

Figure 1.1   *Behind the Green Door*: voyeurs watching the same events unfold as the
             viewer is a common theme in the key exploitation films. (Produced by
             Artie J. Mitchell and James L. Mitchell)

TABOO BREAKERS

First and foremost, exploitation films rationalise images of human behaviour
such as sex and even violence. This approach is often allegorical – with the
spectacle attached to topicality: racial conflict, debates surrounding female
sexuality, gender objectification and interventionist politics. The classical
exploitation film may have cultivated taboo (to some extent) by anticipating a reaction to a rarely seen 'abnormality': venereal disease or sex-change
operations, for instance, but the post-classical form works within boundaries
of greater social recognition. Even the shock of graphic violence is harnessed
within the everyday: the civil rights struggle is front and centre to the early
blaxploitation films, while the Vietnam War can be seen to be allegorised in
the horrors of films such as *The Last House on the Left*. Part of the reason
for this factor is to heighten audience awareness of the taboo being exhibited.
Bordwell mentions that telling a joke about two lawyers in a bar 'wouldn't
be understood in a culture that lacked bars, lawyers, and lawyer jokes'.[14]
Similarly, the horrors of *The Last House on the Left* may have been less

effective – including commercially – were Americans not aware of the fact the film was harnessing (or exploiting) the Manson murders and Vietnam-era ideas of Western savagery. In comparison, the 'head spinning' sequence of *The Exorcist* feels akin to fairy-tale mythology: exploitation sex and violence, however, challenges the viewer to watch.

Rather than a reaction to the abnormal, exploitation treats taboo as part of a contemporary inevitability. The exploitation narrative is chaotic and instances of plot causality can be random; images and situations transpire that force elements of taboo into the lives of initially unprepared characters. Taboo is conformant to its era: exploitation had to transgress fresh boundaries to remain commercial. Facets that are now taken for granted in films were once considered taboo – including nudity of any kind and interracial relationships. Therefore, in looking at the key films selected by this book, a chronology is evident – a graduation towards increasingly more daring exhibitions of hitherto unseen spectacle. Exploitation sells itself on something that is aesthetically or thematically unique from Hollywood. Due to limited distribution (unless, as with *Super Fly*, a major studio bought the rights) exploitation films would usually play territorially and the film prints would then move on to other American states – *The Last House on the Left* opened in just two drive-in cinemas in Massachusetts: 'The independent distributor could not afford to release thousands of prints at once.'[15]

THE B-MOVIE

Another central and important factor in defining exploitation relates to the rise and fall of the 'B-movie' – a term encompassing some of the marginal films referred to by Sconce as 'paracinema' or 'trash'.[16] The B-movie emerged as a cheaply made 'second feature', produced by Hollywood studios during the 1930s, and designed to feature on double-bills with a more lavish (insofar as production values) 'attraction'.[17] Little academic documentation has been done on the B-movie phenomenon and this complicates discussion of the term. For instance, it has been mentioned that the B-movie 'was virtually dead' by 1960.[18] However, the form's most identifiable facets – *generic, cheaply made, double-billed* – ensured that the term continued, and continues, to be referenced.[19] Perhaps it this confusion over the 'B-movie' term that led Bazin to question: 'maybe the notion of the B-film is open to dispute since everything depends on how far up the scale you put the letter A'.[20] This quote relates to the *economy* of the B-movie and the contrast/comparison of its production values with its 'A' counterpart – and this aspect is integral to the term. Indeed, the 'B' in B-movie indicates its (perceived) inferiority to the spectacle of its more expensive correspondent, also the reason why it would typically play on the second half of a double bill. Budgetary limitations are not the sole delineation of the 'B-movie':

exploitation films were also made cheaply and quickly. Both forms also mar-keted themselves within a generic format that was easily identifiable to consum-ers. Speaking of B-movie 'monster films' such as *I Was a Teenage Werewolf* (Gene Fowler, Jr, 1957), Jancovich notes their 'trashiness' (ala paracinema, this is a term that is frequently repeated as some kind of signifier – yet 'trash' is, perhaps, more subjective than just a referent to cheapness) that 'operates as . . . a sign of value for their teenage fans in the 1950s'.[21] This comment necessitates the need to distinguish between the B-movie and the exploitation film. While my own explanation will most likely not be the last word on this, I think it is important to initiate this discourse so that, in future writing, exploitation cinema can be deemed as a separate entity from its B-movie cousin.

Jancovich briefly touches upon the transition of the B-movie from studio productions to low-budget, independently made films by identifying American International Pictures (AIP). The author mentions AIP as the company respon-sible for a resurgence of 'antiquated "formula" pictures' that 'contained nar-rative routes in the old studio system's B picture' and were produced with the intention of following the old 'double bill' pattern.[22] AIP veered into exploitation when they began to be the foremost producer of black action films in the United States, starting with *Coffy* in 1973. The AIP blaxploita-tion films were glossier than previous independent productions but they also proved influential – the genre, after *Coffy*, would generally follow the same structure of morally ambiguous vigilantes and heightened racially motivated violence. AIP was well-established by the early 1970s – with some of their gothic horrors, such as *Pit and the Pendulum* (Roger Corman, 1961) boasting production values not far removed from those of comparable Hollywood films. Nonetheless, outside of their early blaxploitation efforts, such as *Coffy*, few AIP films exhibit explicit spectacles of sex or violence.

As theatres continued to run double-bill programming in the 1960s and 1970s, independent filmmakers drew upon the B-movie mantle with genres that were inexpensive to produce. Predominantly this took on the form of cheap sci-fi, biker and horror movies: *The Little Shop of Horrors* (Roger Corman, 1960), *Rat Pfink a Boo Boo* (Ray Dennis Steckler, 1966) or the AIP likes of *The Mini-Skirt Mob* (Maury Dexter, 1968) and *Frogs* (George McCowan, 1972) are some of the more famous examples. The lower budgets of these films, the short running times and the meagre shooting schedule provided an economic connection to the studio B-movie that existed during the 1930s through to the 1950s. They also, even the AIP films, offer a strangely wholesome entertainment: there may be (hints of) sex or violence (and even drug taking) but the style of these films is not to linger on anything that may cause a commercially risky 'X' (adults only) rating. Therefore, in exploring the relationship between the exploitation film and the B-movie I suggest the following points:

1) *Transgression*: exploitation films instigated their own genres and follow-up titles generally copied the spectacle rather than the thematic. 'B-movie' titles, such as the sci-fi 'alien invasion' production *Plan 9 from Outer Space* (Ed Wood, 1959) were designed to capitalise on the success of Hollywood pictures that had already been commercially successful (in this instance, *The Day the Earth Stood Still* (Scott Derrickson, 1951)). Schaefer has explained that the B-movie of the 'classical' era had 'more in common with the A films of the majors'.[23] Post-1960 and this assertion remains prevalent: the independent production house American International Pictures initiated the decade with a series of Roger Corman-directed films that mimicked the period horror formula of Britain's Hammer Studio: *The Pit and the Pendulum* (1961) and *The Premature Burial* (1962).[24] In comparison, the first horror release that this book views as *exploitation* – *Blood Feast* (Herschell Gordon Lewis, 1963) – invented a genre based around the depiction of graphically gory set pieces set within a contemporary ethos. Correctly dubbed as a 'new wave'[25] – *Blood Feast* would introduce the premise and intention of the horror genre within the exploitation movement: unflinching violence, human protagonists and a camera that does not 'turn away' from gruesome excess. Testifying to its transgressive quality, *Blood Feast* was banned in the United Kingdom until 2001 and only finally permitted to be screened without any censor cuts in 2005 – more than forty years since its premiere.[26] The birth of other exploitation genres established similar innovation: *The Immoral Mr Teas* (Russ Meyer, 1959) was the first film to institute nudity with a storyline and represents a new breed of sexploitation (exposed nudity or sex was not a crucial component of B-movies).[27] *Sweet Sweetback's Baadasssss Song* (Melvin Van Peebles, 1971) introduces a heroic anti-establishment, hypersexual black leading man – instigating the blaxploitation trend. These films set their own benchmarks in that they provide a stylistic model that invents demarcations of their own. *Sweet Sweetback's Baadasssss Song* initiates the style of the blaxploitation film: itself a re-appropriation of the sexploitation spectacle but placed into a thematic of urbanity and violent, racially charged conflict. Subsequent blaxploitation films such as *Super Fly* (Gordon Parks, Jr, 1972) evolved this style but others adapted the concept of the African-American detective into the 'safer' presentation introduced by the Hollywood film *Shaft* (Gordon Parks, 1971): a well-produced, but predictable, actioner. 'B-movie' releases are *indebted* to Hollywood success as opposed to *challenging* it. The grittier and ground-breaking *Coffy* that established a new cycle of female-led, nudity-heavy, blood-soaked blaxploitation cinema, itself

based on subverting the tired macho representations of the genre, represents the exploitation movement because it was doing something new and building on the style of the previous ground-breaking films. To put most simply: *Coffy* had something to *exploit* that audiences had not previously seen.

2) *Revelation*: as I will discuss in more detail in my next chapter, exploitation films centre their narratives upon some sort of visual revelation – a facet designed to 'shock' (the 'exploitable' element) and consequently profit from the salacious curiosity of the audience. This 'revelation' challenges the accepted aesthetic traditions of Hollywood: a 'cut-away' during a scene of sex or violence is rare for the key exploitation films identified by this study. Interracial relationships, which are presented in a relatively non-explicit/non-sexual manner in the Hollywood films of this period, are explicitly shown, and capitalised on, in exploitation productions. B-movies remain indebted to *off-screen* action: death, sex and monstrosity. American World Pictures turned down the opportunity to distribute *Night of the Living Dead*, citing its graphic visuals as being 'too gory'.[28] It did not assimilate with the less transgressive B-movies that the company had become synonymous with producing – such as the identifiable 'trashiness' of *I Was a Teenage Werewolf*. Instead, *Night of the Living Dead* became notorious by 'ignoring decades of cinema convention' and slaughtering its entire cast.[29] The horror-violence in *Night of the Living Dead* is gruesome and prolonged, the style is minimalist and the ending is inconclusive. This is how the narratives of *all* of the key exploitation films discussed in this book function. Audiences were 'promised' that they would see something 'new' in exploitation films: 'Nothing so appalling in the annals of horror' guaranteed the poster for *Blood Feast*. The gradual liberalisation of sex in the cinema reached its conclusion with the eventual revelation of unsimulated intercourse.

3) *Setting*: the setting of an exploitation film is contemporary.
   The narratives of blaxploitation, sexploitation and the exploitation-horror film all take place in modern locations. In addition, where genre conventions dictate that an antagonist is necessary such a figure is always human: the racist police officers of *Sweet Sweetback's Baadasssss Song* (1971), the kidnappers of *Behind the Green Door* (The Mitchell Brothers, 1972) or the psycho-sexual rapists of *The Last House on the Left*. One may be compelled to argue – when looking at examples of exploitation-horror films – that the zombies of *Night of the Living Dead* have supernatural overtones. However, the threat is human-made and the cannibalistic villains have a recognisably human face. In comparison, B-movies would – as their titles indicate – rely

Figure 1.2   *Blood Feast*: an early example of exploitation-horror cinema. (Produced by David F. Friedman)

on a more fantastical theme: *Attack of the Crab Monsters* (Roger Corman, 1957). These are antagonists that do not belong to 'our' world.

4) *Intertextuality*: Returning to Bordwell, Staiger and Thompson's comment: 'the most common sort of intertextual motivation is generic'. Post-1960, when the major studios stopped producing B-movies, low-budget, independently produced copycat films were made to fill the void on double-bill programmes. During the 1970s a number of B-movies channelled the success of *Jaws* (Steven Spielberg, 1975) with other 'nature run amok' films. Examples include *Grizzly* (William Girdler, 1976), *Piranha* (Joe Dante, 1978) and *Alligator* (Lewis Teague, 1980). Audiences were aware of the intertextual 'formula' that these texts were promoting (man vs. beast). By using the word 'intertextual' I want to stress that exploitation cinema was predominantly indebted to its *own lineage* in the same way that post-1960 B-movies were indebted to Hollywood 'A' films. This aspect is most evident in the stylistic similarities between titles within the exploitation movement, particularly their focus on an actualistic simulation of physical excess: sexual discovery, race-domination and/ or horror-violence. Also of note is that exploitation stars rarely, if ever, 'crossed over' to even B-movies – Jamie Gillis, a superstar in adult movies, was a non-entity outside of them. Linda Lovelace may have

been a huge exploitation star for *Deep Throat* but her sole B-movie, *Linda Lovelace for President* (Claudio Guzmán, 1975), was a flop – by all accounts audiences only associated her with the adult cinema that had been so successful. David Hess, the star of *The Last House on the Left*, would generally only appear in similar, sleazy exploitation films, including soundalike films made in Italy (*House on the Edge of the Park* (Ruggero Deodato, 1980)). When the blaxploitation sequel *Super Fly T.N.T.* (Ron O'Neal, 1973) appeared, but with the sex and violence of the original *Super Fly* 'toned down', few were watching. Similarly, auteurism is frequently associated with exploitation cinema – there have, for instance, been books on Wes Craven[30] and Russ Meyer,[31] while filmmakers as comparatively obscure as Radley Metzger have warranted entire DVD 'collections'.[32] Such assumptions of an auteur voice, however, are complicated and interrelated to the intertextual nature of exploitation cinema. Take *The Devil in Miss Jones* as an example. The text evolves the style of the sexploitation film by transgressing elements of generic expectancy (including the sexual presentation of a leading lady nearing middle-age) while still delivering the sensationalism that audiences of the form demand. *The Devil in Miss Jones* is written *and* directed by Gerard Damiano, but – less we forget – any auteurism is interlinked to the demands of the genre, a genre that Damiano would never escape from.

5) *Spectacle*: interrelated to transgression; post-1960 the exploitation film formulates the more conventional narrative of Hollywood, rather than the pseudo-educational pretext of its initial lineage, while maintaining plot and story on the reveal of taboo. This taboo is generally linked to aesthetically exhibiting things that are kept off camera in Hollywood cinema. When Sconce talks about 'an aesthetic of excess'[33] he may be referring to the spectacle of exploitation cinema: although such 'excess' is more than just the focus on taboo imagery. It is the instrumentation of a new aesthetic and thematic approach to such, which only a small number of ground-breaking films can claim to have achieved. Kerner mentions that 'exploitation promises to deliver guilt-free spectacles of violence'.[34] What should perhaps also be established is that exploitation cinema, while commonly progressing and evolving towards greater and more daring spectacles during its 1960s and 1970s heyday, was also inherently cynical. Excess could be and would be shown but only insofar as the narrative could treat such spectacle as a commercial entity that would, in turn, generate profit. That profit, however, was inseparable from a wider cynicism about the viewers themselves that the thematic makes all too clear. The key exploitation films, and much of the cinema that these films influenced,

are actually 'feel bad' movies – the narratives are open-ended as if it promotes a form of communicative action. These are films that do not answer some of the questions posed by the narrative threads that they unravel. As such, to tie-in the 'excess' of exploitation with a supposed balls-to-the-wall desire to entertain ('guilt-free') is, as I will continue to explore, incorrect.

6) *Physical Perversion*: the sexualisation or violation of corporeal beauty. In the post-classical form, a great number of exploitation films graphically connect sex *and* violence as well. The 'shock' element of exploitation is inseparable from the exhibition of bodily distress/destruction/ seduction.

7) *Un-heroic 'heroes'*: as a product of low-budget, independent filmmaking, exploitation titles had to 'sell' something that was different to Hollywood. Even when Hollywood begins to infringe upon exploitation genres – such as with the black-detective films *Shaft* (Gordon Parks, 1971) and *Across 110th Street* (Barry Shear, 1972), there is a considerable divergence. Psychological causality, for instance, in the Hollywood 'black' film, places a heroic African American honouring the system of law. By comparison, blaxploitation films have African-American characters vigilant against any white patriarchal system of control.[35] The B-movie would frequently make the case between 'good' and 'bad' clear even when, as with a Roger Corman production such as the excellent *Jackson County Jail* (Michael Miller, 1976), the 'good' turns out to be a prisoner (who nonetheless sacrifices his life for the sake of the leading lady) and the 'bad' is represented by the police.

EXPLOITATION GENRES

Genre is integral to exploitation cinema: clearly intentioned depictions of horror, violence and sex are manifested in narratives that are fiercely upfront about what is being presented. As aforementioned, *Coffy* begins with a scene of gruelling brutality – the *spectacle*, the sort of film that we are going to witness, is immediately grounded. To clarify my use of 'genre': this study uses the term in the same manner as demarcation, which is to set boundaries and to bring some classification to texts that exemplify similar thematic traits. Allen and Gomery mention that 'genre' highlights 'conventions', which 'then serve as parameters' usually to appease (or sometimes to transgress) 'the expectations of the audience'.[36] This form of artificial organisation allows us to understand what some films *are* and what other films *are not* – even at a basic level (that is, *Star Wars* (George Lucas, 1977) is not a musical). While all films possess influences from outside their foremost generic categorisation, exploitation films base their narratives around carefully constructed set pieces of bodily sensationalism. The 'money shot' in sexploitation evolved into a term for the depiction of unsimulated male ejaculation – proof of an actual orgasm. The prolonged, often agonising, display of murder in an exploitation-horror film or the inner-city violence and hypersexual African American of blaxploitation also became generically expected from audiences who followed these genres. This promise of salacious thrills makes the 'generic' categorisation of these films easier to conclude. For instance, *The Texas Chain Saw Massacre* (Tobe Hooper, 1974), with its title and grisly poster slogan ('who will survive and what will be left of them?'), draws conclusively upon the 'generic conventions' of the horror film. A recent article may have 'read' this production as a western, focusing on its 'rural Texas landscape' and 'the myth of frontier entrepreneurialism'[37] but such theorising is flawed. This reading ignores that (alongside the film's iconic marketing as a horror feature) *The Texas Chain Saw Massacre* portrays generic traits that are completely foreign to the western: the old dark house, the masked protagonist, a 'final girl' who is tormented and chased by a serial killer, an elderly 'Dracula' who sucks the blood of his victims like a vampire. Any hybrid element – such as that of the surrounding 'Texas landscape' – has more to do with reasons of economy.[38] The film's central crux is to frighten and disgust. The generic *intention* of key exploitation texts is also candid: sex to titillate/gruesome violence to horrify/a black action hero for an urban audience to cheer.

It should be noted that exploitation cinema has, occasionally, been seen to achieve the subjective reputation as 'art' (that label that occasionally defies the idea of mere genre). *The Devil in Miss Jones*, one of the key films from the sexploitation genre singled out for attention in this book, was favourably reviewed by *Variety* magazine. The paper wrote, 'With *The Devil in Miss Jones* the hard-core porno feature approaches an art form, one that critics may have a tough time ignoring in the future.'[39] However, regardless of such assumed pretence, these films remain products designed to *engage*, for maximum profit ('exploitability') with taboo imagery within a clear genre narrative. If Hollywood cinema is regarded as 'providing the maximum pleasure for the maximum number to ensure a maximum profit'[40] then exploitation should be viewed as a movement that instigates hopes of *any* commercial return on small budgets. This small return comes from featuring transgressive spectacles. A 'formula' – *'give them something they haven't seen before and they will tell their friends'* – had to exist in order to provide this. Ward argues, 'The supposed needs and wants of a seemingly uncritical audience foreclose analysis of films' aesthetic interest or social significance.'[41] While I am tempted to agree with this statement, I think the two points can also work concurrently – clearly *some kind* of aesthetic value makes a low-budget film a 'hit'. Whereas it is unlikely that it is as simplistic as 'giving them what they want' it *is* probably to do with registering what a sizeable margin of the population is likely to be

Figure 1.3   *Sweet Sweetback's Baadasssss Song*: the film dedicated its closing scroll to a sense of racial brotherhood. (Produced by Jerry Gross and Melvin Van Peebles)

opposed to. Looking at the aesthetics of the most popular exploitation cinema, from *Deep Throat* to *Sweet Sweetback*, it is clear that rather than 'giving them what they want' the films are deliberately defining themselves by what is most likely to cause offence to conservative values and create uproar. This factor is not always thematic (as I mentioned some of these films tow a surprising illiberal line) but in terms of their aesthetic there is a notable desire to be 'offensive' in order to channel word of mouth. Yet this is not to conclude that such offence can be entirely without value – artistic or otherwise.

Exploitation filmmakers would also ride on the coattails of previous successes within the movement in order to stimulate interest from a paying audience. This is perhaps part of why exploitation has become so difficult to define: the movement has so many films that seem to work on a similar trajectory – *The Texas Chain Saw Massacre*, to the layman, may not sound too dissimilar to *The Toolbox Murders* (Dennis Donnelly, 1978). Both may be considered exploitation films, but the latter is merely copying the stylistic originality of the former (while adding a familiar 'B' star in Cameron Mitchell – indicating that the promotion of *just* gory spectacle had begun to fatigue). To say that exploitation, as a movement, is based on a small number of key films is – as mentioned – not to deny that the style was not persuasive enough to flood the market with numerous comparable titles. Moreover, while innovation within the movement was frequent, especially stylistically, such a factor always evolved within the confines of recognisable *generic elements*. *The Devil in Miss Jones* may have made sexploitation 'respectable' to critics, but any artistic subversion took place within the formulaic demands of its own genre: nudity, ejaculation, intercourse, lesbianism – this is what offended some and attracted others (possibly in reaction to the former). Without such generically necessary tropes, the 'arty' *The Devil in Miss Jones* could not function as the profitable entity that it was initiated as. This conclusion is not to insinuate that filmmaking has to be either/or in terms of artistic merit/status as an economic product, but rather to argue that the exploitation *style* is predicated upon delivering taboo spectacle while subverting the predictable elements that genre cinema often delivers.

Unlike other accepted film movements, exploitation cinema boasts a vast number of wide-ranging, generic productions – as opposed to, for instance, the 'two dozen'[42] German Expressionist features. Historically, it is this strict 'containment' that has permitted the identification of a cinematic movement: Bordwell and Thompson speak of Italian neorealism from its prominence in the immediate post-war years, 1945–51.[43] However, the influence of the key neorealist films can still be seen beyond those initial few texts: 'Instead of itself disappearing, neorealism changed its form.'[44] I maintain that the same is true with exploitation cinema and that the sudden market proliferation of blaxploitation, gruesome horror and sexploitation films was influenced by the cheap production values, consequent 'low investment' potential for monetary return and the adaptability of the corporeal spectacle of the form to less aesthetically and thematically complex projects. This book asserts, therefore, that the exploitation *style* remains contingent upon a small number of influential and transgressive productions. Further films may repeat these stylistic traits of the originating influence, but they are best recognised as B-movies in their own right – or at least 'B-exploitation'. Furthermore, if one looks at the cinema that we could deem 'exploitation' following the period of this book – for instance, the slasher thrills of *Friday the 13th* (Sean S. Cunningham, 1980) or the late-night softcore erotica of *Animal Instincts* (Gregory Dark, 1992) – their style is far glossier than anything explored in this book. Even the notoriously violent likes of *Bloodsucking Freaks* (Joel Reed, 1976) and *I Spit on your Grave* (Meir Zarchi, 1978), or the late-in-the-day adult film success *Debbie Does Dallas* (Jim Clark, 1978) are doomed to merely repeat the low-rent, hand-held, spectacle-driven aesthetic and thematic of the films that proceeded them.

Are these exploitation films?

If we accept that exploitation reference some kind of 'guilt free' excess then, yes, undoubtedly they are. In terms of marketing they also know what they are selling: breasts, blood, torture and/or nude girls . . . but in the same way that Roger Corman made Gothic horror to capitalise on the success of Hammer Films. Thematically, however, these later productions lack the cynicism and style of the pioneering titles of exploitation filmmaking and I believe that this very downbeat, grimy and even conservative 'message' was ingrained in the most ground-breaking examples of the movement. It may raise an eyebrow, then, to argue that *I Spit on Your Grave* – which turns a gang rape into an excuse for a 'cut off their dicks' message that sets feminism back decades – is 'merely' a B-exploitation film rather than the 'real deal' but I ask that such a point be considered in the context of previous studies on 'excessive' cinema. Exploitation should not be seen as an indicator of some imagined low quality but should instead refer to key films that played a part in a movement towards a new kind of cinema that, itself, spawned an 'excess' that exists outside of the early aesthetic and thematic of the most ground-breaking texts. That idea of *exploiting exploitation*, as I referred to earlier, undoubtedly exists – but the concept of an exploitation movement belongs to a small number of films. Concluding this chapter, the three central demarcations of this study are now explained in more detail with key films highlighted.

SEXPLOITATION

The exhibition of filmed sex in theatres is a trait that is almost as old as the cinema itself: Kracauer, for instance, maintains that pornography was one of the most popular genres in a post-war Weimar era Germany.[45] It was also during a time of conflict that split popular opinion (Vietnam), and its later fallout, that American filmmakers instigated a similar blockbuster/cultural phenomenon with the success of the explicit sex productions *Deep Throat* (Gerard Damiano, 1972), *Behind the Green Door* and *The Devil in Miss Jones*. Some authors have since argued that watching these films was part of a greater counterculture ethos, a statement of 'free love' against authority: 'a media sensation . . . stoking the interest of socialites, students, swingers and the curious'.[46] In the chapters detailing and discussing these titles, I argue that the key films in the sexploitation genre exhibit a more complex narrative than the popular assumption that interest in screened sex exploded because of their social relevance to a generation of increasing carnal liberality.[47] The mainstream commercialisation of screen sexuality, from foreign imports and exploitation houses to a more audience-friendly 'simulated' alternative (such as *Last Tango in Paris* (Bernardo Bertolucci, 1973)) centres upon numerous factors including the arrival of colour, better distribution practices, more technically adept filmmakers and a brief acceptance of viewing unsimulated sex acts on the cinema screen. All of these factors are considered, alongside the increasing evolution of an identifiable, generic style that permitted sexploitation to be spoken of as 'underground art films'[48] and even compared, favourably, to the 'technical polish' of 'Hollywood product'.[49]

The aesthetic exploration of taboo in the central sexploitation titles would indicate that American society became increasingly liberal, however, the mainstream circulation and popularity of sexploitation was remarkably brief. I will argue that this has to do with the stylistic limitation of the films: once the taboo element of unhiding the sex act was evidenced, the genre moved towards greater thematic ambition with *The Opening of Misty Beethoven* (greater scope of location/storytelling/cast/costumes/spectacle) but failed to recoup its earlier financial presence and return. And as an attempt to offend increased to the extent of presenting unsimulated rape – as in *The Private Afternoons of Pamela Mann* (Radley Metzger, 1975) – the audience was less and less present. As the sex spectacle became the most important facet of the films, stylistic evolution was replaced by the cost-effective presentation of intercourse, leading to the rise and graphic corporeal presentation of the contemporary pornographic film industry. The urge for quick masturbatory satisfaction ultimately became the sole point of the genre, although its reputation for taboo would also drive it underground – away from the cinemas and direct to VHS.

HORROR

Robin Wood was the first author to recognise the American horror film as containing both a Hollywood and an exploitation variation.[50] The horror film, as an exploitation genre, grew out of the pseudo-documentary tradition of the classical exploitation feature, the B-movie form of the 1950s and, to some degree, the success of *Psycho* in 1960. The films singled out as having particular relevance within this genre – including *Night of the Living Dead* (George Romero, 1968), *The Last House on the Left* (Wes Craven, 1972), *The Texas Chain Saw Massacre* (Tobe Hooper, 1974) and *Martin* (George Romero, 1977) – represent a range of provocative, and aesthetically and thematically transgressive, horror cinema. As a genre with intertextual similarities this cycle began to fade from popular view after the Vietnam War and Watergate concluded. These films begin with America in disarray (*Night of the Living Dead*), move on to depicting a country at war with itself and, finally, conclude with the post-war fallout in which, with the passing of the Vietnam conflict and Watergate, disenchantment is now prevalent (*Martin*). A close study of these titles, and a look at follow-up films such as *The Hills Have Eyes* (Wes Craven, 1977), will show that the style of the exploitation-horror film violates the utopian conclusion of its Hollywood counterpart and focuses its imagery upon the most recognisable news stories of the time. The exploitation-horror film graduates, stylistically, towards an attempt to mimic a powerful 'documentary' vérité.

BLAXPLOITATION

The black action film, commonly blanketed under the term *blaxploitation*, has been accused of wallowing in stereotypes: 'the male prostitute ("Sweetback"), the vigilante cops ("Gravedigger Jones" and "Coffin Ed Johnson"); the dope pusher ("Shaft"); and the gangster ("Black Caesar", etc)'.[51] Dunn mentions 'a dominance of ghettoized, underworld depictions' featuring 'hypersexual machismo'.[52] Certainly, the exposure of black sexuality is integral to this demarcation: Sweetback 'the prostitute' uses his sexual prowess to escape to freedom in the inaugural blaxploitation film *Sweet Sweetback's Baadasssss Song* (Melvin Van Peebles, 1971). This 'prowess' is exhibited to the audience in graphic detail: the film's forthright political motif of urban revolution is dichotomous to the demands of the exploitation style: corporeal, sensational-istic, taboo. These elements would be appropriated by numerous 'B' take-offs that drew on the salacity, if not the style, of the key films identified by this book: *Sweet Sweetback's Baadasssss Song* is quickly followed by *Super Fly* (Gordon Parks, 1972) and *Coffy* (Jack Hill, 1973). In previous academic studies, the use of the term 'blaxploitation' has not distinguished between those films made independently, sometimes by a small black film crew, and those financed by significantly more resourceful exploitation producers (such as American International Pictures) or major studios. The relationship between producers, distributors and cinema owners that stood to make money out of blaxploitation movies, and the small African-American film crews who may have had a social message that they wished to convey, also becomes complicated when the latter were replicating the violent and sexual imagery propagated by the former. Here we see issues of 'hyper-masculinity' appearing – the Jack Johnson stereotype critiqued by West for its 'dirty, disgusting and funky' sexuality (as well as the prowess to seduce women of lighter skin colour – a facet of the mentioned blaxploitation films and the prevailing genre).[53] Blaxploitation films venerate and even intensify some of the cultural tropes of the dominant culture that the form is trying to resist. Therefore, any analysis of blaxploitation cinema must pay attention to commodification of race and sexuality within (and behind) these movies. Central to this will be the discus-sion of blaxploitation as a style rather than a term to facilitate discussion of a homogeny of films produced in the 1970s whose sole link to one another is the presence of an African-American leading man or woman.

Further exploitation titles will be introduced in this study to highlight key points. This approach will be evident in Chapter Two, wherein an explora-tion will be taken in regards to the similarities and differences between three cinematic dynamics: the classical exploitation film, Hollywood production and the exploitation movement. Discussing the classical form, I will present how the style of exploitation cinema did not change quite as dramatically as its later 'blockbuster' credentials may insinuate. While, today, we may recognise the original *Night of the Living Dead* as a trend-setting and financially successful film – its own link to the classical period of pseudo-documentary exploitation is clear from its style. Even the hardcore sex of *Deep Throat*, for instance, is framed with a narrative of the 'square up' that indicates a clear attachment to the classical era. These aspects of the form will be discussed next.

Notes

1. For instance, Kenneth Anger's famous book on film scandals *Hollywood Babylon* (Arrow Books Ltd, San Francisco, 1986 [1959]) or the recent documentary *Not Quite Hollywood* (Mark Hartley, 2008).
2. See: Bordwell, D, Staiger, J and Thompson, K, *The Classical Hollywood Cinema* (Routledge, London, 1991 [1985]).
3. Ibid., p. 3.
4. Ibid., p. 375.
5. Robinson, C, 'Blaxploitation and the Misrepresentation of Liberation', *Race & Class* (vol. 40. 1, 1998) – http://journals.sagepub.com/doi/pdf/10.1177/030639689804000101, last accessed 8 August 2017, p. 101.
6. Ibid., p. 101.
7. 'Elvis Presley Filmography',: http://en.wikipedia.org/wiki/Elvis_Presley_filmography, last accessed 20 August 2017.
8. For instance, the USA Blu-ray release of *Zombi Holocaust/Doctor Butcher MD* (Marino Girolami, 1980) features an interview with Levene as he discusses the details of his 'Butcher Mobile' that he trucked around Times Square with fake nurses and doctors promoting the movie.
9. Director Russ Meyer had to spend '$250,000 in legal fees defending, not only [his film] *Vixen*, but the public's right to view whatever they wanted'. Cited in Muller, E and Faris, D, *Grindhouse: The Forbidden World of 'Adults Only' Cinema* (St Martin's Press, New York, 1996), p. 143.
10. *Harpers* magazine review of *The Texas Chain Saw Massacre* (Tobe Hooper, 1974). Cited in Jaworzyn, S, *The Texas Chain Saw Massacre Companion* (Titan Books, London, 2003), p. 90.
11. Janius Griffin on the popularity of *Superfly* (Gordon Parks, Jr, 1972). Cited in Howard, J, *Blaxploitation Cinema: The Essential Reference Guide* (FAB Press, London, 2008) p. 12.
12. Comment from the judge at the trial of Bob Sumner, who was found guilty of breaching New York City obscenity laws for screening *Deep Throat* (Gerard Damianio, 1972) at the World Theatre. Cited in Muller, E and Faris, D, *Grindhouse: The Forbidden World of 'Adults Only' Cinema* (St Martin's Press, New York, 1996), p. 143.
13. Douglas, M, *Implicit Meanings* (Routledge, New York, 2002), p. 261.
14. Bordwell, D, *Poetics of Cinema* (Routledge, New York, 2007), p. 1.
15. Szulkin, D, The Last House on the Left: *The Making of a Cult Classic* (FAB Press, London, 1997), p. 128.
16. For instance, Sconce mentions that 'Ed Wood, Jr's status has long been high in the paracinematic community'. How this can be ascertained when Sconce had just invented the word 'paracinema' is confusing. Indeed, Wood's work is better defined as belonging to the B-movie trend of the 1950s. As I will discuss. Cited in Sconce, J, '"Trashing" the Academy: Taste, Excess and an Emerging Politics of

Cinematic Style'. In Mathijs, E and Mendik, X (eds) *The Cult Film Reader* (Open University Press, London, 2007), p. 114.

17. B-films during the 1930s and 1940s were predominantly westerns – as documented by Reid, J, *Hollywood 'B' Movies: A Treasury of Spills, Chills & Thrills* (LuLu Press, Morrisville, 2005). In addition, Staiger affirms how the term 'western' was considered 'derogatory' in 1939, when *Stagecoach* was released, because it had become synonymous with cheaper product. Cited in Staiger, J, 'Hybrid or Inbred'. In Grant, B (ed.) *Film Genre Reader III* (University of Texas Press, Austin, 2004), p. 193.

18. Bordwell, D, Staiger, J and Thompson, K, *The Classical Hollywood Cinema* (Routledge, London, 1991 [1985]), p. 10.

19. Lisanti uses the B-movie label to include studio films that were not released on the bottom half of a double-bill or produced for this purpose. Examples include *The Lost World* (Irwin Allen, 1960) and *Come Spy with Me* (Marshall Stone, 1967). Lisanti, T, *Drive-in Dream Girls: A Galaxy of B-movie Starlets of the Sixties* (McFarland Publishing, Jefferson, 2003). Betrock, meanwhile, defines *The Fast and the Furious* (Roger Corman, 1964) as representative of 'real B-movies . . . inferior to A-list productions'. Betrock, A, *The I Was a Teenage Juvenile Delinquent Rock'N'Roll Horror Beach Party Movie Book: A Complete Guide to the Teen Exploitation Film, 1954–1969* (St Martin's Press, London, 1986), p. 23.

20. Bazin, A, *What Is Cinema? Vol 2* (University of California Press, Los Angeles, 2005 [1971]), p. 153.

21. Jancovich, M, *Rational Fears: American Horror in the 1950s* (Manchester University Press, Manchester, 1996), p. 84.

22. Ibid., p. 198.

23. Schaefer, E., *'Bold! Daring! Shocking! True!' A History of Exploitation Films, 1919–1959* (Duke University Press, Durham, NC and London, 1999), p. 50.

24. 'For exploitation filmmakers *The Curse of Frankenstein* (Terence Fisher 1957) was a blessing. Produced in 1956 by Britain's Hammer Films and released stateside by Warner Brother in July 1957, the stylish $270,000 horror show earned domestic grosses of nearly $2 million by the end of the year. In the process *The Curse of Frankenstein* fathered the most prolific and durable of all 50's exploitation cycles – the horror teenpic.' Cited in Doherty, T., *Teenagers and Teenpics: The Juvenilization of American Movies in the 1950's* (Temple University Press, Philadelphia, 2002), p. 142

25. Romer, J, 'A Bloody New Wave in the United States'. In Silver, A and Ursini, J (eds) *The Horror Film Reader* (Limelight Editions, New York, 2004), pp. 63–6.

26. See: BBFC information on *Blood Feast*, http://bbfc.co.uk/search/releases/blood%2Bfeast, last accessed 7 July 2016.

27. In speaking about *The Immoral Mr Teas*, authors Muller and Faris confirm that what the film did differently was to showcase female nudity without pretending 'to be educational' or to 'expose nudity as an alternative lifestyle. It was *about* naked women. And it was about *looking* at naked women.' Cited in Muller, E and Faris, D, *Grindhouse: The Forbidden World of 'Adults Only' Cinema* (St Martin's Press, New York, 1996), p. 82; emphasis in the original.

28. Bordwell, D, Staiger, J and Thompson, K, *The Classical Hollywood Cinema* (Routledge, London, 1991 [1985]), p. 705.

29. Newman, K, *Nightmare Movies* (Bloomsbury, London, 1988), p. 1.

30. Robb, B, *Screams and Nightmares: The Films of Wes Craven* (Overlook Press, New York, 2000).

31. McDonough, J, *Big Bosoms and Square Jaws* (Vintage, New York, 2006).

32. American home video label Distribpix, for instance, has grouped together many of

Metzger's films in a five-disc collection – presenting him as an auteur of adult cinema even though he refused to put his real name on the productions, instead helming the films under the pseudonym Henry Paris (see: http://www.distribpix.com/film/henry-paris-collection-5-pack-collectors-box-set/hpc-5-pack-box-set-dvd).

33. Cited in Sconce, J, '"Trashing" the Academy: Taste, Excess and an Emerging Politics of Cinematic Style'. In Mathijs, E and Mendik, X (eds) *The Cult Film Reader* (Open University Press, London, 2007), p. 107.

34. Kerner, A, *Torture Porn in the Wake of 9/11: Horror, Exploitation, and the Cinema of Sensation* (Rutgers University Press, New Brunswick, NJ, 2015), p. 60.

35. That is, *Sweet Sweetback's Baadasssss Song* (Melvin Van Peebles, 1971) and *Super Fly* (Gordon Parks, 1972).

36. Allen, R, and Gomery, D, *Film History: Theory and Practice* (McGraw-Hill, New York, 1985), p. 86.

37. Cumbrow, R, 'After Sunset' (15 August 2011), http://parallax-view.org/2011/08/15/after-sunset/, last accessed 20 August 2017.

38. *The Texas Chain Saw Massacre* was the consequence of a small crew of Austin film school graduates. Cited in Jaworzyn, S, *The Texas Chain Saw Massacre Companion* (Titan Books, London, 2003), p. 33.

39. Lewis, J, *Hollywood v. Hardcore* (New York University Press, New York and London, 2000), p. 211.

40. Maltby, R, and Craven, I, *Hollywood Cinema* (Blackwell, Oxford, 1995), p. 40.

41. Ward, G, 'Grinding out the Grind House: Exploitation, Myth and Memory'. In Fisher, A and Walker, J (eds), *Grindhouse (Global Exploitation Cinemas)* (Bloomsbury Academic, London, 2016), p. 16.

42. Bordwell, D and Thompson, J, *Film History: An Introduction* (McGraw-Hill, New York, 1994), p. 110.

43. Ibid., pp 415–23.

44. Cardullo, B, 'What is Neorealism?' In Bazin, A and Cardullo, B (eds), *André Bazin and Neorealism* (Continuum, New York, 2011), p. 28.

45. Kracauer, S, *From Caligari to Hitler* (Princeton University Press, Princeton, 1974 [1947]), p. 45.

46. Briggs, J, *Profoundly Disturbing* (Plexus Publishing, London, 2003), p. 140.

47. Williams, L, *Screening Sex* (Duke University Press, Durham, NC, 2008), p. 125.

48. Morthland, J, 'Porno Films: An In-Depth Report', *Take One* magazine (vol. 4. 4, March–April 1973), p. 14.

49. Review of *The Devil in Miss Jones*. In *Variety* magazine (21 February 1973, Variety Media, California), p. 34.

50. See Wood, R, *From Vietnam to Reagan* (Columbia University Press, New York, 1986), p. 91.

51. Robinson, C., 'Blaxploitation and the Misrepresentation of Liberation', *Race & Class* (vol. 40 1, 1998) – http://journals.sagepub.com/doi/pdf/10.1177/030639689 804000101, last accessed 8 August 2017, p. 101.

52. Dunn, S, *Baad Bitches and Sassy Supermamas: Black Power Action Films* (University of Illinois Press, Chicago, 2008), p. 84.

53. West, C, *Race Matters* (Vintage Books, New York, 2001 [1993]), p. 120.

2. EMERGING FROM ANOTHER ERA – NARRATIVE AND STYLE IN MODERN EXPLOITATION CINEMA

In this chapter I will discuss the narrative tropes that make exploitation cinema unique during the time period of this book. In doing so, my intention is to discuss the similarities, which have escaped previous discussion of the subject, that exist between the exploitation trend before 1959, in which censorship laws in the United States were dictated by the strict regulation of the Hays Code, and after this period in which the legislation that limited the portrayal of screen sex and violence began to fade. Weiner mentions, 'The early pioneers of exploitation cinema are really the fathers of the modern independent film. These filmmakers were out to "make a buck," and most could not have cared less whether their films were technically or artistically good.'[1] If there is one major difference between exploitation in the classical era and the contemporary period it is that the films begin to show more craftsmanship – something I will further highlight in this chapter. Consequently, exploitation cinema began to be treated a little more seriously by some American critics. It may even be this stylistic element that confuses discussion of exploitation cinema between the pre- and post-censorship periods in America and leads to an assumption that the later films should be classified as an imagined 'grindhouse' or trashy 'paracinematic' entity: halfway between Hollywood familiarity and grungy low-brow generic grime. As I will discuss, the modern exploitation film actually has a far closer lineage to the classical form than its more accomplished style may indicate.

Much like the classical examples, contemporary exploitation cinema was *dependent* on its own epoch, rather than *revelatory* of such – these are films that sell a sense of modern scandal. A classical exploitation text on, for instance, venereal disease was not really a serious and well-meaning investigation into the subject matter. It was instead asking audiences to pay money to see something that may be shocking. In the classical form there is a sense of 'scandal', usually reserved for private discourse (that is, teen pregnancy/marijuana use) that was now liberated by the screen. Or, as Weiner mentions, 'the hallmark of early exploitation films was not necessarily what the films actually showed on screen, but what the audience "might" see if they paid for a ticket.'[2] Hence, just as no one was really going to learn anything about the intricacies of sexually transmitted diseases from a classical exploitation film, or even obtain a morally astute 'lesson' on contraception, the modern examples of the movement are equally contingent on the topicality of what is being transgressed – more so even than crafting a technically proficient sense of spectacle. Discussing this factor further will involve provoking a number of different arguments – related to threads that link the classic and post-classical exploitation cinema together. Generic facets such as the exploitation of African-American dominance, graphic sex and violent corporeality (presented for voyeuristic purpose but frequently deglamorised) are 'sold' with the promise of an aesthetically explicit honesty that is visually – and also thematically – oppositional to the Hollywood alternative. In this sense, the classic and post-classic exploitation film has a great deal in common – a counterculture style that is deliberately subversive.

I should stress that I do not mean 'counterculture' in the sense that Church who, drawing on the work of Sarah Thornton, criticises:

> Supposed distinctions between subcultures and the nebulously imagined 'mainstream' that they define themselves against routinely blur. Even if the shape of a given subculture does not conform to its ideal self-image as an 'underground' cultural formation, certain hip ideologies and competencies (subcultural capital) remain relevant to the policing of imagined subcultural boundaries. This even occurs at the risk of reproducing wider social inequalities (such as gender-based exclusions) that uphold dominant ideological values.[3]

The contemporary fan conception of exploitation cinema as counterculture, borne from books such as Stephen Thrower's *Nightmare USA* (FAB Press, London, 2008) obligates a sense of misguided auteurism – of 'brave' young men and women opposing authority and the rules of censorship in order to realise their masterpiece of skid-row grime that *just so happened* to carry some sort of profound message. In looking at the softcore work of Radley Metzger, for instance, Elena Gorfinkel enthuses about movies that took an 'oppositional stance towards Hollywood' to present some kind of radical sexual treatise.[4]

Nevertheless, despite such perceived stylistic protest the 'oppositional' style of the movement still remained within linear narratives – and Metzger became increasingly reliant on the use of montage in his sex films. The style, in other words, was not as revelatory insofar as subverting Hollywood storytelling as, say, the French avant-garde movement of the 1950s. Furthermore, the idea of some Marxist 'hip' formation of angry filmmakers, deliberately aiming their work at a 42nd Street audience, is difficult to accept: the block itself was just as likely to play major studio movies as 'second-run' features.[5] Furthermore, exploitation films were made prior to any identifiable fan culture that deliberately focused on, and celebrated, B-movie celebrities such as the late Herschell Gordon Lewis – as such, the name value for these texts was in what they sold, not who they were made by. The 'make a fast buck' mentality, then, never disappeared. A filmmaker, such as Lewis, remained producing clandestine and cheap genre fare for the entirety of his career, desperately attempting to 'hit' on something that would keep audiences in the theatres.

Furthermore, some exploitation filmmakers were keen to embrace the mainstream studio system when the chance to work in the system was proposed – that is, Russ Meyer and his *Beyond the Valley of the Dolls* (1970) or Wes Craven and *Swamp Thing* (1982). Both, however, altered the style of their work to appeal to the more lavish expectancies of a bigger audience. On the contrary, the counterculture of exploitation cinema came, quite simply, from an economy of transgression – any message within exploitation films was secondary to selling an audience on paying to see something that would be

Figure 2.1 *The Last House on the Left*: Wes Craven's film shocked viewers in 1972. (Produced by Sean S. Cunningham)

regarded as subversive/scandalous/shocking. Given that a group style emerged from this fiercely commercial activity (and remember that many independent directors were making similar types of films across America) the key films of this book are fascinatingly *of their time*.

NARRATIVE TENDENCIES

Exploitation filmmakers present a narrative of *threat*: specifically, violent or sexual, every small beat concludes with a larger beat of physicality – explicit, often sudden, but nonetheless conclusive. The plot and story are consequently devised around the build-up, and satisfaction, of various set pieces of grand-standing corporeality. Unlike studio narratives, the key exploitation films feature open-endings: conclusions are left without finalisation. The classic three-act structure (or 'restorative three act form'[6]) is either subverted or disregarded entirely – for instance, *The Last House on the Left* has a two-act structure and an open-ended conclusion, ambivalent characters and a clear screenwriter's voice. The anti-violence message of the film, exploited by grue-some horror, takes precedent over the characters on-screen – and, of course, we witness every gruelling detail of the Manson-murder-style horror. In contrast, *Night of the Living Dead* has a one-act structure – as does *Sweet Sweetback* and *Super Fly*.

Schaefer argues that exploitation cinema initially 'came about as the result of restrictions imposed by Hollywood'.[7] To give an example: *No Greater Sin* (William Nigh, 1941) is described by Schaefer as 'a paradigmatic venereal disease tract' in which a 'health commissioner, high school teacher and news-paper man . . . must counter community ignorance' and do so by screening to the locals (and of course the audience) footage of genitals ravaged by sexually transmitted infections.[8] To bypass the censorial dichotomy that existed between educational and exploitation films, *No Greater Sin* presented itself as provid-ing a positive social function while also delivering commercial spectacle.[9] It, as with the bulk of early exploitation films, 'was framed by often-questionable didactic messages meant to prevent the sensational acts depicted'.[10] As censor-ship laws began to fall in the United States, the exploitation film promoted its sensational content within a more traditional Hollywood narrative: slow-building tension, a clear point of view from one protagonist, sequences linked together by a forward moving storyline. Whereas early exploitation films sold themselves on what the audience 'may' see inside the darkened cinema, after 1960 various productions began to explicitly reveal what had only been hinted at. The narrative, therefore, became based around anticipating a repeated sense of spectacle. Hollywood frequently *repressed* what was *expressed* in exploitation cinema – because the subject matters were simply not suitable for mainstream actors and filmmakers. The classic exploitation film existed on the margins of the mainstream and had to offer something oppositional to the studio genre films in order to maintain audience curiosity and financial stability. Exploitation films had to make money, in quick turnaround, based on a spectacle that was immediate, shocking and commercially exciting – something people would speak about. Three interrelated elements bind the narrative of all demarcations within the key exploitation films: 1) the use of shock as spectacle, 2) corporeal indiscretion as narration motivation and 3) the relationship between topicality and taboo.

The Exploitation Spectacle

Schaefer states of the classical exploitation form that moments of spectacle 'bring the narrative to a halt and are geared solely to fascinate the spectator with what, by Hollywood standards, was the forbidden thrill'.[11] The classical exploitation film is also bound by limitations: devised *around* the showcase of salacity but, due to censorship regulations, unable to forthrightly present the very sensationalism being 'sold'. In contrast, Melvin Van Peebles was able to launch the entire blaxploitation boom with his influential *Sweet Sweetback's Baadasssss Song* (1971) by threatening 'lawsuits against Jack Valenti and the MPAA' and using their horrified 'reaction [to the film] for his own ends'.[12] In other words, the counterculture nature of exploitation – after the fall of the ratings system in America (at least as a legal requirement) – was to create commerce out of controversy, much like its classical predecessor. The thrill was no longer 'forbidden' – but taboo could be argued, publicly, as a necessity to fight against what the mainstream represented: stuffiness, repression, sexual and racial hang-ups. Those who supported exploitation cinema such as *Sweet Sweetback* – obviously by buying a ticket – were sold on an image of rebellion that, ultimately, played into the hands (and pockets) of the film's director. The concept of the grindhouse, perhaps, has more to do with the idea that one was making a dangerous decision by walking into the theatre showing a film such as *Deep Throat* or *Sweet Sweetback*. This factor, in turn, allows the films to offer the viewer some form of identity politics (even in retrospect) – however unintentional this may be.

In the classical form, characters frequently enter surgeries to be 'educated' via explicit documentation (an insert of real medical footage) and/or females inhabit lengthy, static camera time to undress for their lover or doctor. The childbirth sequence in *Mom and Dad* (William Beaudine, 1947) takes its 'educational' plot about the 'perils' of premarital sex and merges it with the reality of the forbidden: there is no doubting the validity of what we are seeing. Even when framed within a fictitious story, the authenticity of the stock footage conflicts with the studio-reality that the same era's Hollywood films normalised. Interestingly, this documentary-realism would inspire some later exploitation carny, too. As noted by author Joel Black,[13] the emergence of the Manson Family as legitimate pop-culture figures – and the rumours surrounding their supposed 'snuff' videos of real murder – resulted in a push among independent filmmakers to create faux-reality death movies or to voyeuristically offer a news-style distance from recreated scenes of murder. *The Last House on the Left* would probably never have existed without an understanding of the ghoulish public interest in the details of the Manson crimes, nor the image of the corrupt, murderous, desert-dwelling family in *The Texas Chain Saw Massacre*. In the interim, sexploitation-makers began to offer the sight of genuine penetration, and bodily fluids, while blaxploitation cinema developed shaky-cam realism: mimicking news footage of race-riots and the deliberate abjection of black bodies. In *Sweet Sweetback* one rotund character speaks to the leading man while defecating – communicating an idea of brotherhood between its on-screen African Americans that knows no boundaries of privacy. Again, the scriptwriter's *voice* becomes the foreground in this example of intrusive, documentary-style 'realism'. Unable to be quite as forthright, most of the pre-1960 exploitation productions existed on the margins. These films were based upon the promise of *alternative* thrills but these were thrills that finally concluded the narrative: 'During the childbirth footage, the unwavering camera focuses on the pudenda of a woman, legs splayed in stirrups, giving birth to a baby boy.'[14] When no such stock footage is inserted into the narrative, the classical form fulfils the promise of scandal in other ways: the 'reveal' of scantily clad bodies for inspection in *Escort Girls* (Edward E. Kaye, 1941) or a striptease in *Test Tube Babies* (W. Merle Connell, 1948). Audiences would have to sit through an hour of boring pseudo-documentary morality plays before the 'reveal' provided them with the scandalous image that they were hoping for. Attaching any personal identity to such films was understandably difficult – hence my earlier point about the romanticism of visiting an old grindhouse to see trailblazing exploitation cinema of the modern era.

While Schaefer associates the exploitation-spectacle with 'crumbling continuity' it is also the surprise of some sort of taboo that distracts from the compositional motivation of the narrative.[15] This 'forbidden' element is always allied to factors of social reality that are hidden from public display – *childbirth*, *genitalia*, *sexual disease* and (implied) *intercourse*. The taboo comes from the graphic presentation of issues that were rarely dealt with, and certainly not explicitly visualised, by Hollywood. For example, the frivolous use of stock footage was not typically integrated into a big studio production. It is this documented 'reality' that separates many classical exploitation texts from their mainstream 'other'. In the modern exploitation film, the graphic presentation remains – but it complements the narrative and characters and allows for a more standardised storytelling. Even in the often-ignored hardcore sex films, which I begin to tackle in my next chapter, the characters are defined by their relationship to a repeated sense of spectacle – it would not be enough to 'just' offer a solitary 'real' sex act at the end of the film.

Schaefer's definition of spectacle is something that 'exerts an immediate, effective response in the spectator: loathing or lust, anxiety or amazement'[16] but the author also acknowledges that its function (present too in Hollywood cinema) is to showcase the elaborate. Whereas the classical form either teased (but failed to deliver) sex and/or violence or provided stock footage to satisfy the spectators – the post-classical exploitation film initiates and defines its own genres based on the shock of unhiding the previously hidden. Exploitation cinema during the classical era walked a fine line between body-horror and (intended) titillation – but in the post-classical form we begin to see the realisation of something different. As the movement progresses into the 1970s violence and sex became more interlinked in all exploitation demarcations – such as the graphic, prolonged rape of *The Last House on the Left* or the kidnapping and subsequent sexual acts enforced on the Gloria character (Marilyn Chambers) in *Behind the Green Door*. The narratives feel unsafe because, even in some hardcore films, sex becomes layered with threat. Kleinhans talks of exploitation cinema 'adopting whatever ethical and moral stance it has simply to exploit its subject matter'.[17] While this argument is not entirely incorrect, there is a clear attempt to provide an audience with discomfort in the post-classical exploitation movement – even in sex films, which are frequently as race-exploitative as blaxploitation (that is, *Vixen* and *Behind the Green Door*) or as disturbing as horror texts (that is, *The Devil in Miss Jones*). As a consequence, the 'ethical and moral' stance of the narrative is often in confrontation with the spectacle itself and the evolution of the three exploitation demarcations are frequently interlinked. If the classical films would tease audiences with the promise of an eventual salacious 'reveal' then modern exploitation cinema perhaps shows us too much. The spectacle, by its very prominence in the narrative, including as a function to drive character causality forward, often becomes contradictory to any inherent sense of moralising. For instance, the outright exploitation (inevitably) of women as sex objects may seem sleazy – and not in any ironic sense of the word. However, one could argue that by making this objectification more apparent, even more honest (and thus less symbolic), the inherent voyeurism associated with watching 'exploitative' sex and violence is compromised. The spectator, in other words, is engaging with an expectancy of sexual objectification and/or violent transgression when they pay to see these films. Any such associated sexism or misogyny, then, cannot be accused of creeping into the audience's perspective without the viewer as a willing participant in the act of watching and enjoying. Of course, this is not to say that a discussion on the narrative representations of exploitation cinema should not acknowledge how certain characterisations and situations are subverted. Instead, it is to maintain that these films choose not to hide the objectifications that they present: in exploitation cinema everything is clear and present.

The connection between spectacle and shock in the post-classical exploitation film is further interposed by physical perversity: a 'violation' of humanity, either sexually or otherwise. The spectacle of the body in these films is posited and staged without the social or educational baggage that was once essential in avoiding legal difficulties. This also leads to a certain narrative ambiguity, which is perhaps why many exploitation productions have split academic and critical arguments – allied with both progression and revulsion. The relationship between subjectivity and objectivity/cause and effect/good and bad in exploitation texts is far less obvious than in Hollywood cinema. Sexploitation films, such as *Lorna* and *The Devil in Miss Jones*, may exploit nudity and intercourse, but both films conclude their narratives with a focus on punishment for promiscuity (which connects them to the classical exploitation narrative and its after-the-fact moralising). The explicitness of the sex act may, on the surface, place sexploitation films as oppositional to cultural conservative attitudes but the narratives of the key films are frequently posited upon some form of physical invasion and refute. While the objectification of female bodies may be clear, the conclusions of the narratives are frequently without commentary on the ethical complexities of their own commercialisations. Whether in the classical era or the period discussed by this book, it is not too outlandish to maintain that all of the key American sexploitation texts possess a notable conservative slant.

Themes of the Flesh

The nudity of the first post-classical sexploitation film, *The Immoral Mr. Teas*, would be superseded by simulated coitus in *Lorna* and the logical conclusion of the real act in *Deep Throat*. In each film the storyline comes to a standstill so that visual gratuity can be exhibited to the paying customer – indicating a stylistic bond with *No Greater Sin* et al from the classical era discussed by Schaefer. Williams argues that what became known as the 'money shot' (the conclusion of unsimulated sex with visual evidence of the male orgasm) represents a commodity-fetishism that exists within a Freudian/Marxist dichotomy with the customer paying for an (un)reality that they can never actually own (that is, partake in).[18] I will touch on, and build upon, Williams' work more thoroughly in my next chapter on the sexploitation genre, and its eventual evolution into graphic intercourse, but her analogy of the 'money shot' – or rather what it *represents* – is not something that should necessarily be relegated to just sex films. Hired performers engaging in actual copulation lends weight to Williams' Marxist evaluation of the (literal) exchange – *or invasion* – of body for capital but if taken allegorically ejaculation is replaced by grotesque atrocities (the 'money shot' of bloody violence) in the exploitation-horror film. In both instances, it is the release of bodily fluid that represents the climax of the on-screen spectacle and permits the story and plot to continue. Additionally, the physical superiority of blaxploitation heroes and heroines presents narratives based around the supremacy of violent and sexually dominant personalities and the body-beautiful. The 'money shot' here is also the commodification of the physical: the African American who is defined by his heterosexual prowess in *Sweet Sweetback* and the allure of viewing his muscular torso engaged in intercourse or being bruised and beaten. The exploitation film narrative often homogenises the violation of the body as an instrument of capital. Characters exploit their own, or take and use the bodies of others, and the visualisation of this excess is manifested and sold back to the paying audience. While the 'money shot' has become accepted terminology for the sight of the male orgasm, its innate *function* (rather than representation) – that is to satisfy audience sexual curiosity, and conclude the stylistic debauchery, is analogous to the moments of graphic death/rape/sexual prowess and violent vigilantism that act as the saleable facets within *all* exploitation genres. Each is linked by some form of physical perversion. Upon the arrival of the financially essential 'spectacle' narrative becomes secondary to depiction in exploitation cinema. Without the strict enforcement of a censorship 'can' and 'can't', such as the Hay's Code, exploitation productions could be increasingly more liberal in their approach to 'taboo' aesthetics.

Where the classical exploitation film always reassured audiences about its use of salacious footage – usually via some supposed 'educational' value – its successor exhibited shock without the need for explicit moralising. The result is narrative disorientation. Given that each generic demarcation is not bound by Hollywood decency, the aesthetics of exploitation productions become difficult to predict – the 'excessively obvious cinema' of the studios is replaced by films bound to a formula of one-upmanship. Each taboo is superseded by a new transgression: simulated intercourse in *Lorna* is superseded by acts of incest, lesbianism and dominance in *Vixen*. Unsimulated vaginal sex in *Behind the Green Door* is replaced by anal sex in *The Devil in Miss Jones* and then female-on-male penetration in *The Opening of Misty Beethoven*. This is the most notable disunity between the function of spectacle in classical and post-classical exploitation cinema. With this said, the idea of placing the exploitation narrative within a confine of some form of moralising or actuality continues from the classical era into the 1960s and even 1970s.

The Square Up

Schaefer identifies 'the square up' as a narrative function of the classical exploitation film that exists to reassure the audience that what they are about to see has been produced in order to combat some sort of social evil (that is, teenage pregnancy/sexual promiscuity/drug abuse). 'Beyond operating as an apology or an excuse, the square up ... warned audiences that they were going to see something different ... In most instances, the square-up made claims to authenticity.'[19] Although Schaefer identifies 'the square up' as a uniquely classical function, as with most generic traits it adapted and evolved rather than disappearing completely. Without a Production Code to honour, the square up no longer needed to appeal to fantasies of conservatism or education in order to 'fool' relevant legal avenues. However, retaining 'claims to authenticity' remained common in exploitation films: a voiceover that leads the viewer to believe that what they are going to see is based upon real events introduces *The Texas Chain Saw Massacre*. This further intensifies the element of the macabre.[20] Presenting a manipulated version of 'reality' by assuring the viewer that what they are seeing is an unbiased reflection of actual events is embraced by later horror cinema because the 'true story' angle obviously leant a macabre backdrop to the unreeling fiction. It did not matter that *The Last House on the Left* or *The Texas Chain Saw Massacre* were clearly, *surely undeniably*, works of fiction with editing, actors, soundtrack and so forth, they were still claiming to be based on the outside world (hence: topical). For some viewers, able to immerse themselves in the shaky-cam reality of these films, they were 'unsettlingly believable ... the vérité film style and familiar cast lent an authentic feel to the story'.[21]

The square up would also retain itself via a similar spoken or written 'preparation' – albeit one that served to disorientate the audience. *Sweet Sweetback's Baadasssss Song* has an opening scroll that dictates: 'Dedicated to all the Brothers and Sisters who had enough of the Man' – immediately isolating itself from previous forms of cinema that approached race-relations from a more (at least in aspiration) utopian standpoint. The 'square up', in this instance, also indicates the topicality that exploitation cinema consistently draws upon – 'the man' is obviously referring to white authority making it clear that the film's point of view is from an African-American perspective. Given how rare this perspective was at the time, *Sweet Sweetback* is able to initiate itself as edgy/vital/unique thanks to its adaptation of the square up.

In comparison, the studio film *Guess Who's Coming to Dinner* (Stanley Kramer, 1967), although focused on a mixed-race relationship, plays down any sexual aspect of the partnership – possibly to appeal to mainstream sensitivity. As such, the character played by Sidney Poitier in the film – a well-spoken, well-educated physician – is considered 'acceptable' because he is not presented as a *threat* to white authority. By the climax of the film, Poitier has segregated himself into the same society that initially questioned his suitability for interracial marriage (Poitier's character even refuses to go through with the wedding unless *he* gains the respect of his white fiancée's parents). This presented 'utopia' – that black characters 'do good' by achieving respect within 'white' society – is subverted in *Sweetback*. Poitier, playing a doctor with all the charm and professionalism in the world, is presented as 'an eminently qualified and desirable suitor' for a young Caucasian girl.[22] In comparison, Van Peebles' Sweetback character is a gigolo; hypersexual, promiscuous, confrontational, violent ... The 'square up' in *Sweetback* informs the audience that the film they are about to see is far removed from the more mainstream treatment of race-relations ala *Guess Who's Coming to Dinner*. Indeed, if the final 'reveal' in *Guess Who's Coming to Dinner* is a mere kiss between black and white characters, then stylistically we can see how oppositional exploitation cinema is to its Hollywood counterpart. Mid-way in *Sweetback*, Van Peebles mounts a white woman as a group of onlookers, also white, gaze in amazement at his sexual prowess. The film's most taboo 'reveal' does not even have to wait for the end credits.

Sexploitation, the demarcation evolved from the censorious confines of the classical form that dictated 'the square up', found less use for its conventions as unsimulated sex became the norm but it could still be evidenced. *Deep Throat* begins with an opening scroll that references Freud. With the laws surrounding the depiction of unsimulated intercourse vague, the film demonstrates a connection with pre-1960 exploitation cinema by channelling the language of civic responsibility that the form once specialised in. The director of *Deep Throat*, perhaps aware of the shaky new ground that the depiction of actual sex was trailblazing, would even harken back to the 'square up' in interviews

Figure 2.2   *The Opening of Misty Beethoven*: the adult film industry reached a peak with Radley Metzger's film. (Produced by Ava Leighton)

by arguing that his production was a social necessity: benefiting the sex lives of Americans.[23] In this quote, the 'carny' marketing of the classical form is clearly still present.

Certainly, while the square up may have lost its dominance in the post-classical form of exploitation cinema its ulterior function as narrative displacement, and even as municipal reassurance, would still be drawn upon. In *Behind the Green Door* (The Mitchell Brothers, 1972), for instance, 'the square up' returns in the form of a (filmed) prologue and epilogue that places the narrative within the realms of the fantastical. 'I want to hear that story about a green door you guys have been promising me' asks a chef of two customers in a diner. The square up is to excuse the dubious storyline misogyny (in which a beautiful virgin is kidnapped and subjected to a night of sexual awakening) by confining it within the imagination of a solitary male. At the conclusion of the film it is evident that the narrative has taken place within the storyteller's imagination. Without having to boast questionable claims of academia, the square up function, in the post-classical exploitation film, was to initiate both audience confusion and disorientation: to forewarn of a cinema commercially reliant upon presenting ever greater spectacles of visual taboo. The post-classical square up is therefore foreboding – '*this* is going to be something different' – which, for the key films of this book, initiated an evolving group style that presents a reality of narrative and place aligned to a believable mimesis of the documentary aesthetic.

Topicality

As with the perversion of physicality, topicality is an urgent commodity for the exploitation narrative. The channelling of topicality in exploitation is as transgressive as it is political – providing an aesthetic opposition to the tamer salacity of Hollywood. This is not to argue that exploitation movies do not draw on the topical to make socio-political and/or allegorical statements, rather it is to suggest that any such motivation is expressed within a narrative that also maintains ulterior commercial motives: shock, spectacle, physical perversion. The rapist Krug (David Hess) in *The Last House on the Left* is shown to weep at the sight of his rape victim vomiting in a nearby ditch – but the graphic molestation and torture of the girl, the *exploitable* spectacle, has already been shown to the viewer. The display of shock is complete and the narrative intention of the film, to deglamorise violence (and, topically, to question the viewer's own consumption/acceptance of this material – and of Manson/serial killer 'celebrity'), is only evidenced *after the fact* and, even then, as part of the prevailing show of horror. As the advertising for *The Last House on the Left* would question – 'can a film go too far'? The question is double-edged, acting as a lure to the prospective thrill-seeking viewer and also inviting discourse on where any imagined limits of screen brutality may lie. Either way, audiences will pay to decide upon an answer.

On the other hand, concluding a 'straight' relationship between exploitation and epoch explains little new about these texts because they arguably never hid what they were attempting to sell. To affirm that the blaxploitation narrative mediated the post-civil rights struggle that African Americans faced in escaping from urban deprivation is apparent. To connect the gradual screen leniency in nudity and intercourse with the sexual revolution of the 1960s seems similarly obvious. This 'connection' is perhaps why some of these titles have been subjected to the 'the public-psyche theory': 'basically a quick way to write a story without needing to examine film history or how the film industry works . . . society is vast and multifaceted, and it isn't hard for the critic to make any given film seem to "reflect" some aspect of it'.[24] This approach of a united social unconscious, most interestingly discussed by Kracauer in the films of the German Weimar-era, is also self-fulfilling as it allows for revisionism (that is, Kracauer's argument that the Expressionist films presented a will towards fascism via tyrannical, hypnotic figures such as Dr Caligari). Key films can be reworked to allegorise or anticipate an important social epoch, regardless of whether or not the original productions were 'exploited' within the contingent of this, or any, collectivism. This argument is not to impose 'rules' about what a film can and cannot be seen to do; rather it is to maintain that, by its very nature, exploitation was relentlessly forthright. That people paid to view this taboo imagery is not revelatory: sex and violence has been a profitable part of cinema since the form's inception.

Kracauer speaks of *The Execution of Mary Queen of Scots* (Alfred Clark, 1895): 'the executioner cuts off her head and then holds it in his uplifted hand so that no spectator can possibly avoid looking at the frightful exhibit'. He also maintains, 'Pornographic motifs also emerged at a very early date.'[25] Asking *why* may lead to some interesting conclusions but it has told us little about the style of the films in question. Yet in this topicality and desire to challenge boundaries of what may be termed 'good taste' (at least insofar as it relates to the Hollywood film) a clear visual and narrative approach begins to surface. Schaefer does not venture to make an argument for the classical form of exploitation as representing a 'movement' – most likely because the 'group style' is so divergent (pseudo-documentary films have few stylistic similarities with 'recreated' fiction or burlesque loops). As exploitation enters the 1960s, the productions begin to ascertain facets of classic Hollywood storytelling while rejecting others. The narratives in exploitation films often finalise without any rationality or 'order' restored to the story's confinement. Surprise and disorientation are central to exploitation films: real locations, non-actors, confined settings, hand-held photography and minimal casts and surroundings, along with the revelation of explicit corporeal spectacle, make these productions just as likely to engage in shock as to engage in suspense. While Hollywood cinema would also progress into new narrative trajectories after the fall of the classical era – including parallel time structures, psychological character portraits, the loss of the 'happy' ending, a challenge to the traditional three-act structure and postmodern self-awareness – the modification of the exploitation narrative does not involve any conventions of 'safety'. That is: the low-budget style of the post-classical form has such an effect on mood, setting, plot and story that disorientation is perhaps inevitable, especially to the viewer of Hollywood films in which race (and especially minority depictions of glamour and nudity) or sex and violence is either carefully choreographed or briefly indicated.

In writing about the Czech New Wave, Hames maintains that a cinematic movement evolves from defying past or present conventions through a social dictate that views concurrent practices as restrictive to expression.[26] The author acknowledges that this need not be consequential to an outspoken manifesto and can embrace 'a variety of aesthetic approaches'.[27] Exploitation undoubtedly denied the accepted aesthetic 'rules' of the mainstream Hollywood film but its own subversions and transgressions were undoubtedly inspired by a movement towards presenting a more realistic spectacle. By beginning to look more closely at the demarcations identified by this book, such spectacles will be discussed in greater detail. While exploitation cinema in the 1960s and 1970s gravitated towards a number of spectacles, the most consistent corporeal 'reveal' was that of sex and nudity. As such, a close look at the American sexploitation film and its vast (and frequently overlooked) legacy will follow in my three chapters.

NOTES

1. Weiner, R, ' The Prince of Exploitation Dwain Esper'. In Cline, J and Weiner, R (eds) *From the Arthouse to the Grindhouse: Highbrow and Lowbrow Transgression in Cinema's First Century* (Scarecrow Press, Blue Ridge Summit, 2010), p. 41.
2. Ibid., p. 42.
3. Church, D, *Grindhouse Nostalgia: Memory, Home Video and Exploitation Film Fandom* (Edinburgh University Press, Edinburgh, 2016), p. 13.
4. Gorfinkel, E, 'Radley Metzger's "Elegant Arousal": Taste, Aesthetic Distinction, and Sexploitation'. In Mendik, X and Schneider, S (eds), *Underground U.S.A. Filmmaking beyond the Hollywood Canon* (Wallflower Press, New York, 2002), p. 27.
5. Ward, G, 'Grinding out the Grind House: Exploitation, Myth and Memory'. In Fisher, A and Walker, J (eds), *Grindhouse (Global Exploitation Cinemas)* (Bloomsbury Academic, London, 2016), p. 18.
6. See: Dancyger, K and Rush, J, *Alternative Screenwriting* (Focal Press, London, 2013), pp. 31–9.
7. Schaefer, E, *'Bold! Daring! Shocking! True!' A History of Exploitation Films, 1919–1959* (Duke University Press, Durham, NC and London, 1999), p. 43.
8. Feaster, F, and Wood, B, *Forbidden Fruit: The Golden Age of Exploitation Film* (Midnight Marquee Publishing, Baltimore, 1999), pp. 29–30.
9. To bypass 'the [Hay's] Code and its enforcement . . . producers, states' righters, and

roadshowmen pointed to the educational intent of their films in an effort to lend them an air of responsibility'. Cited in Schaefer, E, *'Bold! Daring! Shocking! True!' A History of Exploitation Films, 1919–1959* (Duke University Press, Durham, NC and London., 1999), p. 327.

10. Ibid., p. 88.
11. Ibid., p. 88.
12. Chaffin-Quiray, G, 'The Underground Trio of Melvin Van Peebles'. In Mendik, X and Schneider, S, *Underground U.S.A. Filmmaking beyond the Hollywood Canon* (Wallflower Press, New York, 2002), p. 103.
13. Black, J, 'Real(ist) Horror: From Execution Videos to *Snuff* Films.' In Mendik, Xavier and Schneider, Steven Jay (eds), *Underground USA: Filmmaking Beyond the Hollywood Canon* (Wallflower Press, New York, 2002), pp. 63–75.
14. Schaefer, E, *'Bold! Daring! Shocking! True!' A History of Exploitation Films, 1919–1959* (Duke University Press, Durham, NC and London, 1999), p. 86.
15. Ibid., p. 80.
16. Ibid., p. 76.
17. Kleinhans, C, 'Porn and Documentary: Narrating the Alibi.' In Sconce, J, *Sleaze Artists* (Duke University Press, Durham, NC and London, 2007), p. 99.
18. Williams, L, *Hard Core: Power, Pleasure, and the 'Frenzy of the Visible'* (Pandora Press, London, 1990), p. 105.
19. Schaefer, E, *'Bold! Daring! Shocking! True!' A History of Exploitation Films, 1919–1959* (Duke University Press, Durham, NC and London, 1999), p. 71.
20. The theatrical poster for *The Texas Chain Saw Massacre* (Tobe Hooper, 1974) even states: '*What happened is true!*'
21. Milligan, S, *Conservative Politics, 'Porno Chic' and Snuff* (Headpress, London, 2014), p. 180.
22. Guerrero, E, *Framing Blackness: The African American Image in Film* (Temple University Press, Philadelphia, 1993), p. 78.
23. Milligan, S, *Conservative Politics, 'Porno Chic' and Snuff* (Headpress, London, 2014), p. 122.
24. Bordwell, D and Thompson, K, *Minding Movies, Observations on the Art, Craft and Business of Filmmaking* (The University of Chicago Press, Chicago, 2011), p. 151.
25. Kracauer, S, *Theory of Film: The Redemption of Physical Reality* (Princeton University Press, Princeton, 1997 [1960]), p. 57.
26. In defining the Czech New Wave, for instance, Hames maintains that 'whereas most Czechoslovakian filmmakers would almost certainly deny the existence of an intentional movement . . . they were clearly united in their rejection of the restrictions of Socialist Realism and the desire to create a more satisfying culture'. Cited in Hames, P, *The Czechoslovak New Wave* (Columbia University Press, New York, 2005), p. 3.
27. Ibid., p. 3.

3. CAN WE CALL IT SEXPLOITATION?

Unlike most other studies that discuss the 'sexploitation' era I have chosen not to separate the trend in softcore films (that is, simulated depictions of sex) from the later boom in hardcore cinema (unsimulated).[1] While I accept that the popularity and prominence of unsimulated sex films did indicate, to quote Church, 'a gradual move from excessive fantasies to permissive realities',[2] I think that the stylistic similarities between the two periods is more profound than many have asserted or discussed. Moreover, it is difficult to draw a line with the appearance of hardcore and conclude that, *just like that*, it eliminated the softcore sex film from theatres. Indeed, only a few years after the accepted trendsetting 'porno chic' classic *Deep Throat* (Gerard Damiano, 1972) audiences were flocking to see – not explicit depictions of oral and vaginal sex – but rather R-rated nudity and simulated intercourse in films such as *Porky's* (Bob Clark, 1981). In 1986 Adrian Lyne's *9½ Weeks* was the new cause célèbre despite being visually tame. As such, the rise and fall of sexploitation – at least within the exploitation movement – requires answers: why is it, for instance, that today audiences flock to *50 Shades of Grey* (Sam Taylor-Johnson, 2015) but not unsimulated sex spectacles? It was the 'excessive fantasies' that audiences ultimately warmed to rather than the hardcore realities of bodily fluids, erections and penetration. In other words: the sexploitation style – from soft to hard – faded from commercial prominence after the audience got to see *everything*. As such, the style of filmmaking that graduated sexploitation from simulations to the 'real thing' was, ultimately, unable to evolve beyond a brave new world of Hollywoodised gloss, home-video cheapness and an ever-decreasing notoriety.

A tension exists between a so-called lowbrow and highbrow approach to marginal cinema (with Arthur Knight arguing that the only difference between art and exploitation screenings is 'the demitasse of black coffee in the lobby of the snootier establishments').[3] Indeed, there is a general understanding that hardcore exists as a *different kind* of exploitation cinema – Gorfinkel, for instance, is careful to separate the softcore films of Radley Metzger from his later, more sexually explicit, work.[4] However, the style of the early hardcore films actually bears comparison to that of the concurrent blaxploitation and horror cinema that were also prominent box-office successes in the United States. The only difference in aesthetic approach, in some cases, is the presence of actual penetration. Moreover, as the verisimilitude of bodily exploitation becomes more extreme in these other genres, the spectacle also evolves in American sex movies.

As such, in this chapter I will introduce five key films that, I propose, progress and ground the sexploitation style. Beginning with *Lorna* (Russ Meyer, 1964) and concluding with *The Opening of Misty Beethoven* (Radley Metzger, 1976), this twelve-year period will be introduced as concurrent with changes in censorship and a graduation of female roles from sexual victim to sexualised predator.

Figure 3.1   *Lorna*: the late Russ Meyer was undoubtedly one of the most influential filmmakers in grounding the modern exploitation style. (Produced by Eve Meyer and Russ Meyer)

Indeed, given the role of women as the foremost spectacle in this cinema, sexploitation's display and transgression of the female body is pivotal to any discussion of these films. Interestingly, gender roles – both male and female – are frequently presented within a distinctly conservative thematic in sexploitation cinema. This factor often confounds the graphic spectacle of promiscuity that the genre exhibits and sells and arguably maintains a cycle of cinema that is far less thematically liberal than it may seem. This thematic of conservative ideas versus an obvious 'excess' may also be why aspects of the genre were more astutely merged with the higher production values, and name actors, of Hollywood studio films. When the exploitation of the body is minimised, the thematic of upholding paternalism and even patriarchy (which films as diverse as *Porky's* or *9½ Weeks* and *50 Shades of Grey* arguably do) feels far less confused because there is a return of abjection (that is, a realm of 'decency') that the hardcore production consistently and aggressively provoke. When Georgina Spelvin, in the blockbuster adult film *The Devil in Miss Jones*, pleasures herself with an enema, for example (even when the seemingly inevitable pay-off is never shown), we understand that a line has been crossed – including one of abjection. It is also a line that Hollywood can never and would never showcase: Kim Basinger can be aroused with ice cubes on her breasts in *9½ Weeks* but the idea that her character would *go further* (or that the ice cubes would be placed into orifices – either male or female) is never in question. Sexploitation films are about 'free' women doing 'dirty' things – before a resolution of monogamy or 'punishment' under male authority. In comparison, the Hollywood sex films that would follow, even Paul Verhoeven's controversial *Showgirls* (1995), allow the female protagonists to be redeemed via their own inherit 'regret' or shame: usually for having sex with the wrong man.

'UNDERGROUND ART FILMS'

In a 1973 article on the increasing popularity of sexploitation cinema, a producer is quoted as suggesting that *Behind the Green Door* (The Mitchell Brothers, 1972) and *The Devil in Miss Jones* be approached 'as underground art films'.[5] The author answers this proposal by mentioning that 'underground films are made specifically for a small, avant-garde audience, porn films go for the lowest common denominator' and, referring to *Screw* magazine's once famous rating system of the 'peter metre': 'the formula neatly excludes that half of humanity born without a peter'.[6] Even today, debate continues surrounding whether or not adult cinema may be worthy of a 'recuperative fan discourse'.[7] Part of the problem of this approach is what has been referred to as a 'defensive formation' in which fans downplay 'the potential for arousal' to try to reclaim the texts as something outside of their originally intended use.[8]

For instance, looking at sexploitation films today, both softcore and hardcore, there are problematic depictions of women and, moreover, an obvious intent at arousal through moments of molestation and 'force'. On the other hand, while the recurring narrative depiction of an insatiable female figure that journeys through numerous physical interactions and pleasures is, doubtlessly, produced for the straight male market, it is possible to argue that this portrayal also maintains the sexploitation actress as the central figure of audience identification. It is this characterisation that also initiates a conservative undercurrent with sexploitation narratives that are frequently more 'feel bad' than 'feel good'. This *feel bad* factor may be considered surprising given the obvious element of arousal surrounding the explicit display of sex and nudity. However, it makes the sexploitation canon more thematically rich than one may at first presume (or, indeed, that has been previously considered).

It is possible to suggest that the reason for this generally dark tone is because the female characters that we are assumed to identify with are shown in oppositional situations to those we, the viewer, would be presented with in Hollywood films. For the journey from virgin to insatiable to take place, each on-screen personality evolves from sexually innocent to sexually confident. The goal-orientation in the key sexploitation films is for the female performer to obtain sexual satisfaction and/or self-assurance. The audience may be expected to 'enjoy' the sex exhibition that these personalities are involved in but their representation, in narratives that objectify them as spectacle, also means that we are intimately exposed to their bodies. This factor arguably becomes most troublesome insofar as the sexploitation female is usually 'punished' or positioned to submit to some form of patriarchy. While this may well condone the argument that the sexploitation film is misogynistic the initial reception afforded to some of these releases indicates that some male viewers were conflicted with respect to the strange dichotomous reaction of (expected) arousal and downbeat outcomes. Commenting on *The Devil in Miss Jones*, its star Georgina Spelvin maintained that it was not a success insofar as its ability to 'turn on' the male spectators: 'guys came out of that film shaking their heads, saying, "I came here to jerk off; I didn't come here to think!"'[9] As the most financially successful and critically acclaimed of all the key sexploitation films,[10] *The Devil in Miss Jones* poses a dilemma. If these productions were posited to erotically excite the male audience, then what may be argued as the genre's grandest achievement succeeded critically through its ability to subvert these very expectations. Scrape further into the sexploitation era, however, and it soon becomes clear that a film such as *The Devil in Miss Jones* is not an anomaly.

As so many scholars of the form now know, for a short time sex films were a mainstream attraction. For instance, Gerard Damiano, the director of *The Devil in Miss Jones* (1973), was taken seriously enough to find himself acclaimed as the 'Samuel Goldwyn of hardcore pornography'.[11] Critics in the early 1970s even began to wonder if eventually mainstream studio directors would adapt the use of genuine intercourse into their own films.[12] That this never took place is probably attributable to the fact that the sexploitation style could only evolve so far. The necessity to 'halt' the narrative in order to exhibit actual penetration and ejaculation is difficult to assimilate into grandstanding Hollywood films in which quick editing and pacing is the rule rather than the exception.[13] Seen today, sexploitation films are slow-moving, and, as hardcore emerged, the need to showcase prolonged images of genitals (to 'prove' the existence of intercourse) hampers the forward causality of plot and story. It is this stylistic dead end that, I would argue, also resulted in the marginalisation of the sexploitation film only shortly after the collapse of censorship permitted the reveal of unsimulated sex.

On the other hand, a more, let's say, Foucaultian approach may ascertain that, without censorship laws to react *against*, the spectacle of 'hardcore' sex, and the easy availability of such material, was why the majority of the films that followed the blockbuster *The Devil in Miss Jones* failed to gain the same level of notoriety and acclaim.[14] For instance, Lewis mentions that, in 1973, a course could be taken to study the social significance of the explosion in popularity of unsimulated sex films in New York. He states, 'The Academy's confirmation of the cultural significance of porn affirmed the fact that by 1973 hard core was no longer so significant anymore.'[15] This statement also supports my point that all exploitation genres needed to remain oppositional to the mainstream in order to sustain commercial curiosity – but to remain oppositional also involves furthering the reveal of new taboo content rather than relying on repetition of past ideas.

It is also worth noting that the landmark court case, *Miller v. California*, which permitted a state-by-state ruling of 'obscenity' (that is, a film could be outlawed in Texas as 'obscene' but legal in New York), resulted in the 'theatrical exhibition of hard core . . . pretty much eliminated nationwide by the end of 1973'.[16] While *Miller v. California* permitted each US territory to decide whether or not sex films could play in local cinemas, there is evidence to suggest that Lewis's conclusion is incorrect. For instance, a post-trial article in *The New York Times*, with the headline 'Film Pornography Flourishes Despite Court Ruling', states: 'It is still possible to see blue movies and purchase graphically explicit books in virtually all major cities.'[17] Muller and Faris also mention, 'Despite early trepidation on the part of filmmakers that the Miller decision might destroy their industry, nothing could have been further from the truth.'[18] Thus, evidence that, after 1973, a sizeable audience still existed for sexploitation is highlighted by the fact that films that featured unsimulated intercourse continued to display higher production values. This aspect presumes an ambition and intention of appealing to larger audiences that many previous studies have avoided discussing. The general acceptance, per Lewis, is that *Miller v. California* resulted in hardcore becoming cheaper and nastier before finding its inevitable audience on home video where masturbation could be carried out in private and favourite sex scenes re-watched at will. An alternative conclusion could well maintain that audiences were simply no longer interested in the spectacle of real intercourse. Once it had been seen, it was almost immediately stripped of taboo.

On the other hand, my reason for concluding the sexploitation style with *The Opening of Misty Beethoven* is because it aspires to evolve the gritty and pragmatic presentation of previous sex films to an ambition of greater locations (including filming on the streets of Paris and Rome), lavish set design and costumes and numerous characters (typically the genre focuses on only one or two central protagonists). There is also a frequent use of montage – which compromises the length of its actual sex scenes. While Hollywood failed to galvanise an interest in merging hardcore with its studio films, it took a talented sexploitation-maker such as Radley Metzger to take this action for himself. This belated attempt to work the sexploitation style into a more accessible and normative Hollywood presentation failed to function commercially: *The Opening of Misty Beethoven*, while acclaimed as a classic today by many 'cult' cineastes, was not a crossover hit. Testifying to this, in 1977 *Variety* magazine decided to stop reviewing unsimulated sex films altogether. In doing so, a clear boundary was drawn between 'legitimate' Hollywood, independent films and what would become the pornographic underground (which, by the turn of the 1980s, had found its home on videotape).[19] *The Opening of Misty Beethoven* was perhaps far too ambitious – not to mention colourful and even boisterous – to fit into the type of sexploitation that had defined the genre unto that point. This conclusion may, of course, be relying on a lot of hypothetical reflection, but exploitation cinema undoubtedly had less to challenge in the post-Vietnam, post-free love and post-civil rights period: a reason – even – for the growth in anti-porn feminism. What was once used as a forum for critics (and audiences) to discuss the limits of acceptability and challenge censorship became the subject of protest for its normalisation of promiscuity and the female body as masturbatory objectification. Church affirms how even today's adult VHS industry censors some 'of its "rougher" or more "taboo" past'[20] – but this past has largely gone without any comment. As I will go on to discuss, sexploitation from the 1960s also provoked audiences with the idea of rape as an erotic proposition – and this threat became further integrated into the horror and even blaxploitation films of the 1970s. While problematic, it is impossible to ignore the fact that the most successful texts of the exploitation period frequently focused on the idea of bodily violation – even if, as in *The Opening of Misty Beethoven*, a concluding set piece sees a handsome male penetrated by a strap-on worn by the slender leading actress.

Evidence indicates that sex film directors *did* want to believe that lightning may strike again and that, once more, adult cinema could – *would* – break back into the mainstream – even as the 1970s progressed into the 1980s.[21] However, when exploitation cinema exhausts its own spectacle pushing any further aesthetic and thematic boundaries is challenging due to the expected repetition of generic spectacle. As such, while a film such as *The Opening of Misty Beethoven* could exhibit an ambition that was as admirably epic as any cinema of the time, it was – nonetheless – hampered by the inevitable display of hardcore sex that, once satiated years prior, now seemed only to appeal to male voyeurs willing to face the shame (or willing to embrace the 'taboo') of entering into an adult theatre. When this denomination became clear to adult film producers, narrative would be stripped back and the repeated and graphic *act* of sex would, eventually, define the modern porno.

NAKED AMBITION

As previously maintained, *The Immoral Mr. Teas* (Russ Meyer, 1959) is the first American film to present nudity within an identifiable narrative structure. The production also remains greatly indebted to the nudist camp travelogues and the pseudo-documentary approach of the classical exploitation period. *The Immoral Mr. Teas* is without dialogue and its flimsy story of a peeping tom spying on girls exists solely to carry the viewer from one scene of (comedic) nudity to the next. This loosely formed narrative indicates that the pragmatic presentation of screen nudity and sex (that is, featuring a plot and story grounded in any semblance of believable causality) presented challenges for filmmakers who had previously documented only episodic vignettes during the classical era. This pseudo-documentary approach, however, became what would define sexploitation due to the requirement to prove that sex – or at least some kind of physical reality – was actually happening. If, in the classical era, this meant childbirth footage or revealing genitals plagued by a sexually transmitted disease (STD) it was only inevitable that eventually censorship dictates would crumble and the real thing would be exhibited. This demand for documentary 'proof', then, is inseparable from sexploitation – and it is also the reason that the demarcation is the most stylistically influential of all the exploitation movement. From the initial agitprop approach of blaxploitation and the focus on the African-American body (including the penis) in *Sweet Sweetback*, to the much-commented upon 'documentary' style of the central exploitation horror texts, the 'it really happened' tactic of sexploitation became the most desired spectacle across the movement.

According to Winston, drawing on Grierson's famous quote of documentary as 'the creative treatment of actuality', the form itself was always beholden by a tension between 'truth' and 'evidence'. States the author: 'Clearly, documentary needed to make a strong claim on the real but at the same time Grierson did not want it to be a mechanical, automatic claim arising from nothing more than the very nature of the apparatus . . . The supposition that any "actuality" is left after "creative treatment" can now be seen as being at best naïve and at worst a mark of duplicity.'[22] This factor becomes increasingly important to the style of sexploitation films during its evolution from simulated acts to unsimulated acts. The 'truth', the 'reality', is that sex acts are becoming edgier and – eventually – actually happening, but as with documentary itself, the narrative approaches seek, in their own various ways, to try to fix a greater sense of verisimilitude to the inherent fantasy. Pornography, as with documentary, is based around showing us some kind of revelation – a 'proof' that something has happened that transforms opinion and thought – and, as such, the debate surrounding this mix of actuality and fiction has created confusion, debate and discussion. Withdrawn for eight months as a result of obscenity battles, *The Immoral Mr. Teas* indicated that any 'creative treatment of actuality' in the sex film would, like documentary, be treated with cynicism.[23] Eventually released, uncut, to America cinemas, the censorship victory of *The Immoral Mr. Teas* led to the emergence of other filmmakers who began to exploit the cinematic exhibition of sex without the tenuous justification of an educational purpose. The group style of the exploitation movement was developed during this early period of sexploitation films, building upon the success of *The Immoral Mr. Teas* and venturing into aesthetic and thematic areas that featured displays of nudity and carnal relations beyond what Hollywood was prepared to exhibit.

It is director Russ Meyer's later film *Lorna* that is indicative of the first example of a contemporary and deliberate *style* within the sexploitation form, focused between the aesthetic grandeur and psychological complexity of the foreign 'art house' and the thematic causality and generic inevitability of the classical Hollywood form. More influential than it is credited, *Lorna* draws upon the exhibition of nudity but shows evolution from *The Immoral Mr. Teas* insofar as its use of a linear narrative. In other words, there is a defined story and plot surrounding the exhibition of nudity, rather than just a loose series of comedic asides based around women undressing. For instance, *The Immoral Mr. Teas* has, outside of its credits, no identifiable beginning, middle and end – the film concerns a middle-aged man who imagines every woman he meets without clothing. Each documentary-style travelogue of exposed female flesh is played for comedic effect. In contrast, *Lorna* introduces a more sizeable cast, features a prologue to the main story and exhibits sex for reasons of character development *as well as* titillation. The film is *about* sex but there is more to the story than *just* sex – even if all sex acts are captured with a documentary-style approach: shaky-cam, intrusive long shots (including to cover-up the fact that intercourse is not really taking place) and frantic close-ups. This is important to stress because the key titles in the sexploitation pantheon follow this approach. *Lorna* also shows an artistic progression from the lurid 'peep show' perversity of *The Immoral Mr. Teas*: sombre black-and-white photography captures the solemn mood of the feature, minimal locations evoke the claustrophobia of Lorna's frustrated marriage and male sexuality is presented as either submissive or sinister. The character, 'Lorna', is introduced as dominant to her husband although secretly wishing to be domineered. This comes to pass in a rape-fantasy with an escaped convict. Although attributable as thematically misogynistic in its conclusion (Lorna is murdered for her dalliances outside of marriage – caught in a knife fight between her lover and husband), the film has a more transgressive approach towards female sexuality – insofar as it acknowledges male impotence (Laura's hapless husband) – than any comparable Hollywood releases of the time.

When this new kind of sexploitation was released into American theatres, critics were unsure of how to respond. *Variety*, for instance, referred to *The Immoral Mr. Teas* as: 'Nude comedy with touches of art appeal. Can do very well in an art house run.'[24] In contrast, *The New Leader* magazine described its director, Russ Meyer, as 'a brothel keeper with delusions of intellectual grandeur'.[25] Once more we are faced with a highbrow/lowbrow attitude towards a genre that is, at once, fiercely commercially orientated ('nude women!') and, on the other hand, still indebted to a more subversive filmmaking approach. Regardless of whether one concluded that this was 'art' or 'exploitation', the reception to Meyer's film indicated at least one thing: the form demanded an opinion and the presentation of explicit nudity or sex met with either a defence ('art') or castigation. The *style*, in other words, confounded critics – but the word-of-mouth and resulting discussion assisted in a growing commercial prominence. Had sexploitation productions been mere provocations of desire then, presumably, a less complex reaction would have sufficed. Moreover, the contemporary debates around reclaiming these films as 'art' indicate that this argument never faded.

It is worth briefly highlighting the five key films that progressed and grounded the sexploitation style – from softcore to hardcore and from grime to grandstanding ambitions of widescreen studio sets and sophisticated costumes and locations. In doing this, I do not want to fall into a defensive mechanism of, to quote Church, 'trying to take ostensibly "low" culture seriously'.[26] However, the author's assumption that this is a contemporary phenomenon[27] is incorrect – as shown by the confused reception to *The Immoral Mr. Teas*. As such, I do not want to take a highbrow/lowbrow approach to these films. Instead, by maintaining that their reception was addressed, by some, as concurrent to the mainstream cinema of the time, I instead want to argue that this period was not necessarily initiated – by either viewer or critic – as a tension between an identifiable indie-counterculture and a defined 'studio' mainstream. For some years, exploitation cinema *was* a mainstream proposition – and only by understanding this can we address the films as something *of their time* rather than, retrospectively, as entities that just so happened to deal in an 'excess' that is naturally suited to a 'low' culture.

THE KEY SEXPLOITATION FILMS

1) *Lorna*: The story concerns a beautiful newlywed who is sexually unsatisfied by her student-intellectual husband. She finds sexual satisfaction after being attacked by an escaped convict, whom she subsequently welcomes into her bedroom. Her husband discovers the affair and, as the two combat one another, Lorna is accidentally stabbed and dies. *Lorna*, the first sexploitation film to present coherent narrative causality; the stark black-and-white photography, non-studio, outdoor locations, amateur cast and synthesis of suppressed masculine violence with rape/sexuality evoke foreign art cinema.[28] Reviewing *Lorna*, the trade journal *Variety* considered the film as 'a sort of sex morality play'.[29] This astute observation anticipates the genre in its entirety and this is something I want to ascertain throughout the following chapter. Despite the obvious oppositional stance to normative censorship or taste boundaries (something that can be argued as foremost necessitated by financial concerns) the genre, as aforementioned, is frequently more conservative than its explicit corporeality may indicate. Muller and Faris discuss *Lorna* as 'the bible, wrapped in a *Playboy*'.[30] This dichotomy of liberal sexual presentation and conservative thematic is evident in all of the key sexploitation films – and, arguably, it remains within pornography today.[31] The adaptation of the 'square up' (from the classic era, here appropriated by an on-screen narrator who 'frames' the action), the promotion of nudity, alongside the eroticisation of rape (a tableau quickly disregarded by the form), designate *Lorna* as a key exploitation film.

2) *Vixen*: the first X-rated sexploitation film.
Narrative causality has matured: goal-orientation is made clear as it relates to the main character (*Vixen* aspires to increasingly more daring sexual experiences, depicted in a chronology based around the explicitness of each act), the sex spectacle is treated as a greater part of the story and advances the plot – 'how far will she/*can she* go?' The film concludes with more cohesion than *Lorna*. In the interim period Meyer had directed and produced several more films that built upon the minimalist black-and-white aesthetics of *Lorna*.[32] The use of colour in *Vixen* – and further loosening of censorship barriers – provides freedom to include more acts of sexuality, including lesbianism and an allusion to mixed-race partnership. Generic elements from

Figure 3.2   *Vixen!*: thematically conservative, this film indicated the common
juxtaposition of sexploitation – liberal depictions of nudity and sex
combined with patriarchal punishment and/or conclusions for the
depicted promiscuous women. (Produced by Russ Meyer)

other commercial cinema are introduced to the sexploitation narrative:
a black character plays a major role in the genre; horror and violence are present, socio-political allegory and the female-dominatrix.
Misogyny is still prevalent: Vixen is presented as loudmouthed and
untameable – she *'asks for it'*. Narration is present to 'open' the film
and establish its setting, once more alluding to the generic 'square up'
and its appropriation outside of the classical era. The story focuses on
a woman with an insatiable appetite, although she is disgusted by the
local presence of an African-American draft-dodger. The plot introduces a conservative discussion about the threat of communism and
the American youth's expectance to fight against the threat in Vietnam.
This social commentary is possibly included to maintain *Vixen* as a
film that may avoid any local obscenity charges (that is, a film of artistic merit) although the film's conclusion also indicates that the Vixen
character is the sole spokesperson for (perceived) American values (in
this case a clearly reflexive anti-censorship thematic). These values are
also, insofar as her character is presented, the right to live a sexually
promiscuous lifestyle without interference, economically or morally,

from the state. The film confounds its own jingoistic conclusion, however, by indicating that Vixen's lifestyle is entirely dependent on the earnings of her pilot husband. As an attempt to produce an explicit (but simulated) sex film with forthright social commentary *Vixen* is an evolution of the style seen in *Lorna* but indicates an uncertainty of how to effectively marry the spectacle with lengthy political diatribes (the film's monotonous dialogue eventually dominates over the more marketable depiction of nudity and fornication).[33]

3) *Behind the Green Door*: the first wide-release hardcore (unsimu- lated) pornographic film but the crossover from *Vixen* to *Behind the Green Door* is not fanciful. Narrative causality is weakened by the novel focus on unsimulated sex acts, but story and plot continue to be misogynistic: the main female character is not permitted dialogue to express disillusionment/enjoyment/satisfaction. The character of Gloria (Marilyn Chambers) is a female, abducted from the streets of San Francisco and introduced to a stage orgy – initially against her will – that seems to be presented as a kind of radical 'performance art' (complete with clowns and mime artists). Gloria is not permitted to speak: an answer to (and even a reflexive criticism *of*) the mouthy *Vixen* character. The audience also intermingle. A coda reveals that this 'fantasy' is all within the mind of a local businessman. The 'square up' remains present, in this case to contextualise the graphic inter- course: the film begins and ends with the author of the fantasy. The film is about a male wish-fulfilment, the possession of a female and her journey from a virgin to insatiability. The fact that the male figures in the film can never obtain a subservient idealised female in *actuality* maintains the movement of sexploitation from the sexually available beauties of *Lorna* and *Vixen* to the unobtainable 'reality' of Marilyn Chambers in *Behind the Green Door*. The genre is now self-aware as 'fantasy'.

4) *The Devil in Miss Jones*: aesthetic and thematic elements of the genre are now utilised to sustain mood/shock/suspense and surprise. The group style of the exploitation movement remains prevalent: locations are few, verisimilitude of surrounding and corporeality are central to narrative inference, performers are unknown. The spectacle of intercourse is used almost entirely for story purpose rather than eroti- cism (the actors are mature/unattractive, body hair is visualised, brief homosexuality between men is introduced, the sex acts are presented within an explicitly religious narrative that finally idealises monog- amy). The film has a middle-aged spinster commit suicide but, trapped in purgatory, she is permitted to explore her sexual fantasies before being damned to hell. Sex is presented as the hidden that becomes

unhidden: shameful, punishable *and dirty*. It feels as if the audience is being damned for enjoying the spectacle of young Playboy Playmate blonde Marilyn Chambers being ravaged for *our* pleasure in *Behind the Green Door*.

5) *The Opening of Misty Beethoven*: the conclusion of sexploitation as a movement towards an appropriation of mainstream ambition within the form's style: extravagant costumes, sets, spectacle and an increase in cast and production values are introduced. *Behind the Green Door* and *The Devil in Miss Jones* present their spectacle through a series of linked set pieces but narrative in *The Opening of Misty Beethoven* is even more superior. The sex is briefer, montage is prevalent, the plot and story are grander and aesthetically the form now aspires to comparison with its Hollywood 'other': lavish sets, expansive foreign locations, colourful costume design and extensive use of montage. Furthering this increasing breakdown between what may be considered 'mainstream' and 'lowbrow': *The Opening of Misty Beethoven* owes its plot to *My Fair Lady*: only in this instance a sexually inadequate French prostitute is taught by a bourgeois male how to satisfy an upper-class clientele. Sets have been built to mimic interiors of nightclubs and aeroplanes: brief unrealities that attempt to produce Hollywood illusions. The genre's misogyny – as well as its masculine authority and class dichotomy – is, however, finally, but only slightly, subverted (the female becomes *penetrating* rather than *penetrated*, takes charge of her former teacher and also acquires his business, albeit remaining favourable towards the concept of prostitution as sexual liberation). The tone of the film is lighter than its predecessors. This is possibly because Hollywood had capitalised on the 'seriousness' of the sexploitation form with *Last Tango in Paris* (Bernardo Bertolucci, 1972). *The Opening of Misty Beethoven* reverts back to the comic-sexuality of *The Immoral Mr. Teas* in an attempt to break from generic norms – the popularity of *The Devil in Miss Jones* led to similarly themed sex-guilt productions.[34] This tone of *The Opening of Misty Beethoven* insinuates a genre that wants to marry its spectacle with the production values of the mainstream, but subsequent sexploitation titles struggled for commercial recognition. In the year that *Variety* stopped offering coverage to the genre, they commented, in a review of *Autobiography of a Flea* (The Mitchell Brothers, 1977), 'There is usually on the hardcore circuit an inverse relationship between the level of production value and the quality of the film. The more lavish the budget, the worse the pic.'[35] In other words: the attempt to marry the high production values and ambition of the Hollywood spectacle seen in *The Last Tango in Paris* with the

unsimulated imagery and prevalent style of the sexploitation genre, evidenced by *The Opening of Misty Beethoven*, had been a failure insofar as both critical *and* commercial appeal.

Of course, the sexploitation narrative is based around both the set piece of nudity and/or graphic intercourse and the libidinous autonomy of a female who progresses from innocence to insatiability. Thematic intertextuality between films can, therefore, be illustrated through a discussion of its heroines. I will begin this discourse in my next chapter by focusing on how the sexploitation female of the 1960s (softcore) progressed into the sexploitation female of the 1970s (hardcore) and the interim influence of both foreign and Hollywood cinema. The resulting depiction will indicate a genre that adapts stylistic elements of both forms. The reason I have concluded with *The Opening of Misty Beethoven* is because it looks and plays like the last final gasp of a form hoping against hope that Hollywood may choose to pay attention (it has a story based on *My Fair Lady*). It takes what Meyer initiated and places the peeking and perversions into an aesthetic and thematic of such huge scope that it could not possibly have proved influential. As with other exploitation genres, what sold with sexploitation was the spectacle – *the sex*. And to depict that you don't need to have a cast and crew in Paris, or a dedicated set dresser, you simply need to pay two actors.

From *The Opening of Misty Beethoven* onwards, there was no further evolution of the sex film trend (unless we take into account 'gonzo').[36] Instead, as ascertained by Church, the form would – in returning to its naturally confrontational beginnings – highlight more 'illicit acts'.[37] Some of the later, better known adult films, such as Damiano's *The Story of Joanna* (1975), *Waterpower* (Shaun Costello, 1976), Metzger's *Barbara Broadcast* (1977), *Pretty Peaches* (Alex de Renzy, 1978) and *Taboo* (Kirdy Stevens, 1980), feature everything from rape, enemas, urination, squirting, BDSM, male-on-male acts and even (narrative) incest. Censored for decades after their theatrical stints, such films could only have played the grimy downtown cinemas reserved for such fare – where increasingly more grandstanding depictions of abjection and a bizarre merging of body-horror with titillation made the spectacle ever more central to the narrative. In such cases, the anticipation of even the current era of short-attention Internet porn is realised. Are *these* strange adult movies also exploitation films? In daring to show content that few were willing to engage with, and that still provoke censors to this day, they were undoubtedly challenging boundaries of accepted taste. But as a movement, sexploitation surely fatigued with the innovation of *The Devil in Miss Jones* and *The*

Opening of Misty Beethoven. These later titles are merely a spectacle of kink-play that could never and would never register with a wider population.

NOTES

1. For instance, Church acknowledges the 'shift from 1960s sexploitation to 1970s hard-core films'. Church, D, *Disposable Passions: Vintage Pornography and the Material Legacies of Adult Cinema (Global Exploitation Cinemas)* (Bloomsbury Academic, London, 2016), p. 214.
2. Ibid.
3. Quoted in Betz, M, 'Art Exploitation Underground'. In Jancovich, M, Reboll, A, Stringer, J and Willis, A, *Defining Cult Movies: The Cultural Politics of Oppositional Taste* (Manchester University Press, Manchester, 2003), p. 204.
4. Gorfinkel, E, 'Radley Metzger's "Elegant Arousal": Taste, Aesthetic Distinction, and Sexploitation'. In Mendik, X and Schneider, S, *Underground U.S.A. Filmmaking beyond the Hollywood Canon* (Wallflower Press, New York, 2002), pp. 26–39.
5. Morthland, J, 'Porno Films: An In-Depth Report', *Take One* magazine (vol. 4. 4, March–April 1973), p. 14.
6. Ibid.
7. Church, D, *Disposable Passions: Vintage Pornography and the Material Legacies of Adult Cinema* (Bloomsbury Academic, London, 2016), p. 154.
8. Ibid., p. 156.
9. Cited in McNeill, L and Osborne, J, *The Other Hollywood: An Uncensored Oral History of the Porn Film Industry* (HarperCollins, New York, 2004), p. 131.
10. See Lewis, J, *Hollywood v. Hardcore* (New York University Press, New York and London, 2000), p. 212.
11. O'Reilly, Bill, 'The Devil Behind *The Devil in Miss Jones*' (26 August 1974); originally available at http://thephoenix.com/Boston/news/107158-devil-behind-the-devil-in-miss-jones/?page=1#TOPCONTENT – page offline, referenced at: http://boingboing.net/2010/08/26/bill-oreilly-reviews.html, last accessed 20 August 2017.
12. See: Morthland, J, 'Porno Films: An In-Depth Report', *Take One* magazine (vol. 4. 4, March–April 1973), pp. 12–16.
13. Russ Meyer's major studio film *Beyond the Valley of the Dolls* (1970), for instance, traded the explicit nudity and simulated but graphic sex scenarios of *Vixen* for ambitiously staged musical numbers, lavish set design and (very) brief sexual encounters.
14. Foucault famously discusses how a 'prudish' society births 'more centres of power' for sexual discussion and display. See: Foucault, M, *The Will to Knowledge* (Penguin Books, London, 1998 [1976]), p. 49. My own argument is that as soon as unsimulated imagery was normalised (insofar as one could at least access it), the sexploitation form lost its presence as a commercial force. In other words, the 'taboo' of seeing imagery that was 'forbidden' (and unsimulated sex films such as *Deep Throat* were subjected to legal trials), once revealed and followed by numerous similar productions showing the same spectacle, made people evidently less interested.
15. Lewis, J, *Hollywood v. Hardcore* (New York University Press, New York and London, 2000), p. 269.
16. Ibid., p. 265

17. *The New York Times*, 'Film Pornography Flourishes Despite Court Ruling' (on 4 November 1973)
18. Muller, E and Faris, D, *Grindhouse: The Forbidden World of 'Adults Only' Cinema*, (St Martin's Press, New York, 1996), p. 143.
19. See McNeill, L and Osborne, J, *The Other Hollywood: An Uncensored Oral History of the Porn Film Industry* (HarperCollins, New York, 2004).
20. Church, D, *Disposable Passions: Vintage Pornography and the Material Legacies of Adult Cinema (Global Exploitation Cinemas)* (Bloomsbury Academic, London, 2016), p. 135.
21. Marilyn Chambers made a comeback in *Insatiable* (Godfrey Daniels, 1980), which features helicopter shots, locations in London and extravagant cinematography.
22. Winston, B, *Claiming the Real: The Documentary Film Revisited* (BFI Publishing, London, 1995), p. 11.
23. 'The film stayed on the shelf for eight months' until a member of the motion picture censorship board 'approved the film on the spot'. Briggs, J, *Profoundly Erotic: Sexy Movies that Changed History* (Plexus Publishing, London, 2005), p. 150.
24. Review of *The Immoral Mr. Teas*. In *Variety* magazine (27 January 1960, Variety Media, California), p. 22.
25. As quoted in Briggs, J, *Profoundly Erotic: Sexy Movies that Changed History* (Plexus Publishing, London, 2005), p. 151.
26. Church, D, *Disposable Passions: Vintage Pornography and the Material Legacies of Adult Cinema (Global Exploitation Cinemas)* (Bloomsbury Academic, London, 2016), p. 82.
27. Church mentions, with an ironic sneer, that director Radley Metzger has been redeemed as a purveyor of 'erotic art' in recent years: 'unwittingly celebrating hetero-male sexual and aesthetic tastes, on the part of both filmmaker and fans' (ibid., p. 82). I would argue that due to the 'kink' element of Metzger's work it is better understood within the exploitation movement and its desire to shock/create scandal (admittedly financially driven) than any such 'hetero-male sexual and aesthetic tastes'. Indeed, a bisexual scene within *Misty Beethoven* – which features a male being anally penetrated – is surely confrontational to the hetero-normative pornography of its era making a claim of Metzger as a champion of 'hetero-male sexual and aesthetic tastes' perplexing.
28. Especially *Contempt* (Jean Luc Godard, 1963): I explore this in more detail later in this chapter.
29. Review of *Lorna*. In *Variety* magazine (30 October 1968, Variety Media, California), p. 6.
30. Muller, E and Faris, D, *Grindhouse: The Forbidden World of 'Adults Only' Cinema* (St Martin's Press, New York, 1996), p. 100.
31. For example, sex scenes conclude with male orgasm and not female orgasm. I will move on to discuss this.
32. Such as *Faster, Pussycat! Kill! Kill!* (1965) and *Mudhoney* (1965).
33. At least one critic labelled the film's politics as 'unnecessary vitriolic' and 'poorly conceived' while praising the sex spectacle as 'far more efficiently directed than the norm in this field'. Cited in McGillivray, David, '*Vixen* Review', *Monthly Film Bulletin* (vol. 4. 568, May 1981), p. 98.
34. Gerard Damiano would later direct the similarly maudlin *Memories within Miss Aggie* (1974) and the sadomasochistic themed *Story of Joanna* (1975), which ends with the male antagonist committing suicide.
35. Review of *Autobiography of a Flea*. In *Variety* magazine (9 February 1977, Variety Media, California), p. 11.
36. The 'found footage' style of adult cinema where an 'amateur' performer is picked

up on the street and seduced into making a sex film – famously spoofed in *Boogie Nights* (Paul Thomas Anderson, 1997). However, this became the norm of video directors such as Simon James Honey (Ben Dover) and purposely leant its style to the VHS format.

37. Church, D, *Disposable Passions: Vintage Pornography and the Material Legacies of Adult Cinema (Global Exploitation Cinemas)* (Bloomsbury Academic, London, 2016), p. 133.

4. SEX MORALITY PLAYS:
CHARACTER IN ADULT CINEMA

In the Russ Meyer film *Lorna*, the title character (played by Lorna Maitland) is trapped in a loveless marriage and only becomes 'liberated' after she is attacked, and raped, by a handsome convict during a walk in some woodland. She comes to embrace the man but at the end of the film Lorna is killed after stepping into the middle of a fight between her husband and her new lover. As mentioned in my last chapter, the trade journal *Variety* found *Lorna* to be 'a sort of sex morality play'. This factor is most evident in the image of the 'good' housewife rebelling against sexual conformity but – in breaking with tradition and the role expected of her – 'punished' in a tragic climax. *Lorna*'s affirmation of rape with male empowerment and female submission, alongside the allegory of property territorialism/marriage, would prove influential in both the sexploitation thematic and also Hollywood cinema.[1] And it is this thematic – the uneasy relationship between the spectacle of sex and the 'taboo' of the act – that defines the sexploitation genre and frequently gives it conservative overtones.

As with his later film *Vixen*, Meyer indicates that it is in the rural backwoods that sexual rebellion and true social-liberal values are held. What Crane mentions, referring to the director's work, as 'white-trash yokels who care, unlike their refined, careering city brethren, to hang fire and chase earthly pleasures'.[2] In comparison, when the sex film turns to unsimulated depictions of coitus, the protagonists are from the city: *Behind the Green Door* is set in San Francisco, and *The Devil in Miss Jones* and *The Opening of Misty Beethoven* both begin in New York.

Figure 4.1   *The Devil in Miss Jones*: sexploitation goes blockbuster. (No producer credit)

Responding to Meyer's assumption that liberated sexuality comes from the 'hidden' mountainous and lakeside townships and villages, these later unsimulated sex films indicate that sexual tension and frustration is born from the cityscapes of the modern day (concurrent blaxploitation films would also promote this idea). Interestingly, the female characters are more alone in these populated densities than Lorna and Vixen are in their comparative wilderness. This movement of sexuality from the rural to the urban, from the 1960s to the 1970s, complements the grimy and gritty style of the increased depiction of spectacle: a factor that theorists have generally not discussed. Later sexploitation films, for instance, prey upon the displacement of both viewer and character in immediate settings of modernity that are presented as lonely and even anonymous. It is a stylistic evolution that adds to the rawness of the aesthetic: the dirt and grime (and in *Behind the Green Door* even the crime) of cities and nightclubs is arguably more evocative than the beauty of the outdoors.

Thematically, *Lorna*'s presentation of marital frustration provokes questions surrounding monogamy and permits the character to express sexual disappointment and desire – facets of female personalities that American cinema had previously shied away from. *Lorna* indicates that the sexploitation heroine, and the cinematic females that followed her, were not beyond becoming consumed by lust. This would be the case even when, as with Amy in the controversial Hollywood film *Straw Dogs*, the consequences would surmount only further insecurity.[3] In contrast with another contemporary Hollywood example: Faye Dunaway's Bonnie in *Bonnie and Clyde* (Arthur Penn, 1967) chooses to maintain her relationship with Warren Beatty's Clyde, regardless of his impotence. Lorna, and the Hollywood women inspired by her – such as Amy in *Straw Dogs* – are at least permitted to break away from their sexual frustrations rather than abide by monogamy or abstinence. It is the sexploitation heroine that instigates this rebellion but the 'sex morality tale' aspect of the film concludes in her punishment.

Lewis mentions that films that did not show unsimulated intercourse but dealt explicitly with sex 'routinely involve some sort of pathology: rape/ coercion, guilt, ulterior motives'.[4] It is notable that *Lorna*, *Vixen* and more mainstream films such as *Straw Dogs* and later *Last Tango in Paris* and *Emmanuelle* all feature sequences in which the leading female character is violently attacked and raped (or, as in *Vixen*, experiences an attempted rape). The presumed cultural desire to suppress the very female sexuality being sold in these films can be seen to confound the notion that American cinema was comfortable in the liberation of on-screen intercourse even when the act was still being simulated. Williams affirms, referring specifically to *Last Tango in Paris*, that: 'Americans needed to learn to screen sexual pleasures tinged with the emotional tenor of threat and violence.'[5] The more recent controversy surrounding *Last Tango in Paris*, and its director Bernardo Bertolucci, in particular the revelation that the director may have convinced Marlon Brando to perform an unsimulated rape on actress Maria Schneider, perhaps indicates that it was not just Americans who could boast of this perspective.[6] Concurrently, then, both Hollywood and sexploitation films – for a few years – share a similar dichotomy: the saleable and titillating visual presentation of the lustful woman juxtaposed with her being 'tamed' for the sin of monogamy.

However, the sexploitation *style* itself meant that this 'threat and violence' could not evolve into unsimulated intercourse and still appeal to a large audience. Imagery of rape, mixed with genuine penetration, could be argued to (quoting Bazin) evoke a presentation of 'true obscenities that the cinema should not show'[7]: a 'reality' of sex mixed with a simulation of agony, blood and terror. As a result of these boundaries, socially constructed as they may be, when sexploitation films graduate into revealing genuine intercourse, the violent nature of the form fades, although the narrative thematic of a 'sex morality play' remains. What I propose is that the later, most successful unsimulated sex films be seen to transgress the concept, instigated by *Lorna*, that the insatiable woman had to be 'tamed' by force rather than by consensual physical satisfaction. The change in setting also benefits this thematic: whereas Lorna is tamed by the wilderness (represented by the yokel convict who dominates her, at first violently) later sexploitation heroines are defeated by their urbanity. The climax of this reading is with *The Opening of Misty Beethoven*, where the character of Misty must seduce the top proprietor in New York to prove her sexual worth. As Misty enters what looks not unlike an imagined picture of the future Trump Tower in Manhattan, the sex film really does prophesise its coming of age and its fatigue: there is nowhere left to go now it has reached the high life and become culturally accepted as ever-present.

In Meyer's later *Vixen*, the Lorna character has been replaced by Vixen Palmer (Erica Gavin) – one half of a couple living in the Canadian Rockies. Vixen's liberal sexual lifestyle does not embrace different races: a flirtatious African-American draft-dodger, in fact, actually incurs her rage. During the film, Vixen has sex with another woman, her own brother, one of her husband's friends and others. Taboo is broken down in the character's search for increasingly more transgressive acts of sexual liaison. At the conclusion of the story Vixen encourages the draft-dodger to return to America after thwarting a hijack attempt in which her pilot-husband is almost forced to fly to Cuba. As a character, Vixen is racist, loud-mouthed and war-mongering and the film's story also makes anti-communist thought explicit with a final showdown between the heroine and an armed Fidel Castro sympathiser. While Lorna goes from serving one domineering male (her husband) to serving another domineering male (her rapist), Vixen uses racist language and openly speaks against the anti-Vietnam movement. Her affairs take place behind her husband's back but at the end of the film she remains with him. The fact that he works and she does not attests to the film's chauvinism: Vixen maintains a free lifestyle through dependency, despite Meyer's attempts to use her as his own voice of conscience.

Men are at least used by Vixen for sexual purposes – the rape-fantasy of *Lorna* now distanced. The focus of the sexploitation female is therefore within two distinct areas: her domestic conservatism and her sexual liberalism. The disharmonious conclusion to *Lorna* indicates that the two personalities are incompatible, while *Vixen* maintains the opposite. As I will discuss, when the simulated sex film evolves into scenes of unsimulated intercourse this thematic still maintains present: in all instances the *threat* of something (in *Lorna* it is her rapist, and then returning to marital status quo; in *Vixen* it is the idea of embracing the very counterculture that her swinger lifestyle may indicate sympathy with) forces the sexploitation heroine to undergo a journey of sensual awakening. In each case she is either punished (*Lorna*) or finishes the narrative with a single 'loyal' partner (as in *Vixen*). In both cases the status quo of patriarchy wins – male authority is ultimately retained.

To understand the thematic of Meyer's films, however, it is worth mentioning the influence of the so-called 'arthouse'. Concurrent to the depiction of the sexploitation female in *Lorna* and *Vixen* are two influential foreign films, a factor that seems to have bypassed any previous study of Meyer's work.[8] Godard's *Contempt* (*Le Mépris*, 1963) can be considered a thematic influence on *Lorna*: a failed marriage, promiscuity, delineated locations, cold and alienated characters and bedroom insecurity. Betraying its 'high' art-house credentials, Brigitte Bardot's cleavage is stressed on the theatrical posters to *Contempt*, just as the statuesque figure of Lorna Maitland is exploited on the advertising to the Meyer film. Such carny marketing was nothing new for an apparent 'art' release: states Betz 'the 1959 marketing campaign for Louis Malle's *The Lovers* goes to considerable lengths to capitalize on the rapturous possibilities of the foreign or art film. Jeanne Moreau is pictured in medium close-up from the side, her head reclined and buried in pillows, neck arched, eyes closed, lips parted, right hand clutching the sheets by her head.'[9] Yet it is in the stories of some of these art films – perhaps because of their apparent campaign towards a more bourgeois audience – that we can see some grounding for later exploitation cinema to rebel against. For instance, *Contempt* is filmed in cinemascope, and with colourful set design, while *Lorna* is more subdued – its solemn black-and-white photography and minimal locations mediate the claustrophobia and entrapment of the story. Given how similar both stories are, it is not unimaginable that Meyer made a decision to aesthetically oppose the very appearance of Godard's character study. Certainly, despite the aesthetic differences, *Contempt*'s character study of sexual anxieties and libidinous dominance is radiated in *Lorna*. Furthermore, in both films, the marketing focused on the heaving chest of the respective leading ladies: Brigitte Bardot and Lorna Maitland. Those who formulate debate on these films around a highbrow/lowbrow dichotomy may, as I mentioned in my last chapter, be surprised to note such similarities.

A probable influence on *Vixen* is the Swedish production *I Am Curious (Yellow) (Jag är nyfiken – en film i gult)* (Vilgot Sjöman, 1967). As well as sharing *Vixen*'s woodland setting, the film mixes political commentary with sexually explicit imagery.[10] The comical tone of *I Am Curious (Yellow)* is also echoed in *Vixen*. Thematically, *Vixen* can be seen as a right-wing response to the radical left-wing student (played by Lena Nyman) of *I Am Curious (Yellow)*, who fantasises about castrating her two-timing lover, reaches sexual maturity through an affair with an older man and falls into making a documentary that reacts against contemporary conservative ideas. By contrast, Vixen (the character) rallies against her American draft-dodging neighbour, conflicts with an Irish communist and concludes the film with the 'freedom' to practice her liberal lifestyle. In both films the spectacle of sexual intercourse is worked *into* the plot and *around* the social commentary.

The women of *Lorna* and *Vixen* are conflicted between the housewife and the lustful, free-spirit caricature of the hippy lifestyle. *Vixen* more forcefully confronts this: the character is sexually liberal but politically conservative (although she lives in Canada it is clear that her politics are concerned with America, in particular her support of the Indochina conflict). As a response to *I Am Curious (Yellow)*, *Vixen* is logical – the film argues that sexual liberalism needs not to be synonymous with left-wing politics. The 'curious' element is also carried over from foreign cinema – *Vixen*'s poster asks us, 'Is she woman or animal?' This obviously panders to another chauvinistic fantasy of the uninhibited female, but it also relates to the sexploitation female post-*Lorna*: *is she housewife or whore?*

Both of Meyer's films endeavour to sustain their generic spectacle within a haphazard series of sexual encounters, as well as character and narrative causality that appropriates the gender politics of such films as *Contempt* and *I Am Curious (Yellow)* into a more accessible exploitation narrative. By sustaining a conservative approach to gender – the punishment of the liberated woman in *Lorna*, the racial-disgust and right-wing politics of *Vixen* – each film, with their more mature females, indicates that sexual freedom is not just the champion of the youthful sociology student of *I Am Curious (Yellow)*. They also maintain a thematic from which the unsimulated sex film is born: that sexual utopia for the female within a patriarchal society can only ever be imaginary or sustained within a masculine totalitarianism. Lorna is killed for her dalliances while Vixen is reliant on her husband's income to maintain her sexually liberal lifestyle.

Speaking about cinema as social representation, Allen and Gomery explain:

> Furthermore, however, indirectly and obliquely movies are social representations. That is, they derive their images and sounds, themes and stories, ultimately from their social environment. In fictional films, characters are given attitudes, gestures, sentiments, motivations and appearances that are, in part at least, based on social roles and on general notions about how a policeman, factory worker, debutante, mother or husband is 'supposed' to act.[11]

The sexploitation female journeys from preyed-upon (*Lorna*) to predator (*The Devil in Miss Jones*) and from race-hate (*Vixen*) to racially liberal (interracial sex takes place in lengthy unsimulated form in *Behind the Green Door*). The 'attitudes, gestures, sentiments, motivations and appearances' of these characters indicate a gradual thematic progression. As sexploitation furthers its aesthetic premise away from the simulated, the genre's initial demonisation of female sexuality as lurid and submissive (and the *she asked for it* undercurrent – present in both *Lorna* and *Vixen*) also advances. The more covert lesbianism of *Vixen* is replaced by a presentation of same-sex relationships in *Behind the Green Door*, *The Devil in Miss Jones* and *The Opening of Misty Beethoven* that allows for social representations that are more daring and revelatory: at least insofar about the potential for sexual pleasure. As much as these films are 'sex morality plays' the spectacles they present are concurrent with the transgression of the taboos of their time. For instance, *Vixen* teases at interracial coupling but refuses to *go there*. In contrast, *Behind the Green Door* allows for an African-American actor to penetrate and satisfy the blonde white female, typical of Western ideals of female beautification. Indeed, when the sexploitation film moves into depicting unsimulated intercourse, the spectacle threatens to outweigh the narrative.

Behind the Green Door is one long sex sequence in which Gloria, a kidnapped virgin given not even a single line of dialogue, is taken to a private member's club (the 'Green Door') in San Francisco and 'ravished' by a group of women, an African-American man and then a gang of men who take turns ejaculating on to her body. The story attempts to defend the chauvinism by presenting the plot as the figment of male imagination: *this never actually happened*. Unlike the hugely influential *Deep Throat*, which was the result of several short sex sequences – many pre-existing – spliced into 61 minutes of film,[12] *Behind the Green Door* was the first concerted and wide-distributed attempt at making a sexploitation feature with unsimulated love-making.

Gloria is reduced to a spectacle in *Behind the Green Door* but the overriding thematic can be seen to indicate a more wishful era: sexual freedom aligned with casual, non-committal sex. However, *Behind the Green Door* maintains the patriarchal conservatism of *Lorna* and *Vixen*: Gloria is 'rescued' from the Green Door by a male in the audience and pleasures him as the film comes to an end. Gloria is not permitted to be a 'character' with a voice of her own; she is simply a spectacle: a body who *submits*. Hollywood's answer to *Behind the Green Door* was *Last Tango in Paris* that introduces Marlon Brando as Paul, a middle-aged man who has an affair with a 19-year-old stranger, Jeanne (Maria Schneider). [13] As with Gloria in *Behind the Green Door*, Jeanne is 'used' for pleasure – she is objectified and humiliated by her lover. *Last Tango in Paris* was received by some critics as a simulated attempt to register the success of *Deep Throat* and *Behind the Green Door* but with a name actor and a respected filmmaker at the helm. For instance, Klemesrud pointed out that *Last Tango in Paris* was charging $5 a ticket in Manhattan: 'porno house prices . . . But since Brando is in it, the film has been deemed art.'[14] The same critic would label its star, Maria Schneider, as 'the Establishment's Linda Lovelace',[15] indicating the perceived social acceptances between *actual* sex and *simulation*. These social acceptances, however, never really happened: outside of a very brief curiosity, hardcore sex was pushed away by the mainstream public. The more cinematic simulations of *Last Tango in Paris*, which could be presented with real actors and an arthouse director working with a Hollywood budget, proved to have stylistic longevity.

The difference between Gloria in *Behind the Green Door* and Jeanne in *Last Tango in Paris* is that Gloria is forever trapped in a fantasy she can never escape: destined to forever appease the male imagination. Williams describes her as 'the most (misogynistically) extreme utopian solution' to the working men's club in the film – her body offering these labourers 'escape from the real world'.[16] Williams views *Behind the Green Door* as failing to deal with the emerging awareness in the early 1970s of 'the unspecified desires of females who might not wish to be consumed objects and who certainly did not wish to be ravished or raped'.[17] Williams' argument is supported by the film's narrative but what I propose is that *Behind the Green Door* is also reflexive: by acknowledging its own fantasy world the production indicates that the very notion of an insatiable female – *objectified, speechless, willing* – can only transpire, and be fulfilled, within the male imagination. Gloria *is* the ultimate sexploitation 'heroine' in that she *never says no*: indeed, she does not even speak. The film invites its audience to watch people watching unsimulated sex and, through this device, permits a consistent acknowledgement of 'it's only a movie'. *Behind the Green Door*, in its own way, predicts the challenge of gender politics as unsimulated intercourse becomes a normative stylistic element within the sexploitation form. A genre aimed specifically at a male audience will struggle to deliver a screen presentation of equal relations: especially as demand for the sex spectacle becomes more audacious (which *Behind the Green Door* satisfies with increasingly more bombastic imagery).

Gloria concludes *Behind the Green Door* by sleeping with the film's 'narrator' who has cast himself in the story as her savour from the public orgy she has been coerced into. Jeanne, by contrast, leaves her obnoxious lover in *Last Tango in Paris* to die after shooting him. This sexual nihilism, presented through a torrid affair that dehumanises both male and female, is taken to another extreme in *The Devil in Miss Jones* – a story that opens with a middle-aged virgin committing suicide. As a social representation, *The Devil in Miss Jones* is bold because it suggests that an older generation has been denied the sexual liberation that cinema has given its youth. The film ends with a nightmare scenario – the liberated female trapped by a patriarchal punishment: doomed to spend eternity with an impotent male, her pleasure interrelated to the masculine. *The Opening of Misty Beethoven* concludes the key films of the sexploitation genre and its story finally allows the form to exploit what it condemns without narrative excuse or any thematic 'guilt'. Misty, a street prostitute, is 'trained' to become a 'Golden Rod Girl', the most lusted-after escort in the world, as part of a challenge between a rich playboy and a female colleague. In the Pygmalion-style scenario of the story, Misty works her way up the social ladder until she finally becomes the penetrator instead of the penetrated and sodomises a New York entrepreneur with a toy-phallus. *The Opening of Misty Beethoven* allegorises the wealth of the upper classes with the exploitation of the poor. For instance, Misty's first attempt at seducing an impresario takes place in a toilet cubicle with her bent over the lavatory. This sex scene takes on a more humiliating ethos as it represents the film's wider undertones of upper-class dominance (possibly a comment on the lowbrow/highbrow arguments that were prevalent at the time regarding these films). At the close of the narrative, the playboy finds himself falling in love with Misty as she gains her own sexual confidence. In the final scene he is depicted as *her* slave: a prisoner to the monogamy he initially opposes, while Misty runs his prostitution service.

The 'sex morality play' of these films, introduced by *Lorna* and carried through to *The Opening of Misty Beethoven*, is a recurring thematic element of sexploitation and an overriding influence on the consequent aesthetic style. *The Opening of Misty Beethoven* takes the sexploitation film's image of the virginal female as increasingly more insatiable (until her body and orgasmic spasms *become* the spectacle on offer) to an interesting conclusion. With the character of Misty, the sexploitation heroine becomes what she has otherwise resisted – a masculine subordinate who dominates in both the business world, however dubious that 'business' is, *and* the bedroom. To reach this epiphany and escape patriarchal dependence she becomes a figure of transsexuality – impressing her employer to the extent that he surrenders to her control. The role of the female in these films, especially as 'social representation', maintains an evolving concern about gender equality. From the rape-punishment of *Lorna* through to the allegorical display of Misty's resultant reinvention as a penetrative dominatrix, sexploitation often condemns what it exploits. The exposed female bodies may be there, on the screen, to titillate but the films refuse their female characters any sort of liberation outside of a consistently present male patriarch.

This point is not to argue that the sexploitation film is threatened by female empowerment. These films approach the role of women from a perspective of both wish-fulfilment – given the veracious sexual appetites of the characters – and patriarchal defeatism. The men in sexploitation films may control the destiny of the female but it is rarely to their benefit. *Lorna* is a film that ends in tragedy. In *Vixen*, Vixen's husband pays for her lifestyle, but her promiscuity is presented as untameable, and the man who 'saves' Gloria from the Green Door club can only have her in his fantasies. Miss Jones is banished to hell because she can no longer be 'controlled' and Misty ends the film in charge of the very business that made her America's greatest seducer. These characters indicate that the sexual politics of the sexploitation genre are more provocative of gender subversion than the imagery of graphic nudity and intercourse may suggest.

Notes

1. For example, the Lorna character would be repeated in the notorious major studio film *Straw Dogs* (Sam Peckinpah, 1971).
2. Crane, J, 'A Lust for Life: The Cult Films of Russ Meyer'. In Harper, G and Mendik, X (eds) *Unruly Pleasures: The Cult Film and its Critics* (FAB Press, London, 2000), p. 97.

3. The film ends with a siege in which Dustin Hoffman's previously pacifistic math-ematician character must now arm himself to protect his home and his wife.
4. Lewis, J, *Hollywood v. Hardcore* (New York University Press, New York and London, 2000), p. 228.
5. Williams, L, *Screening Sex* (Duke University Press, North Carolina, 2008), p. 364.
6. https://www.theguardian.com/film/2016/dec/09/bertoluccis-justification-for-the-last-tango-scene-is-bogus-its-called-acting-for-a-reason – last accessed 20 August 2017.
7. Bazin, A, *What Is Cinema? Vol 2* (University of California Press, Los Angeles, 2005 [1971]), p. 174.
8. The only biography on Meyer to date makes no mention of this: McDonough, J, *Big Bosoms and Square Jaws* (Vintage, New York, 2006)
9. Betz, M, 'Art Exploitation Underground'. In Jancovich, M, Reboll, A, Stringer, J and Willis, A, *Defining Cult Movies: The Cultural Politics of Oppositional Taste* (Manchester University Press, Manchester, 2003), p. 217.
10. The disdain towards communism in *Vixen* may also be representative of a reac-tion *against* the French New Wave that became synonymous with an allegiance with the young leftism of the 1968 student riots. As mentioned, exploitation is fundamentally about the turning of profit through commercial exhibition of taboo. That *Lorna* can claim influence from a form that later became synonymous with an oppositional ideology to Meyer's exploitation of sex and violence is represented by *Vixen*'s anti-communism thematic. The French New Wave as a leftist dogma of socio-political revolution is discussed in Cowie, P, *Revolution, The Explosion of World Cinema in the 60s* (Faber and Faber, London, 2004), pp. 197–207.
11. Allen, R, and Gomery, D, *Film History: Theory and Practice* (McGraw-Hill, New York, 1985), p. 158.
12. *Deep Throat* is undoubtedly an exploitation film but not a key example of the movement due to its short running time and the fact that its style is unique – it began as a series of short pornographic loops until the producers recognised that it could be edited into an hour-long feature. Often uncommented upon is how, as a consequence of this, the end film is slapdash and barely holds any kind of discern-ible story together.
13. *Last Tango in Paris* was directed by an Italian (Bernardo Bertolucci) and with several foreign crew, including renowned cinematographer Vittorio Storaro. However, the film was released first in America and marketed on the strength of Marlon Brando's star power.
14. Klemesrud, J, 'Maria Says her Tango is Not', *The New York Times* (4 February 1973), p. 117.
15. Ibid.
16. Williams, L, *Hard Core: Power, Pleasure, and the 'Frenzy of the Visible'* (Pandora Press, London, 1990), p. 161.
17. Ibid., p. 161.

5. THE BODY IS EVERYTHING: SEXPLOITATION SPECTACLE

Linda Williams recognises that contemporary debate surrounding the sexually explicit image has typically centred upon 'the feminist rhetoric of abhorrence' – a factor that has permitted only for the question 'of whether pornography deserves to exist at all'.[1] Noting that this discussion is unhelpful in contextualising or understanding any of the generic elements of the sex film, the author concludes by stating, 'I wish to ask just what the genre is and why it has been so popular.'[2] In her well-regarded book *Hardcore*, Williams discovers the divergence and variety between sex films but also 'the difficulty hardcore films have in figuring the visual "knowledge" of women's pleasure'.[3] It is this later point that the author pays particular attention to in her study – especially as regards the 'money shot' of male ejaculation that often signifies the conclusion of sex scenes in the hardcore sex film: what Williams dubs the 'frenzy of the visible'. The author notes, referring to softcore productions such as *Lorna*, 'Sexploitation producers were so terrified of resembling hardcore pornography – and they did constantly skirt prosecution for obscenity in their vulnerable position outside the Code – that they would frequently displace the energy of genital coupling into a more generalised orgasmic abandon of the female body.'[4]

While Williams distinguishes between the two types of films – using sexploitation to affirm simulated on-screen intercourse and hardcore to relate to the eventual unhiding of the sex act – there is still a notable aesthetic cohesion between the two despite the fact that one is 'real' and the other is not. Indeed, the 'orgasmic abandon of the female body' that Williams sees in softcore films such as *Vixen* is also present in the later hardcore releases (*Behind the Green Door* has a lengthy sequence of intercourse that finalises by studying, in close-up, the orgasmic face of Marilyn Chambers – penetration is not even in shot). The evasion of showing penetration does, as the author confirms, force choreography of simulation in films such as *Vixen*, but – similarly – by having the freedom of showing erections, ejaculation and so forth, later sexploitation filmmakers still struggle to evoke an on-screen stylistic signifier of *pleasure*. The intercourse is undoubtedly happening in *Behind the Green Door* and *The Devil in Miss Jones* but – as with *Lorna* and *Vixen* – the style remains conclusive on facial expression and reaction, even when the release of semen indicates the closure of the sequence and the restoration of the 'normal' narrative. In a horror film, by comparison, the biggest challenge to any verisimilitude of mood and tone lies in the presentation of death – at least insofar as exploitation cinema wants everything to appear as genuine as possible (and an obvious special effect is likely to draw the viewer away from the action). Similarly, for a sex film, the challenge remains aesthetic – capturing a believable simulation of female orgasm. In this sense, then, the aesthetic goal of both soft and hardcore sex films is identical.

Indeed, in the unsimulated sexploitation film, the avoidance of highlighting genitals feels strangely uncinematic: the physical coupling could supply evidence of penetration but by having to avoid this depiction, the verisimilitude that the genre evokes is never quite satisfied. To break the sex film into a *soft* and *hard* equation complicates the obvious evolution from one to the other and the reason behind this genesis as well as the stylistic consequences. While providing commercial appeal was the most obvious factor behind the growing explicitness of the sex film – from *The Immoral Mr. Teas* to *Vixen* and eventually to the graphic group sex and lesbianism of *The Devil in Miss Jones* – there is also a graduation of technical sophistication.[5] Moreover, we may even consider the decision to 'unhide' the 'obscene' element of on-screen sex as partly, at least, based on progressing a style that was hampered by simulation. Certainly, there was a similar corporeal spectacle present within other exploitation genres that progressed towards an ever-greater screen reproduction of veracity: from the gruesome simulation of murder in the exploitation-horror film to the ghettos and vérité gangster brutality and hypersexuality of blaxploitation cinema. For instance, reviewing the simulated sex film *Fleshpot on 42nd Street* (Andy Milligan, 1973) *Variety* magazine commented, 'with all the hardcore competition, the old meagrely budgeted softcore sexploitation pic has been floundering'.[6] In other words: for a brief period, critics noted that audiences *wanted* to see the sex act rather than have it hidden and, more so, per this quote, understood that softcore sexploitation had led to, and been superseded by, the hardcore film. Answering this factor, Vincent Canby would also argue that the hardcore film 'threatens . . . the Puritan conscience and our traditional sexual taboos, which we all have . . . and which have nothing to do with the mind, but with emotions'.[7]

If we think of sexploitation as triggering these 'emotions', based purely on a cultural line related to a larger Puritanism (unsimulated pornography still cannot be legally screened in several democracies, while the softcore version remains perfectly above board[8]), then it explains why the hardcore form could not sustain its own commerciality. Ultimately, if we all, to some extent, enjoy provocation then there is only so far that real sex, once seen, can continue to push any proverbial buttons of either 'acceptance' or even perhaps titillation and taboo. This is not, however, the narrative that has often been written about the 'porno chic' period. Crane, for instance, states that 'the success of hardcore in America . . . relegated its immediate predecessor, the softcore film, to the dustbin'.[9] Yet, Russ Meyer made three softcore projects during the period of *Deep Throat* and *The Devil in Miss Jones* while *Emmanuelle* was successful enough to span numerous sequels and cash-in titles (that is, the famous Italian *Black Emanuelle* (Bitto Albertini, 1975)). Meyer's films, such as *Beneath the Valley of the Ultra-Vixens* (1979), did evidence a gradua-tion towards increasingly graphic full-frontal nudity during its (simulated) sex scenes but the director clearly just could not bring himself to let the full-thing take its place in his motion pictures. Perhaps this is why there is, as mentioned in the last chapter, an identifiable thematic 'puritanism' in films such as *Lorna* and *Vixen*.

Koch also factors censorious aspects into her discussion of the sex film – but adds, 'We also see that in the course of time, settings, stereotypes and characters change even in pornographic cinema in order to conform to newer fashions, especially about what is considered sexy.'[10] An ever-expanding aesthetic sexual liberalism (if not thematic sexual liberalism) is evident in the progression of the sexploitation style: interracial intercourse, forced inter-course, group sex and homosexuality are also approached and depicted. This diversion occurs as the American sex film graduates from softcore (simulated) to hardcore (unsimulated). However, in countries that had less lenient censor-ship laws, some hardcore films were released in a softcore format. A review of the hardcore sex film *The Story of Joanna* (Gerard Damiano, 1975), for instance, appeared in the UK film journal *The Monthly Film Bulletin*: 'Like the kind of horror movies it resembles, the film relies on atmosphere, decor and lighting and on its physical immediacy as drama to carry off a nonsensical conception.'[11] Without the distraction (if we can call it such) of intercourse and ejaculation, this review approaches *The Story of Joanna* as intertextual with the horror film. The 'reveal' of penetration is not the only point of interest in these films – as evidenced; they could still play without these moments in place and, without the hardcore elements to 'distract' the audience, the style was perhaps more evident. A title such as *The Story of Joanna*, based around a master–slave relationship, or *The Devil in Miss Jones* are remarkably similar to horror films such as *The Last House on the Left* in their barren, provocative, low-fi style. The cinematic element was, consequently, more credible than Williams' separation between soft and hard as demarcation may acknowledge. This factor also leads to a further question of style and how, even without the sight of actual intercourse, these films were still exhibited and acclaimed. The 'money shot', for instance, which Williams concentrates on evaluating, can be argued as less important to the causality of the unsimulated sexploitation film than has been previously discussed.

THE MONEY SHOT

Everyone who has ever seen a hardcore sex film will know the money shot: the sight of actual male ejaculation that signifies the closure of a sex scene. Once the semen is revealed, characters continue within their ongoing narrative struggles or dilemmas – usually as if nothing has ever happened. Stylistically, the money shot is the main holdover from the 'porno chic' period – even today it is that key element of 'realism' that *proves* finality – the exhaustion of the male and the release of actual orgasm. The show, simply, *cannot go on*. Williams, in her writing, approaches the money shot from a Marxist perspective but not from the position of physical-exploitation. Instead, the author introduces an intriguing argument from the perspective of commodity-fetishism, which she also links with that of Freud. Marx's fetish, argues Williams, is one of industry: 'a form of delusion whereby the workers who produce a commodity fail to recognize the product of their own labour'.[12] Williams relates this industry-fetishism to the idea of reifying a commodity so that it has a value over-and-above its own subjective status by initiating a discussion of phallic-power and 'the money shot'. In the hardcore film we see masculine interpretations of the feminine – a phallic-worship that can never visualise the female satisfaction that it desires, frustrating the stylistic ambition of total sexual realism. This factor is adjoined to Freud's 'fetish as delusion' taken from his famous case of Dora and her son Hans, 'a little boy who does not want to surrender the belief that his mother has a penis'.[13] Inevitably, perhaps, Williams also acknowledges Marx's attribution of a capitalist society's devaluation of women.[14] And she further maintains Freud's 'castration disavowal'.[15] Her conclusion affirms that both of these elements factor an important part in the popularity of the hardcore 'money shot' – 'forms of repressive power'.[16] Therefore, Williams factors the phallic conclusion of the sex film's generic commerciality (the visual climax of a set piece) as a substitute for the female orgasm that cannot be screened – hinting at the stylistic frustration of a genre predicated on realism. The female orgasm thus becomes synonymous with male lack *as well as* masculine oppression: the woman is marginalised by the spectacle of ejaculation. And this can surely be viewed as a stylistic inevitability. However, this 'inevitability' does not necessarily mean that sexploitation films are bound by misogyny – that is, that the male orgasm always concludes scenes – and offers only the male viewer a relatable climax (even concurrent to their own) – at the *expense* of the female equivalent.

Let me explain this argument further. Williams is careful to distance her readings of various sex films from the vicarious disgust at the mere idea of the genre that comes from some of the most noted anti-porn feminists, such as Andrea Dworkin. *Deep Throat*, for instance, is discussed and enjoyed by Williams despite 'all its silliness and obvious misogyny'.[17] The author clarifies this misogyny by mentioning that in one sequence from *Deep Throat* the film's leading female 'Linda' (Linda Lovelace) discovers that her lover is 'unable to meet her demands for more sex . . . the spectre of the insatiable woman has been shown to take its toll on more limited men'.[18] In this instance the 'money shot' has been exhausted: there is *no more*. This focus on 'the spectre of the insatiable woman' (dichotomous to the exhausted male) may, however, be argued as working against a reading of 'obvious misogyny' and phallic-empowerment. Were this scenario reversed and the exhausted female was to be begrudgingly having to satisfy her husband then it would be far closer to the 'misogyny' that Williams maintains in the visage of the 'insatiable' Linda Lovelace in *Deep Throat*. As such, I want to argue that the 'money shot' may also be seen as a progressive stylistic function and that thematic is everything – even in sexploitation. And by demonstrating this, I hope that even the hardcore sex film may be viewed in a new light – that is, one that, thanks to its stylistic attributes, is sometimes more corporeally complex than previous readings may have concluded.

As such, let us take a closer look at the film *The Devil in Miss Jones*. In this ground-breaking sexploitation film the money shot should be seen to represent, through the use of close-up, the *weakness* of the penis rather than its strength. If, as Luckett mentions, 'female power is generally linked to breast size'[19] in the films of Russ Meyer (and one can argue this is because the simulated sex production could not offer close-up depictions of male or female genitals) then the money shot's focus on the penis may be argued as more subversive than an argument of male lack, and female marginalisation, may indicate. Luckett, for instance, maintains that in any Meyer films 'small breasts highlight marginalisation, failure, even utter villainy'.[20] In other words, on-screen depictions of the physical *can* be perverted and even allegorised outside of the initial 'reveal' and the (most obvious) function of nudity and sex as 'arousal'.

Williams introduces 'Pornotopia' to define the real–unreal binary of the mechanical reproduction of the actual sex act. Pornotopia is the sex act made cinematic but, related back to Williams' theory of *seeing* the 'money shot' via the male gaze and the resulting commodification of the female, it 'solves the problems of the male viewer in ways consistent with a dominant phallic, heterosexual economy'.[21] Yet, 'Pornotopia' is not always so easy to define. Williams confirms as much: proposing three different screen 'utopias' suitable to the genre: *Separated Utopias* ('the most obviously escapist'[22]), *Integrated Utopias* (confrontational and aware of sexual problems/niches[23]) and *Dissolved Utopias* (where 'Pornotopia is already achieved'[24]).

The author maintains:

> Because hard-core fantasy offers symbolic solutions to problems that viewers perceive as real, in order to 'solve' these problems contemporary pornography has had to 'talk to itself' about sexual relations, to acknowledge that sex is more of a problem than we have ever before admitted.[25]

These films certainly talk about sex, and form their narratives around the spectacle of sex, but this does not mean that they necessarily seek to 'solve' the problems of sexual repression and sexual anxieties. It is notable that Williams avoids discussion, aside from very briefly, of *The Devil in Miss Jones*, despite it being the most commercially successful of all sexploitation films. Williams' states, in the short paragraph in which the title is mentioned, that *The Devil in Miss Jones* takes place in a Dissolved Utopia: the character of Miss Jones is cast into purgatory, after committing suicide, and permitted to fulfil a brief period of passion before being sentenced to damnation. Thus, the sexual spectacle is hers: she can do as she pleases.

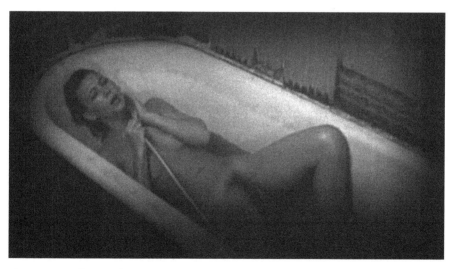

Figure 5.1   *The Devil in Miss Jones*: actress Georgina Spelvin became an unexpected sexploitation superstar at age thirty-seven. (No producer credit)

Williams' relative exclusion of *The Devil in Miss Jones* may be because if utopia indicates a sense of perfection/pleasure then the film fails to present such.

Aside from focusing on a middle-aged character, with a less-than-perfect screen body, the title has a conflicted attitude towards sex (the film *exploits* graphic intercourse but seems uncomfortable doing so: especially as Miss Jones is punished to damnation following her interlude of promiscuity). The success of *The Devil in Miss Jones* allowed its director, Gerard Damiano, to helm two subsequent films with a similar perspective towards sexual freedom: *Memories within Miss Aggie* (1974) and *The Story of Joanna* (1975). The former, despite becoming the second top-grossing film in New York during the week of its release, receives no mention from Williams and the latter, as with *The Devil in Miss Jones*, is discussed only briefly in her famous book *Hardcore*. [26] I have chosen to single out *The Devil in Miss Jones* as its two successors repeat the guilt/repression/anti-consumptive themes of the original film and thus fail to progress the style of the original production. Nonetheless, all three of these exploitation films indicate a move away from the sexual utopia that Williams discusses: in fact, they indicate that, just as a feature dealing with violence need not be pro-violence, nor should a film dealing with the spectacle of explicit sex necessarily condone promiscuity.

The Devil in Miss Jones also highlights the most explicit crossover of the exploitation style: thematically and even aesthetically it takes aspects from the horror film (the entire opening sequence has Miss Jones slashing her wrists and bleeding to death before being expulsed to damnation/the grimy surroundings when she finds herself in purgatory). 'Not for the squeamish or the tasteful' commented one critic of the time, obviously attempting to understand this most *unsexual* of sex films.[27] *The Devil in Miss Jones* takes the actualisation of intercourse and uses it to *complement* its thematic of claustrophobia, objectification and the initial thrill of consumption. Sex in the film, for instance, takes place in confined, claustrophobic and dimly lit areas of an old mansion while the soundtrack is forever, with its sounds of wind and orchestration, ominous. However, the film concludes with a 'message' that is oppositional to the sex spectacle being exploited. Miss Jones goes from fellatio to penetration to sodomy to lesbianism and finally to group sex (each explicitly presented to the viewer), but the film ends with her locked in hell, in a state of insanity, with an impotent man sat next to her for eternity. This damnation is her 'punishment' for daring to enjoy the sex she engages in. The star, Georgina Spelvin, comments of the film's 'message': 'To wit: abuse it; you lose it.'[28] The film's own evolution of graphic spectacle may even be seen as subtext: an attempt to oppose the very exploitation style itself and an argument that greater corporeal excess will eventually damn cinematic ambition.

A visual link between horror and sex films has been noted by Williams who builds upon Bazin's contrast of the execution of Chinese communist spies with cinema's potential gravitation towards capturing unsimulated intercourse. Both of these examples are viewed by Bazin as a perversion of the physical: 'the obscenity of the image was of the same order as that of a pornographic film. An ontological pornography. Here death is the negative equivalent of sexual pleasure, which is sometimes called, not without reason, "the little death".'[29] This acknowledgement of Freud's famous pleasure principle is noted by Williams, who argues that the death throes of the convicted man may be contrasted with the spasms of the sexploitation actress, 'This French petite mort links the involuntary shudder of pleasure to the involuntary shudder of death – both spasms of the ecstatic body.'[30] By avoiding greater discussion of *The Devil in Miss Jones*, Williams does not approach the idea that the horror of the sex image, literally in this case (that is, Miss Jones frantically masturbating in the film's climax as her onslaught of insanity begins), may indicate a deliberate stylistic gravitation towards what Freud calls 'impelling' sensations.[31] Given that such presentation is in the context of a *sex* film (suggesting 'sensations of a pleasurable nature'[32]), what may also be concluded is that Bazin's fears of the exhibition of unsimulated intercourse as uncinematic is unfounded. Instead, the use of this generic trope is utilised by *The Devil in Miss Jones* to deliver a sex spectacle and to transgress (male) audience arousal by presenting a final 'punishment' for partaking in it. The character we have identified with throughout the narrative is left unsatisfied and tormented. This provocation of emotions, and the critical success of *The Devil in Miss Jones*, teases at how the spectacle of sex *could* have been used as something other than just a form of arousal.

Rather than contrast, as Williams does, the 'spasms of the ecstatic body' with death and orgasm, I instead suggest that *The Devil in Miss Jones* indicates the potential of the exploitation style to subvert its own generic tropes via a more studied and explicit use of spectacle. Analysis has been given to the way that horror films often forthrightly present feminine body-horror, for example, how 'the vampire questions the nature of phallic sexuality'.[33] However, the idea that a sex film, the 'lowest common denominator', may also subvert the expectancy of 'pleasure' has avoided analysis. The 'ecstasy' in *The Devil in Miss Jones*, for instance, graduates into a spasm of insanity and fear, *not* orgasm. The film appropriates this newfound display of explicit sex into a narrative and spectacle that questions the very consumption of this graphic imagery. Similarly, by having a star that is middle aged and not glamorous, *The Devil in Miss Jones* also indicates that the sex film need not pander to a general acceptance of American beautification.

With *The Devil in Miss Jones* the 'pornography' of the unsimulated image becomes a central stylistic function – replacing the close-ups on faces and breasts that typify the unreal recreation of intercourse in *Lorna* and *Vixen* or the square up of 'this is all a fantasy' that excuses the sexism of *Behind the Green Door*. To indicate this stylistic use of unsimulated sex as a function of character and plot development, I want to highlight how, in the two concluding sex sequences in *The Devil in Miss Jones*, the male face is entirely obscured. Instead, the penis is now objectified solely as an instrument for its virginal star (discovering intercourse for the first time and at a late age) to pleasure herself with. In these instances, the masculine is represented solely as genitals and 'the dominant phallic, heterosexual economy' that Williams focuses her utopias upon is subverted. In this approach, the exploitation style reaches a peak of visual intelligence. The journey from the buxom female (exposed breasts being the first 'reveal' of the post-censorship era in *The Immoral Mr. Teas*) to represent what Luckett describes as 'the dominance of the feminine body'[34] in *Lorna* and *Vixen* to the close-up on genital arousal and penetration is not *just* to prove that sex *is* happening. The marginalisation of the male, in *The Devil in Miss Jones*, were it replaced with a similar marginalisation of the female (that is, if all that were on-screen were *her* genitals and two lustful men) could be argued as misogynistic in its explicit objectification. On the contrary, the presentation of the objectified male, in *The Devil in Miss Jones*, indicates the development of Miss Jones and her attitude towards men. At first, she is a virgin, afraid of erections and penetration, but now she consumes what she at first fears. As the sexual predator, by the film's conclusion, she is taken from her Pornotopia and punished. Even the 'money shot', rather than an unconscious representation of 'male lack', is indicative of an awareness of male objectification: of the uselessness of the masculine sexual appendage outside of an erection. After the 'money shot', featuring an anonymous male, takes place, Miss Jones and another woman express visual disappointment that the potential for further satisfaction is now gone and lick and grope the flaccid penis with clear desperation – they want the erection to return, however futile. It is this reflexivity, this *awareness* of what the sex image *can* represent and how a stylistic subversion permits a different presentation, that makes *The Devil in Miss Jones* a pivotal achievement (arguably *the* key film above all others) in the sexploitation genre. It confuses a reading of even the generically necessitated 'money shot' as either climax (the sequence continues for some time after ejaculation) or as representative of male dominance.

The consumption that Miss Jones partakes in is also allegorically approached in an instance in which the 'money shot' of fellatio segues into the character devouring fruit. This works on two levels: to ascertain her free sexual consumption (denied to her in the 'real' world) and, in her banishment to hell, a conclusion that the 1970s female struggles to gain the wealth of expenditure that patriarchal-capitalism provides for the masculine (on her entry to purgatory Miss Jones is told that she will be 'watched' by a businessman-like male, dressed in a suit, working from an office). In other words: feminine desire is revealed to be *oppositional* to the patriarchy that functions within an Anglo-Christian society. The Pornotopia of *The Devil in Miss Jones* is unattractive: described by Canby at the time of the film's release as emphasising 'guilt and repression ... Sex is bad. Sex is dirty. It is something to be disinfected, one way and another.'[35] What this 'sex is dirty' thematic indicates is that the sexploitation style evolved to the extent that even the conclusive 'money shot' could represent *something else* – a feeling in the viewer that is oppositional to arousal.

Perhaps indicating its own unique placement within the sexploitation genre, the theatrical poster for *The Devil in Miss Jones* did not advertise or display an image of the female star. Instead, in heavy white lettering on a plain black backdrop, the cinemagoer was exposed to four reviews from upmarket publications that managed to reference the film alongside Modigliani, Sartre and the Marlon Brando blockbuster *Last Tango in Paris*. And at least one critic argued that *The Devil in Miss Jones* did not function as titillation, stating that the film 'seemed so repugnant ... But I think that means it was at least an *effective* film, since it was supposed to be a sexual horror story.'[36] This conclusion may be because the film features a middle-aged performer engaged in graphic sexual acts (in one sequence a female performer even reveals unshaven underarms). In revealing this image, the feature presents the idea of sexuality outside of the perfect physicality of which audiences were/are comfortable. This liberation of a more aged body, and accepted (expected?) grooming, proved unrivalled in its commercial appeal: *The Devil in Miss Jones* was 'the leading grosser of all porn films'.[37] In order to challenge the beautification of its era, *The Devil in Miss Jones* permits its middle-aged spinster to replace the more recognisable figure of the young girl (that is, Gloria in *Behind the Green Door* or Misty Beethoven) who loses her innocence and matures into a sexualised figure. Was this casting decision a commercial move or a socio-political one? To conclude in the latter would bring us back to the tiresome discussion of whether or not one is, indeed, attempting to reclaim pornography as 'highbrow' – and yet it is surely impossible to avoid the impression that those involved in the film *were not aware* that sexploitation cinema consistently provided audiences with youthful bodies.

At the outset of the film Miss Jones is a suicidal frustrated housemaid. Her embrace of Pornotopia (before she is damned to hell) allows her transformation into the insatiable. In the aforementioned sequence where the male is objectified solely by his penis, we also hear Miss Jones speak to another, mysterious, female: 'You're going to taste it and then me', 'Put it in me', 'I want to feel it in my cunt'. The use of *it* indicates the character's perception of men: they are used only for sexual gratification. The objectification of the male replaces the earlier objectification of the female. No longer is Miss Jones the timid, inexperienced, unsure middle-aged woman. In her first sexual encounter her male partner guides her through the experience – *orders her, controls her, patronises her*. The style of this scene is important: the close-up of the penis in *The Devil in Miss Jones* provides characterisation (we are made to associate with the female character's insatiable lust) and moves, however crudely, towards allegory (the denouncement of patriarchy to a master–slave relationship, itself anticipating the film's conclusion).

What makes this technique uniquely 'exploitation' is also the *duration* of the close-up. Whole sequences in *The Devil in Miss Jones* develop and progress and conclude in close-up. While the move to unsimulated sex insisted on evidence of actual penetration, the close-up of the face is a consistency of the sexploitation style – the intrusive nature of such patterning, perhaps, to the voyeuristic element of spectatorship. The close-up of the sexploitation film may pertain to an explicit corporeality that some will find vulgar or, as Bazin predicted, even as uncinematic – that the capturing of an actuality fails to assimilate with a form that provides illusion, no matter how 'real' that illusion may be received. In the unsimulated sex film, such as *Lorna* or *Vixen*, the close-up of flesh, breasts, thighs and orgasmic faces allow for statuesque females to become palpable: glamorous beings presented for titillation but with buxom physical perfection that outgrows their characters and conveys a chauvinistic fetish-idealism. Williams, referencing Meyer's films, describes how the simulated sexploitation form frequently displaces 'the energy of genital coupling into a more generalised orgasmic abandon of the female body . . . with jiggling breasts . . . female sexuality in these films verge on clinically hysterical'.[38] This 'hysterical' presentation is because the 'orgasmic abandon' is subject to the limits of its own fakery. What Williams does not discuss is how the sexploitation female physically transforms from the exaggerated to the understated as the films progress from simulations to actualisations of penetration. The female form is large in the Meyer features: big breasts, big hair, big lips: whenever characters enter into discourse in *Vixen* it is almost consistently in a close-up of these areas that reminds us of the voyeuristic undertones at work. If, as mentioned, the close-up exists in the sexploitation film, foremost, as titillation then it must also provide us with fascination – purposing that sexual arousal. For simulated sex this fascination can only be a tease, the close-up hinting at what *could be* rather than *what is*, and the breasts – the sole sexual appendage that can be exploited – are fetishised as a consequence.

Rather than Williams' assumption that the 'money shot' represents an attempt to negate female presence, and visualises a phallic-idealism for the male viewer, therefore, I propose that its eventual generic prominence has more to do with visual storytelling and the growing importance of the close-up to the style of these films. The money shot represents a *beginning, middle* and *end* – albeit with physical causality as *plot* and *story*. As established, the conclusion of the sex act in *Lorna* and *Vixen* (and in Hollywood films) is frustrated by how to identify satisfaction – male *or* female. In these cases, music cues or facial satisfaction stand-in for the visual proof that orgasm has taken place. It is telling that as sex films begin to show unsimulated intercourse the 'money shot' is instigated as either a special effect (as in *Behind the Green Door* or *Deep Throat* – wherein stock footage of a rocket taking off is juxtaposed as a comical allegory) or as representative of a character's sexual and sensual lust (as in *The Devil in Miss Jones* where semen is consumed). It is only as 'hardcore' emerges from sexploitation – in the binary of presuming spectacle in place of narrative, as afore-referenced – that filmmakers utilise male ejaculation as a generic understanding of the conclusion of spectacle.

Koch mentions that the 'aesthetic of the pornographic film relies on an underlying metaphor of the body as machine'.[39] If a film made for an adult (predominantly male) audience, such as *The Devil in Miss Jones*, fails to replenish the body and if the body is exhausted and the narrative conclusive in this regard, then we can perhaps maintain that some genre films, from this era, perversely fail to celebrate the very spectacle being sold. *The Devil in Miss Jones* is a key example. *The Devil in Miss Jones*, as its 'sex is dirty' conclusion reveals, is reflexive to Williams' definition of Pornotopia – that a 'dominant phallic, heterosexual economy' leaves minimal place for the female expression of sexuality (let alone the generic expression of an unshaven, unlikely sex star in a middle-aged woman – making the film's commercial success surprising and begging questions of the audiences of 1973). The film has a dystopian approach to the on-screen love-making: the voyeurism of the viewer is occasionally interrupted by the business-like juror of purgatory, reminding Miss Jones that she has only a little time left until she is sentenced to damnation. There is a message in *The Devil in Miss Jones* and it is clearly not one of sexual liberation. Perhaps, in its own reflexive manner, the film is predicting an era when sexploitation itself will be 'banished' or exhaust its spectacle. It certainly anticipates an era of body-shaming and ageism. Hence the fact that its older starlet is consistently reminded, by a male patriarch, that punishment is forthcoming.

It is important to point out that as sexploitation furthers its aesthetic premise away from the simulated and towards the 'hardcore', the genre's initial demonisation of female sexuality as lurid and submissive (and the 'she asked for it' undercurrent) becomes more domineering and confident – albeit within self-aware and/or cautionary stories. Pornotopia in the 1970s is distinguishable from Pornotopia in the 1960s – even if the style shows a notable intertextual lineage: the use of close-up, the convulsing female body, the narrative of threat – either from rape or invasion or from insatiability, dissatisfaction, excess, claustrophobia and a search for satisfaction in an empty modernity. Sexploitation probably does not exist as an attempt to allow us 'to believe in the utopian possibility that "enlightenment, liberation, and manifold pleasures" are all linked – for example, that making love . . . may actually have something to do with opposing war'.[40] This argument was attempted in the past: 'None of them that day bombed a peasant village, created a Brownsville or a South Bronx, or poisoned a river' stated *The New York Times* of the *Deep Throat* audience and concurrent legal problems of watching sex films in the cinema.[41] As a commercial form exploitation films had to maintain a spectacle that delivered what Hollywood could not and the cinematic exhibition of unsimulated sex was always inevitable. The *where*, *when* and even the visceral nature of the sexploitation spectacle is less important to understanding the form (and its relation to both the art house and Hollywood) as is a discussion about the *depiction* of sexuality, surroundings and gender roles.

It is important to maintain, therefore, that the thematic of the sexploitation 'group style' is frequently as dystopian as it is utopian and the insatiability of the sex act itself is not always treated as idealistic. Monogamy, for instance, is occasionally championed and even when orgiastic pleasure, presented in a film such as *Behind the Green Door*, is emphasised, it is as a fantasy unobtainable outside of Pornotopia itself. Pornotopia, it could be argued, drawing on Williams' definition, is about the *safety* of the cinema screen: sexual anarchy outside of social stigma, the *fantasy* that the male characters in *Behind the Green Door* can never have as they imagine group sex, lesbianism and multiple ejaculations. It is a stylistic function that also allows for more flexibility, given the fantasy nature of the intercourse (even when simulated), than Williams credits: my example of *The Devil in Miss Jones* and its particular use of the close-up may indicate this conclusion. The key sexploitation titles can be seen as self-aware as regards their own shortcomings – that is, possibly drawing on the fantasy–reality binary of *The Immoral Mr. Teas* (wherein Mr. Teas can only *imagine* sexually available women), these productions may *exploit* sexual liberation, but they only do so within cautionary stories. These films deal with sex in a forthright manner – both visually and thematically removed from the approach of Hollywood – but there remains a hesitance in promoting sexual liberation. This argument could be seen as a cultural one: as sexploitation became the mainstream (that is, trade magazines such as *Variety* reviewed the films and the box office crossed over to rival Hollywood financial takings) the productions were no longer completely taboo. The key films, therefore, enshrine a certain heteronormative value even while the exhibition of the sex spectacle is removed from mainstream cinematic approaches.

CONCLUSIONS ON STYLE

The sexploitation style is, foremost, of course, about the 'reveal' – the exhibition of nudity or the proof that real intercourse is happening. This 'reveal' is perhaps why the close-up plays such a key role in the narrative progression of these films. Titillation and verisimilitude document the evolution of the genre: initially in simulating sex via graphic nudity and eventually in the mechanical reproduction of penetration and ejaculation. The close-up is also associated with allegory: initiated by the Russian social-realist cinema, of which *Battleship Potemkin* (Sergei Eisenstein, 1925) is perhaps the most famous. Eisenstein's close-ups of maggot-infested meat in *Battleship Potemkin* is used to symbolise the top-down financial distribution of the capitalist state, the vermin made allegorical with the sailors who revolt against their leaders after being directed to consume the disgusting and rotten food. By providing sharp edits and stressing the visual connection between the close-up of flesh and the close-up of his disgusted cast, Eisenstein delivers an aesthetic of class warfare: the sailors as maggots feasting, in this case literally, on the spoils of the dominant class.

Scenes of love-making, especially in Hollywood cinema, rely on montage to depict a progression of assembly. In comparison, the sexploitation equivalent can appear crude: close-ups on exposed flesh and genitals are voyeuristic in nature – although this element of the form's style also provides a distinctly un-Hollywood use of the technique, especially – as discussed – with respect to plot-time. For instance, the opening of *The Devil in Miss Jones* documents the running of bath water, the undressing of actress Georgina Spelvin and her getting into the bathtub *as it happens*. As with Bazin's appraisal of the presentation of time in *Umberto D* ('life itself becomes the spectacle'[42]), a similar mimesis of 'real' time is frequently evidenced in sexploitation films, especially when the sex act, or more explicit nudity, can finally be revealed.[43] The running water in *The Devil in Miss Jones*, for instance, flows until the bathtub is full. There is no evidence that brief cuts to the actress undressing have interrupted the *actual* time that the bath would take to fill. Acts of sex are not rushed, or compromised by having to hide the intercourse: often (although not always) they can take place in a realistic documentation of undressing/ foreplay/intercourse/ejaculation (of the hardcore films discussed only *Misty Beethoven* plays with montage during sex scenes – perhaps to complement its Hollywood ambitions). These aspects of the sexploitation style have little parallel in mainstream American studio cinema and they stand removed from the subtle eroticism of international comparables. While functioning as a genre, the sexploitation films that provide evidence of a progressive and unique group style are difficult to assimilate as either art house or as products of the mainstream. The explicit use of spectacle results in a raw and provocative aesthetic while thematic elements clearly evolve into more allegorical and complex depictions of female sexuality.

For instance, a Hollywood film will typically utilise montage to depict the development of the sex act because it *is* a simulation. To prolong this simulation would further indicate the lack of actuality. Kracauer would famously critique the theatricality of Georges Méliès: 'The train in *Arrival of a Train* is the real thing, whereas the counterpart in Melie's *An Impossible Voyage* is a toy train as unreal as the scenery through which it is moving.'[44] This fabricated 'unreality' is also the difference between the simulation of sex and the close-up of an actualisation of the act: the former strives towards presenting a depiction of believable intercourse while the latter allows audiences to see it in explicit detail. In *Lorna* and *Vixen*, the sex acts are never fully realised. Close-ups of the female body may deliver titillation but there is a consistent feeling of frustration: when the camera pans across bodies engaged in intercourse it must still eventually focus on something else revealing a notable falsification. We become aware that the actors are not actually engaged in coitus and the simulation draws attention to the mise en scène – the strategically placed bed sheets or the positions that cover the explicit reveal of genitals. As maintained by Morthland: 'when you get right down to it, these films have never gotten right down to it'.[45] The sexploitation style indicates a desire to go further – the sex in *Lorna* is not as explicit or as varied as the sex in *Vixen* – but the genre only found the ability to utilise the close-up as a dramatic function, and arguably as artistic technique, when concerns about believable simulations were replaced by actuality. It may have been discussed at the time, when *Deep Throat* and *The Devil in Miss Jones* became a phenomenon, but hardcore sex *could* have married with Hollywood stylistics – as evidenced by *The Opening of Misty Beethoven*. However, were this accomplishment to succeed in the long term it would surely have taken a very patient audience. The need to exhibit hardcore sex, involving the real-time complexities (foreplay/oral/vaginal/ejaculation), means that narrative pace is almost always compromised. However, the key films discussed in this chapter undoubtedly build and progress their characters, as good as in any other exploitation cycle, even outside of their spectacle.

This assertion would, again, challenge Bazin's idea that the unsimulated sex act would, when reproduced on the screen, create a documentary aesthetic without any cinematic worth: 'it is clear that if we wish to remain on the level of art, we must stay in the realm of imagination'.[46] Ironically, to return to an earlier point, an example of a Hollywood sex scene maintains that presenting intercourse within the 'realm of imagination' necessitates the use of montage – something that Bazin believed was oppositional to (what he saw as) the depiction of spatial realism in cinema.[47] The coupling between actors Donald Sutherland and Julie Christie in the Hollywood film *Don't Look Now* (Nicolas Roeg, 1973) is represented by the actor's faces and close-ups of hands, flesh, lips and breasts and is further intercut with a flash*forward* in which the two dress themselves. Genitals are obscured and sharp edits clearly indicate that the performers are not actually making love. As sexploitation evolves into unsimulated intercourse, this montage of camera angles to dictate the passing of time becomes less necessary. The *time-spectacle* in the exploitation film provokes a more believable presentation of occasion.

Sex scenes in the simulated form remain relatively brief (if still longer than Hollywood would permit) but the spectacle becomes more protracted when unsimulated intercourse is introduced. In *Behind the Green Door* we see the undressing of Gloria (played by Marilyn Chambers), foreplay, penetration, orgasm and so forth – all of which takes place in a mediation of actual time. In contrast, the time-spectacle of *The Opening of Misty Beethoven* is less extravagant: montage is introduced to indicate the development of character as we view Misty go from sexless call girl to expert lover across a space of several days: the sex, as a result, is plentiful but also exhausting (possibly analogous to the Misty character's own 'trial and error' as she discovers sex with multiple men).

In *The Devil in Miss Jones* the time-spectacle is more confused because various sex acts are introduced without any prelude – the viewer is placed within the midst of undressed bodies. In each example the close-up is imperative to both titillation and to character development.

The style of the sexploitation film does not so much change in its move from softcore to hardcore sex – rather it allows the close-up to tell us more through revealing more. The tease of the softcore, wherein the displayed physicality is exaggerated at the expense of any sexual actuality – both Lorna and Vixen have large breasts – is diluted in the unsimulated sex film. Gloria in *Behind*

Figure 5.2   *The Opening of Misty Beethoven*: stock characters and location filming
indicate the ambition of late-period sexploitation and a desire to evolve
the style into Hollywood standards. (Produced by Ava Leighton)

the Green Door and Miss Jones and Misty in *The Opening of Mist Beethoven* boast a slight physicality; small breasts have replaced the buxom figure of the simulated form. The depiction of intercourse is now the prime element of titillation rather than the 'tease' or genitals or the display of flesh. The bodies are more normative, less exaggerated. The poster image for *Behind the Green Door* stresses this: *The All American Girl* – the 'everyday' figure/spectacle/environment.

Pornotopia in the 1970s aspires to engage: verisimilitude is synonymous with more than just actual locations and intercourse – even the heroines appear more plausible: Misty Beethoven's charismatic but naïve and ambitious prostitute, for instance. Unlike the often centred compositions of Hollywood cinema, depth in the sexploitation film is defined by the body, the exposing of flesh, the bedroom. This style continues with the unsimulated spectacle, wherein the close-up is used as proof of intercourse. The sexploitation film stands to dissimulate time in a way that the classical form does not, and the close-up is integral to this. It may be that the form's actualistic locations and unknown actors also supply the sexual veracity that the genre demands. The ordinariness of the sex environment – such as the woodland location of *Lorna* or the grubby nightclub of *Behind the Green Door* – only becomes subverted when *The Opening of Misty Beethoven* ambitions a closer marriage between Hollywood and exploitation: sex in aeroplanes, lavish parties, cityscapes. Nonetheless, its longest sex act still unfolds in a grubby bedroom. With *The Devil in Miss Jones* sexploitation was appreciated as a *cinematic* attraction: the use of spectacle *as* narrative indicated that graphic intercourse and ejaculation could function as part of the genre's style. Everything in the sexploitation film is about the *reveal*: after graphic intercourse became accepted, and *The Devil in Miss Jones* was a success, only *The Opening of Misty Beethoven* indicates a further evolution of the sexploitation style. However, perhaps because audiences had already become familiarised with a style that was based on minimalism, and shades of darkness (both *Behind the Green Door* and *The Devil in Miss Jones* over pallid colour palettes), the idea of a glitzier sexploitation was always going to be a difficult sell. Metzger, after *The Opening of Misty Beethoven*, championed this style in further films, to ever-decreasing returns, but it was clear that the genre was struggling to maintain interest. While the genre would still produce interesting productions – *Insatiable* (Stu Segall, 1980) features very high production values, *Café Flesh* (Stephen Sayadian and Mark S. Esposito, 1982) has a dystopian postmodern narrative – neither evolves the aesthetic attributes of the form. The sex, when it takes place (and this is the same for all further sexploitation films) is shown in the same pattern depicted by the key texts explored here. Close-ups of genitals, a brief variation of positions and a sense of time-spectacle – and the all-important 'money shot' – result in an unavoidable artistic dead-end. Whatever narrative virtues these, and other, films have are hampered by the demands of genre. Perhaps just as importantly, outside of adult cinemas or VHS rental shops, no one was watching, and mainstream outlets were naïve to their existence. As such, in light of *The Devil in Miss Jones* and its success, it may not be too surprising to see sexploitation re-emerge as something such as *9½ Weeks* – where American audiences could once again be made to feel guilty for even daring to have curiosity about such filth as sex on the screen.

To sum: *Lorna* initiates a film about sex being about more than *just* sex. The lonely housewife, her domination and eventual death, the allure of her nude beauty: the sexploitation film is initiated by solemn visuals, minimal locations, natural light and the close-up as a technique for titillation. Sex defines character and story: men want it, women supply it but, in both *Lorna* and *Vixen*, the simulation of the act never provides a marriage of what the genre demands – spectacle *and* thematic. These films are driven by lust but as long as the end result of this lust is never revealed, the sexploitation style feels stripped of the verisimilitude it seeks to unhide. *Behind the Green Door* and *The Devil in Miss Jones* (and to a lesser extent *Deep Throat*) answer this – penetration can now be seen. Previously, characters such as Lorna and Vixen were distinguished by films that concealed the very act that defined their personalities and operated as part of the narrative causality.

In this chapter I have argued that the sexploitation film introduces a style that is based upon an increasingly actualistic display of the sex act. In *Lorna*, nudity is utilised as part of a narrative that boasts art-house elements: minimal locations, actual surroundings, natural light, unknown actors and stark black-and-white photography. The film's ending indicates a 'punishment' for the same physical and sexual inhibitions that the Lorna character breaks from. In *Vixen*, the sex is more graphic but still simulated. The plot introduces comedy and politics, but the story maintains itself around star Erica Gavin and her increasingly more adventurous sex life: incest, lesbianism, the possibility of interracial coupling. The style is frustrated by a lack of realisation. *Lorna* and *Vixen* may demonstrate a believable simulation of environment, time, spectacle and the use of close-up to detail the female body, but by refusing to show intercourse they remain indebted to the expectancies of the Hollywood style: to hide the true obscenities of penetration. With *Behind the Green Door* and *The Devil in Miss Jones*, the revelation of unsimulated sex provides the genre with the 'reveal' it has evidenced evolving towards. The sight of the 'real thing' allows the style of the sexploitation film to be less indebted to quick edits or intrusive simulations of spectacle (that is, carefully placed props to cover genitalia). In addition, the sex permits characterisation: Gloria in *Behind the Green Door* and Miss Jones in *The Devil in Miss Jones* become personified by their insatiability. The screen corporeality works in binary with the experience of each character's journey from virgin to voracious. With *The*

Opening of Misty Beethoven, the final marriage between sexploitation and the Hollywood style is complete. Less a collection of set pieces, the film allows for greater locations, the occasional set, extravagant costumes and numerous acts of penetration. Evident that the mainstream is not going to abridge the use of unsimulated intercourse, there is nowhere else for sexploitation to go. In 1977, when *Variety* stops reviewing these films, they become spectacle rather than narrative (for instance, 1978's memorably titled *Debbie Does Dallas*, which is *all about* repetitive and badly framed scenes of intercourse) eventually produced solely for videotape.

Williams has been criticised for approaching the sex film through the point of view of a male spectator, with Champagne claiming that 'the money shot is not in fact a fetishised substitute for visual evidence of female pleasure but the apotheosis of the search for male knowledge of male pleasure – which is, after all, no more "self-evident" or "visible" than female pleasure'.[48] This criticism could also be labelled at myself and, in conclusion, I want to defend this decision. Indeed, while women undoubtedly did see titles such as *The Devil in Miss Jones*, the audience for sexploitation was assumed, even by those who made the films, to be male (that is, the 'peter metre' rating of *Screw* magazine). The form's celebration, and celebrity, of its female stars indicates that the popular commodification was of the actress and not the actor.[49] Champagne also criticises Williams for leaving no room for a reading of gay pornography.[50] This is a criticism that could also be factored here; however, films such as *Boys in the Sand* (Wakefield Poole, 1971) failed to cross to the mainstream and were not exhibited outside of theatres defined by their exhibition of homosexual features. Even today, gay sex films – rightly or wrongly – are left out of the anti-sex discussions of Dworkin and her contemporaries. Perhaps, and this is just hypothetical, they just complicate *everything*.

With this said, while there may be an argument that homosexual pornography from the 1970s is distinguished by a group style, such a style did not register with the mainstream in the way such as, for instance, *The Devil in Miss Jones* and, consequently, productions aimed at the gay market are representative of a more specialised, and certainly far more marginal, area of the exploitation dichotomy.[51] The reason that films such as *The Devil in Miss Jones* command scholarly understanding is because for a short period they were compared to their Hollywood 'other' and competed against such at the box office. Of *The Devil in Miss Jones*, *Variety* wrote, 'If Marlon Brando can be praised for giving his almost-all in *Last Tango in Paris*, one wonders what the reaction will be to ... Georgina Spelvin ... her performance is so naked it seems a massive invasion of privacy.'[52] Such critical attention (rightly or wrongly) simply does not exist for *Boys in the Sand*.

The sexploitation films I have discussed not only succeed in providing voyeurism and a close-up 'invasion of privacy'; they also highlight a surprising conservatism. The sex is graphic, but the characters are defined by threat: Lorna is raped and eventually killed; Vixen is confounded by the possibility of an African American lusting after her; Gloria, in *Behind the Green Door*, is presented as mute – she exists as a willing victim in an orgy; Miss Jones is damned to purgatory for her promiscuity; and Misty becomes the aggressive penetrator – impressing her 'teacher' and settling into monogamy. As I will go on to demonstrate with discussion of the exploitation-horror film and the blaxploitation genre, this 'threat' of physical dominance is a key facet of the exploitation movement and its style. Sexploitation is unique in being able to *show* the threat and realisation of its spectacle. By next discussing the exploitation-horror film I will indicate how another pivotal genre in the movement provided its audience with the unhidden transgressions that Hollywood refused to abridge. In doing so, intertextual similarities with the sexploitation films discussed here will be further maintained.

NOTES

1. Williams, L, *Hard Core: Power, Pleasure, and the 'Frenzy of the Visible'* (Pandora Press, London, 1990), p. 4.
2. Ibid., p. 4.
3. Ibid., p. x.
4. Williams, L, *Screening Sex* (Duke University Press, Durham, NC, 2008), p. 91.
5. I will explore this in more detail later in this chapter with specific focus on *The Devil in Miss Jones*.
6. Review of *Fleshpot on 42nd Street*. In *Variety* magazine (12 July 1973, Variety Media, California), p. 24.
7. Canby, V, 'The Screen: "Censorship in Denmark" Begins Run' (1970), http://www.nytimes.com/1970/06/17/archives/the-screen-censorship-in-denmark-begins-run-derenzy-is-director-and.html?mcubz=0, last accessed 20 August 2017.
8. For instance, in South Korea or Taiwan – and the UK up until the millennium!
9. Crane, J, 'A Lust for Life: The Cult Films of Russ Meyer'. In Harper, G and Mendik, X (eds) *Unruly Pleasures: The Cult Film and its Critics* (FAB Press, London, 2000), p. 89. It is worth noting that the success of *Emmanuelle* and *Last Tango in Paris*, in particular, would indicate the opposite – but in the former case distribution was aimed at areas in which hardcore was illegal and, in the latter example, Brando undoubtedly assisted in the curiosity/box-office appeal. Meyer, of course, could not afford big-name stars on his meagre budgets.
10. Koch, G, 'The Body's Shadow Realm'. In Gibson, P and Gibson, R (eds), *Dirty Looks: Women, Pornography, Power* (BFI, London, 1993), p. 27.
11. McGillivray, D, '*The Story of Joanna* Review', *Monthly Film Bulletin* (vol. 44. 522, 1977), p. 154.
12. Williams makes the following clarification, acknowledging the differing academic locations of Marx and Freud: 'Although Marx and Freud define their fetishes very differently, they both share a common will to expose the processes by which individuals fall victim to an illusory belief in the exalted value of certain (fetish) objects.' Cited in Williams, L, *Hard Core: Power, Pleasure, and the 'Frenzy of the Visible'* (Pandora Press, London, 1990), p. 105.
13. Ibid., p. 103.

14. Marx and Engels maintain that the bourgeois fear a 'community of women' on equal standing and removed from their status as 'instruments of production'. Cited in Marx, K and Engels, F, *The Communist Manifesto* (Penguin Classics, London, 2002 [1888]), p. 240.
15. Williams, L, *Hard Core: Power, Pleasure, and the 'Frenzy of the Visible'* (Pandora Press, London, 1990), p. 118.
16. States Williams: 'Indeed, these close-ups of remarkably long, perpetually hard, ejaculating penises might seem to be literal embodiments of this idealized fantasy phallus which Freud says we all – men and women – desire. The ejaculating penis of the money shot could, in this sense, be said to disavow castration by avoiding visual association with the woman's genitalia.' Cited in ibid., p. 118.
17. Williams, L, *Hard Core: Power, Pleasure, and the 'Frenzy of the Visible'* (Pandora Press, London, 1990), p. 110. It is worth pointing out why this chapter does include *Deep Throat* as one of the key sexploitation films. The reason is that the film is made up of individual sex loops and, consequently, does not actually indicate a deliberate style of filmmaking (it is, in its form of vignettes stuck together, more of a throwback to the primitive and threadbare narrative structure of *The Immoral Mr. Teas*).
18. Ibid., p. 111.
19. Luckett, M, 'Sexploitation as Feminine Territory'. In Jancovich, M, Reboll, A, Stringer, J and Willis, A (eds), *Defining Cult Movies: The Cultural Politics of Oppositional Taste* (Manchester University Press, Manchester, 2003), p. 151.
20. Ibid.
21. Williams, L, *Hard Core: Power, Pleasure, and the 'Frenzy of the Visible'* (Pandora Press, London, 1990), p. 163.
22. Ibid., p. 160.
23. Ibid., p. 170.
24. Ibid., p. 174.
25. Ibid., p. 154.
26. Canby, V, '*Memories within Miss Aggie* Review', *The New York Times* (23 June 1974), http://movies.nytimes.com/movie/review?res=9E0DE4DA113BE53ABC4B51DFB066838F669EDE, last accessed 20 August 2017.
27. O'Brian, Glenn, '*The Devil in Miss Jones*', *Interview* magazine (vol. 33, 1973, New York), p. 42.
28. Spelvin, G, *The Devil Made Me Do It* (Little Red Hen Books, Los Angeles, 2008), p. 166.
29. Bazin, A, *What Is Cinema? Vol 2* (University of California Press, Los Angeles, 2005 [1971]), p. 173.
30. Williams, Linda, *Screening Sex* (Duke University Press, Durham, NC, 2008), p. 65.
31. See Freud, S, *The Ego and the Id* (W.W. Norton & Company, New York, 1989 [1960]), p. 15.
32. Ibid.
33. See Creed, B, *Phallic Panic* (Melbourne University Publishing, Melbourne, 2005), p. 27.
34. Lorna as a 'dominant' character is debatable, but it is inarguable that her buxom physique is presented as irresistible to the film's masculine characters. Cited in Luckett, M, 'Sexploitation as Feminine Territory'. In Jancovich, M, Reboll, A, Stringer, J and Willis, A (eds), *Defining Cult Movies: The Cultural Politics of Oppositional Taste* (Manchester University Press, Manchester, 2003) p. 151.
35. Canby, V, '*Memories within Miss Aggie* Review', *The New York Times* (23 June

1974), http://movies.nytimes.com/movie/review?res=9E0DE4DA113BE53ABC4B
51DFB066838F669EDE
36. Morthland, J, 'Porno Films: An In-Depth Report', *Take One* magazine (vol. 4. 4, March–April 1973), pp. 13–16; emphasis in the original.
37. *The Devil in Miss Jones* 'turned a neat $6,604,067 in less than half the time it took *Deep Throat* to struggle over the $5 million mark'. Cited in Morthland, J, 'Porno Films: An In-Depth Report', *Take One* magazine (vol. 4. 4, March–April 1973), p. 16.
38. Williams, L, *Screening Sex* (Duke University Press, Durham, NC, 2008), p. 91.
39. Ibid., p. 35.
40. Ibid., p. 13.
41. Review of '*Deep Throat*', *Film Facts* magazine, 1972 compendium (vol. 15. 18, AFI, New York), p. 647.
42. Bazin, A, '*Umberto D*: A Great Work'. In Bazin, A and Cardullo, B (ed.), *André Bazin and Neorealism* (Continuum, New York, 2011), p. 116.
43. Ibid., p. 116.
44. Kracauer, S, *Theory of Film: The Redemption of Physical Reality* (Princeton University Press, Princeton, 1997 [1960]), p. 32.
45. Morthland, J, 'Porno Films: An In-Depth Report', *Take One* magazine (vol. 4. 4, March–April 1973), p. 13.
46. Bazin, A, *What is Cinema? Vol 2* (University of California Press, Los Angeles, 2005 [1971]), p. 174.
47. Bazin, A, *What is Cinema? Vol 1* (University of California Press, Los Angeles, 1967), p. 51.
48. Champagne, J, 'A Foucauldian Reading of Hard Core' in *Boundary 2* (vol. 18. 2, summer 1991, Duke University Press, Durham, NC), p. 201
49. In the article in *The New York Times* that coined the famous term 'porno chic', Blumenthal stated, '*Deep Throat*, with its star Linda Lovelace, has grossed over $3.2 million in more than 70 theatres across the country.' Cited in Blumenthal, R, 'Porno Chic', *The New York Times* (January 1973), p. 25. Note how Linda Lovelace is singled out as the 'star' – something that would set a precedent for all sexploitation: the female was the 'celebrity' in this genre and not the male. When *Variety* came to review *The Resurrection of Eve* (The Mitchell Brothers, 1973), the reviewer mentioned that the cinema was 'nearly SRO [sold right out], mostly with midtown businessmen'. 'Review of *The Resurrection of Eve*', *Variety* magazine (17 October 1973, Variety Media, California), p. 12.
50. Of Williams book, Champagne criticises: 'its elimination of a space for gay or lesbian pornography, or gay or lesbian readings of "straight" pornography'. Cited in Champagne, J, 'A Foucauldian Reading of Hard Core', *Boundary 2* (vol. 18. 2, summer 1991, Duke University Press, Durham, NC), p. 182. Williams actually does acknowledge gay pornography, however, but maintains: 'Because lesbian and gay pornography do not address me personally, their initial mapping as genres properly belongs to those who can read them better.' Cited in Williams, L, *Hard Core: Power, Pleasure, and the 'Frenzy of the Visible'* (Pandora Press, London, 1990), p. 7. In her later book *Screening Sex*, however, Williams does focus on gay pornography, including a critique of *Boys in the Sand* (Wakefield Poole, 1971): Williams, L, *Screening Sex* (Duke University Press, Durham, NC and London, 2008), pp. 143–54.
51. Take, for instance, *Variety* magazine's review of an obscure gay sex film called *The Devil and Mr. Jones*: 'gay carbon copy of *The Devil in Miss Jones* but with no box office resemblance'. Even in the trade papers, there was a separation made between films made for a homosexual audience (and their minimal appeal) and

the phenomenon of the early hardcore sex films, which were among top-grossing releases in America. 'Review of *The Devil and Mr. Jones*', *Variety* magazine (19 March 1975, Variety Media, California), p. 36. Further, while an exploration of the history and group style of (what may be called) gaysploitation is a worthy and necessary academic endeavour, it is beyond the remit of this discussion.

52. '*The Devil in Miss Jones* Review', *Variety* magazine (21 February 1973, Variety Media, California), p. 24.

6. EXPLOITATION-HORROR CINEMA

In my previous three chapters I maintained that the sexploitation style was grounded within a small pocket of influential features: a controversial statement but one, I think, which can be justified with the conclusion that this style finally exhausted the opportunity for any grand progression. My own argument is that once a trend based on stimulating interest by, to a large extent, transgressing boundaries of aesthetic and thematic acceptance is exhausted, there is little where else to go. In my sexploitation chapter, for instance, I indicated how sex films would later – as with *9½ Weeks* – return to the old formula of 'teasing' the audience with the promise of, but not realisation of, something salacious – an approach that has more in common with the classical era of sexploitation, as documented by Eric Schaefer. To suggest a similar trajectory – the eventual exhaustion of spectacle and style – from the American horror film, however, may seem ridiculous. In the 1980s there were a number of international censorship scandals surrounding horror cinema – from the video-nasties scandal in the UK to critics Siskel and Ebert famously berating *Friday the 13th* for its gruesome on-screen murders. Clearly, horror still caused shock.

What I want to suggest is that the demarcation we call 'the exploitation-horror genre' began, grew and fatigued as an entirely different entity from these glossier and better-realised films that typified the sequel-mania of the 1980s (*Friday the 13th, Sleepaway Camp*) and, to a larger extent, the video-rental period. Just as the likes of *Behind the Green Door, The Devil in Miss Jones* and *The Opening of Misty Beethoven* took the sexploitation style defined by the classical era and then Russ Meyer and evolved both narrative and spectacle, so too does the exploitation-horror film represent a progression of aesthetic and thematic elements. That this style later became, as with *Friday the 13th* or even the more cheaply produced Troma productions, adapted into something more grandstanding – *all about the spectacle* in other words – does not necessarily indicate that the films themselves should be considered to be 'just the same' as those of this chapter.

On the contrary, the early exploitation-horror films have more stylistic similarity with the sexploitation genre than to these later, glitzier and certainly more garish examples of the form – including an increasingly more ambitious attempt at imparting a gritty verisimilitude of both spectacle and environment. In singling out the key titles, I will begin with *Night of the Living Dead* (George Romero, 1968), move on to *The Last House on the Left* (Wes Craven, 1972) and *The Texas Chain Saw Massacre* (Tobe Hooper, 1974) and conclude with *Martin* (George Romero, 1977). However, I would also argue that Craven's *The Hills Have Eyes* (1977) and Romero's later *Dawn of the Dead* (1978) represent the conclusion of the exploitation-horror style coupled with more comfortable financial resources – resulting in experienced casts, larger scope and more shocking special-effects artistry. It is these films, alongside the studio ambitions of *Halloween* (John Carpenter, 1978) – a blockbuster independent that looks as slick and lavish as any Hollywood 'A' picture – that bridge the gap between the rougher exploitation movement and its mainstream 'other'. By the time of *Friday the 13th*, arguably the most influential of the 1980s horror cycle, the documentary-style voyeurism of Romero and Craven finds itself placed within a similar polish to that of *Halloween*.

Even the grottier *I Spit on Your Grave* (Meir Zarchi, 1978), which to all extents and purposes apes the studied, threadbare and travelogue aesthetic of *The Last House on the Left* fails to register as a pivotal title in terms of its stylistic presentation. As mentioned, this is not to say that *I Spit on Your Grave* is *not* an exploitation film – but it *mimics* rather than *develops* the style of the movement. It should be noted that I am also attempting not to identify the exploitation-horror form just by way of its marketing – as tempting as this may be. This aspect, more than any other, is what has probably confused previous studies – mainly because *all* exploitation has become conspicuous by the nature of its of-the-time advertising extravagance, 'warnings' and ballyhoo. *I Spit on Your Grave*, of course, may well be one of the most famous examples of this – but stylistically the film itself is shoddier realised than even the most loathsome of B-movies, which is probably why a seemingly endless, but easily fakeable, gang rape takes up so much of its running time.[1]

Continuing the idea of similarities between sex and horror films, it is worth discussing how the 'money shot' in sexploitation grew towards proof of actual orgasm: evidenced by the reveal of male ejaculation. Interestingly, the 'money shot' in exploitation-horror is similarly based upon revealing something that Hollywood cinema (at the time) would refuse: the human body in its final, agonising moments and, often, subsequent mutilation or molestation. Speaking about *The Last House on the Left* and *The Texas Chain Saw Massacre*, Crane mentions, 'Now, even when ultra violence is eschewed, we know what could have been.'[2] Hollywood films of this era may have been violent, such as *The Wild Bunch* (Sam Peckinpah, 1969) and *A Clockwork Orange* (Stanley Kubrick, 1971) but they carefully edit the very spectacle of death being showcased. We do not see the rapes and beatings of *A Clockwork Orange* in any detail (they either take place off-screen or in distanced long shot and montage) while the shoot-outs of *The Wild Bunch* do not infer anything but a cartoon sensibility: characters may die but their agony is never presented – the impact of a bullet wound never detailed in any believable mimesis of the 'real' thing.

In comparison, the bodies of the exploitation-horror film *suffer*. The violence is 'feel bad': we are made voyeurs to protracted sequences of struggle and/or death. Characters in these films do not 'die' without a fight to cling to life. These films exhibit a far more daring and repellent spectacle than Hollywood could or would aspire to – and not necessarily through intricate make-up work. Unknown actors, documentary-style filming techniques, prolonged spectacles of horror and torture and narratives that claim to present 'true stories' further simulate a permeable atmosphere of dread and disgust. While the 'proof' of death in the exploitation-horror film is simulated, the group style of these features showcases a notable cinematic evolution towards the believable recreation of this fiction. Of course, unlike sexploitation, a horror film cannot present us with 'reel atrocity' but this does not mean that, concurrent to the X-rated productions that were proving popular, other genre producers did not attempt to exploit the concept that what was being unspooled in the cinema was indeed *genuine*. Furthermore, all indication from the era suggests that viewers – less technically 'informed' than today – were occasionally fooled by what was marketed and handled as actual murder footage.

Hallam and Marshment theorise that 'viewers are well aware of the fictional status of fictional texts'[3] and that the spectator will analyse 'a text's realism in terms of their own idea of what constitutes a plausible fictional world'.[4] An obscure example from the history of this era complicates this assumption. As detailed by authors Kerekes and Slater, the release of the film *Snuff* (Horacio Fredriksson and Michael Findlay, 1976) was advertised upon the basis that the feature concluded with an actual on-screen murder: 'Filmed in South America ... where life is CHEAP!'[5] *Snuff* was originally an unfinished Argentinian-American production.[6] It is not a key exploitation film: it was produced in South America, under the title *Slaughter*, as an attempt to cash-in on the notoriety of Hell's Angels biker gangs, or perhaps even the Manson Family, but evidences little stylistic similarity with the key titles of this chapter. Rather than spectacle or 'taboo', what is 'sold' is the cult practices of a youth gang. In its initial realisation, *Snuff* – or *Slaughter* – is more akin to a B-movie variant on *Easy Rider* (Dennis Hooper, 1969).

However, by the time this footage appeared as *Snuff* it had been looped into English in post-production. Shelved for years, due to its inability to find a distributor (possibly because of the poor quality of the filmmaking), *Snuff* was purchased by a New York company, Monarch Releasing, who added a marketable coda: the narrative terminates without any storyline conclusion and the spectator is suddenly guided to a sequence that takes place 'behind-the-scenes'. This 'square up', which ascertains an obvious connection to the classical exploitation form, indicates how – by capitalising on the more studied and gruelling acts of mortality depicted in such horror as *The Texas Chainsaw Massacre* – *Snuff* exploited the whole concept of the *exploitation movement* itself. By eliminating the social cues that remind viewers of their invigoration in fiction (such as credits), *Snuff* disorientated its audience. This meta-exploitation is evidence of how the style of the form, and its reputation for believable simulations of corporeality, permitted intriguing commercial opportunities for producers. It also indicates why such theorists as Carroll, and his assumption that audiences do not mistake cinematic representations 'for the referents those images portray', is incorrect. Indeed, despite the fact that the final sequence of *Snuff*, portraying an actual killing, is shot from underneath the torso of the screen killer (indicating a point-of-view-shot *from* the victim), audiences were willing to be suckered in, perhaps *because* sex films now showed real sex (further indicating the stylistic concurrencies within the exploitation movement). In such an atmosphere why couldn't something like *Snuff* be genuine? Consequently, this ludicrous, but cinematic, approach to staging a moment of screen horror managed to draw protests and horrified crowds and even encouraged government investigation.[7] The simulated murder at the film's conclusion was also mistaken for a real event by British playwright Sarah Daniels.[8] Released briefly on videotape, *Snuff* was later banned outright in Britain.[9] Furthermore, the film's distributor was pressed by *Variety* magazine to confirm that the on-screen bloodshed was not genuine.[10] In a similar vein, *The Texas Chain Saw Massacre* was banned in the UK with the head censor concluding: 'Its documentary air makes it even more severe and even more distressing to watch than *The Last House on the Left*.'[11] Given that all exploitation cinema marketed itself upon veracious spectacle, and corporeal sensationalism, the presentation of such was commercially essential. That some audiences, and censorship boards, 'believed' that these elements were real, or looked 'real' – and were certainly dangerous enough to warrant prohibition – leads to an inevitable question about what this tells us about the relationship between exploitation cinema and the *form* of verisimilitude that it presents.

As seen with the discussion of *Snuff*, then, filmmakers of this period would service the 'tricks' of the classical exploitation period if it could result in audience confusion about the perceived 'reality' of the spectacle (that is, taking a documentary travelogue approach to the action or offering a 'square up' that indicated what was about to happen actually took place). Certainly, the controversies that many exploitation-horror productions encountered upon their release was grounded upon the basis that the spectacle was too invigorating and consequently too unbearable. *Night of the Living Dead* – despite being today viewed as a classic – was even described as 'the pornography of violence',[12] a blatant indication of an intertextual similarity between sexploitation and the films of this chapter.

A New Breed of Horror

It should be noted that other authors have discussed a sort-of 'fleshy excess' that may be seen to link horror and sex cinema. For instance, McRoy acknowledges that in many sex films narrative is subservient to spectacle: 'thinly developed and highly derivative plot lines'[13] that function primarily to ground the acts of intercourse. While my own discussion of the key sexploitation films indicates that they are frequently more studied than this criticism may indicate, it would be foolish to deny that the genre's ability to titillate generated much of its appeal and affect. McRoy also makes a subsequent comparison between horror and the hardcore film, briefly touching upon the use of 'extreme close-up' and 'the application of disorientating editing effects' in both.[14] Instead of singularising any stylistic similarity between key films, however, McRoy expresses a general commonality between contemporary sex and horror productions based upon the explicit invasion of the human body. This generic factor is reasoned to disturb the viewer's sense of an organised world and physical identity.[15] The author argues that this disorientation of accepted 'mainstream' presentations of corporeality allows 'viewers to experience a sense of psychic dislocation and the thrill of transgressing boundaries that were always illusory'.[16] Such a presumptive link between viewer reaction, and the provocation of films that provide explicit depictions of physical transgression, is centred upon an analysis of two productions that share little in common with each other outside of the spectacle of badly reproduced gore-effects: the cheaply made American horror *Dr. Gore* (J. G. Patterson, Jr, 1973) and the Spanish slasher *Pieces* (Juan Piquer Simón, 1982). McRoy concludes that these films act as 'social resistance' against 'the artificiality of socio-cultural paradigms informed by modernist myths of organic wholeness'.[17] It is a nice idea, but one that – under further scrutiny – simply does not add up.

First: by choosing to focus on two films, from two separate countries and decades, that highlight badly reproduced moments of death and 'splatter' effects, McRoy complicates his own argument. These productions would have been seen under different circumstances and even context (*Pieces* can trace its lineage back to a legacy of Spanish horror that begins with *The Awful Dr. Orloff* (Jess Franco, 1962)). In addition, the poor technical qualities of each film are unlikely to permit his questionable assumptions of 'social resistance' to take form: even audiences of the most explicit unsimulated sex films are likely to be disinterested in anything *but* the spectacle itself. Further, as detailed in my last chapter, the sexploitation style is based upon a verisimilitude of more than *just* the act of sex. Finally, were these boundaries 'always illusory' then there would be no taboo to engage with in the first place: indeed, as I have explained, the transgressive elements of exploitation cinema have just as much to do with a disorientation of narrative causality as it does simply showing us gory or sexy moments of corporeality.

Ultimately, the key exploitation-horror films function as something other than just a succession of gruesome effects. While the rapid sequencing of gory dismemberment in a film such as *Pieces* may indicate a curious engagement between the film and its audience – that is, the intentional viewership of productions that shatter normative presentations of the human body – McRoy's approach typifies the loose 'paracinematic' reasoning of cinema that has often grounded academic analysis of these films and horror cinema in general. As such, diverse texts are blanketed together under a wider argument that disregards any sort of timeframe, production history or even context – almost as if 'all horror movies are the same'. Yet not every film identified by obvious generic elements (for instance, the chainsaw killer and severed limbs of *Pieces*) *is* the same and the notion that *all* horror films provide – or even attempt to provide – the same effect is flawed.

Robin Wood was the first author to initiate the use of the term 'exploitation-horror' to refer to independent, low-budget films that retained generically identifiable elements but remained aesthetically and thematically distinct from their Hollywood other.[18] This definition has all too frequently been disregarded as labels such as 'paracinema' and even 'grindhouse' have begun to be used interchangeably with 'exploitation'. Recently, per my introduction, some authors have made an astute attempt to ask what 'grindhouse', as an example, now refers to given that present representations of the term bear little similarity to how filmmakers and distributors originally approached so-called 'grinder' theatres. As Ward mentions, 'Perhaps if we approach grindhouse on the basis that it never uncomplicatedly existed, we might arrive at a fuller understanding of why we wish that it did.'[19] The reason that I find this quote important is because, as indicated by McRoy, there has been a tendency to offer more power to films – even something as unassuming and ridiculous as *Pieces* – than they initially possessed and part of this may be a wish-fulfilling desire to create a 'paracinematic' or 'grindhouse' culture of reflexive awareness that neither the filmmakers nor the audience was aware of at the time.

Nonetheless, it is Wood's definition that, arguably, allows us to consider a group style among a small number of key films and, indeed, there is some crossover between the films identified by Wood and titles discussed in this chapter. Therefore, Wood's arguments are important to acknowledge, even if his analysis of the films he deems 'exploitation-horror' lead the author to conclusions that are different from myself. For instance, each film selected by Wood is appropriated to appeal to his reasoning that 'in a society built on monogamy and family there will be an enormous surplus of repressed sexual energy, and that what is repressed must always strive to return'.[20] It is this 'return of the repressed' that Wood sees *expressed* in the narrative of the films that comprise his discussion on the 'American Nightmare': *Night of the Living Dead*, *The Last House on the Left*, *Raw Meat* and *The Hill Have Eyes*: 'all centred on cannibalism, and on the specific notion of present and future (the younger generation) being devoured by the past'.[21] Wood's argument – that the exploitation-horror films of the Vietnam/post-Watergate era represent a

Figure 6.1   *Night of the Living Dead*: Duane Jones was a rare black hero back in 1968, although his race is never mentioned. (Produced by Karl Hardman and Russell W. Streiner)

liberally motivated wish-fulfilment regarding the collapse of patriarchy and capitalism – does not, however, analyse much stylistic similarity between films.

In addition, *Raw Meat*, the British film appropriated for Wood's hypothesis, does not maintain nationality with the other productions he discusses (admittedly, it does share an American director but even in its cast it has name veterans – Christopher Lee and Donald Pleasence). Nonetheless, by acknowledging that a small number of independently produced, low-budget horror cinema are sufficiently different from their mainstream 'other' to warrant a separate categorisation, and by arguing that these films contain a consistent theme (suggesting a movement, of sorts), Wood's model provides more coherence than the vague labels and confusing terminology that, as an example, Jeffrey Sconce has introduced.

Certainly, Wood's treatment of *Night of the Living Dead* (1968) as the über text of a 'new' kind of horror is also concurrent with other critical perspectives.[22] Moreover, the style of *Night of the Living Dead* can almost certainly be seen as introducing unique visual and thematic elements that influenced the exploitation-horror films that followed in its wake. As the range of dates for the key films of this chapter indicate, and given the unavoidable demands for violence within the horror narrative – including the national fallout, both morally and politically, of the era – war plays a considerable part in the analysis of these films. Not just the newsworthiness of Vietnam, as is often stated by critics (mainly in retrospect), but the fact America was also expanding its reach into Africa in its fight against communism: backing South Africa militarily, anti-leftist forces in Angola and attempting to broker peace in Rhodesia.[23] The country as a major force, across continents, was in the public eye – and it is difficult to avoid the sense that these films are at least making an effort to speak about how American exceptionalism – including the use of violence, especially once it is normalised within society as a suitable response to confrontation, can become difficult to suppress again.[24] In this sense, exploitation-horror has another thematic commonality with sexploitation – the idea of unleashing a proverbial Pandora's Box – a corporeal taboo that can never function within the realms of 'decent' America. Not for nothing do exploitation-horror films frequently give us mirror images – the 'civilised' versus the 'uncivilised', those who no longer contain their urges meeting those who have never had to respond to, or deal with, violent behaviour. This thematic also interrelates with aesthetic spectacle: the deglamorisation of violence, which troubled censors and critics of the time, is in stark contrast to the more technically virtuosic accomplishments – and subsequent lack of verisimilitude – that typify Hollywood horror productions such as *The Exorcist* (William Friedkin, 1973) and *The Omen* (Richard Donner, 1976). The famous head-spinning of *The Exorcist*, or the gruesome decapitation of actor David Warner in *The Omen*, are presented as spectacles of effects wizardry – they are to be marvelled at within the context of stories of super-natural *un*reality.

The 'journey' of character across these films is also relevant to the exploitation-horror film's evolution of spectacle and thematic. As discussed, the female role in the sexploitation film progresses, with respect to her sexual self-assurance, with each title: from Lorna, the housewife, to Vixen, the temptress, and the insatiable figures of the unsimulated form – culminating in the penetrative, seductive, domineering Misty in *The Opening of Misty Beethoven*. The sex spectacle that surrounds them also becomes increasingly more ambitious and graphic, interrelated with narratives that maintain each physical encounter as a progression of both character and story. These films may be *about* sex, but they are also about how their female personalities react and contribute to (or take from) the lustful encounters they engage in. The sex or nudity is presented in close-up, actual locations are used, bodies and, eventually, genitals and ejaculation are documented: the environment and 'real time' of the carnality on show frequents a raw, and occasionally unglamorous, presentation of physical spasms, lustful faces, clenched hands, open mouths. With the exploitation-horror films, violence is also documented in close-up. The physical reaction to threat is once more the focus of the spectacle. In place of sexual spasms are those of the mortal body in its death throws.

Were exploitation-horror films about more than just graphic violence, however? Of course they were. Otherwise we would have seen mondo cinema – travelogue faux-documentaries that provoked audiences with footage of genuine animal or human death – become consistently huge draws at the American box office. Brottman, with a comparison of softcore and hardcore sex scenes, argues that simulations can frequently be 'more effective, more arousing'.[25] Although Brottman's reasoning is subjective, the popularity of latter 'erotic' films, such as *9½ Weeks* or *Two Moon Junction* (Zalman King, 1988), released when the presentation of unsimulated sex had faded from mainstream exhibition, indicates the wider popularity of sanitising the act of intercourse. The actual deaths captured in the pseudo-documentary mondo films, such as *Africa Addio* (Gualtiero Jacopetti and Franco Prosperi, 1966), likewise, also enjoyed only a brief period of commercial success.[26] The unflinching reproduction of an autopsy or execution may disgust but such imagery exists outside of any any effective narrative construction: character, plot and story are disregarded. Exploitation-horror films, on the other hand, such as *Night of the Living Dead*, present spectacles of murder and death within the cinematic trajectory denied by the mondo productions. As with sexploitation films – which would eventually spawn an industry that recorded nothing *but* the act of sex (comparable to the mondo 'shock' documentaries, which would become, as with pornography, better suited to the video market) – the exploitation-horror film bases its style *around* the gruesome imagery it captures in close-up detail. But this corporeal depiction coincides with a larger threat of physical intrusion that each production narrates.

Night of the Living Dead introduces characters who fail to coexist under violent crisis, resulting in their deaths as the terror outside makes its way into a barricaded farmhouse. In *The Last House on the Left* two parents regress into the primal – slaughtering their daughter's killers until a solemn dénouement indicates that their humanity has been purged alongside their vengeance. *The Texas Chain Saw Massacre* introduces the viewer to a family of backwoods cannibals, led by a local businessman who runs a small gas station. They feast on stranded roadside passengers – in this case a group of five young teenagers. The final girl, Sally (Marilyn Burns), escapes from the cannibals but her exposure to violence has driven her to madness. Finally, with *Martin*, a 17-year-old boy, raised by an abusive uncle who insists that the teenager is a vampire (and has convinced him he must drink blood to survive), is both antagonist and protagonist: his violence is connected to the hopelessness of existence in a post-industrial, post-war, small American town. In each of these films, exposure to violence – and its introduction to 'normal' lives – is presented as miserable, desexualising, degrading – the later *The Hills Have Eyes* and *Dawn of the Dead* would continue this theme, until the more 'rollercoaster' thrills of *Halloween* and *Friday the 13th* indicated that terror, rather than outright disgust, was perhaps more 'fun' and appealing. Stylistically, the latter movies are also less challenging – they don't feel too out of place alongside even the mega-budgeted *The Exorcist* or *The Shining*. On the other hand, up until the gradual introduction of effects work in *Martin*, there are no 'cathartic' magic tricks to marvel at: the exploitation-horror film sells a spectacle of the unpleasant – cannibalism, molestation, rape, conflict and extended mental abuse. In these films we are faced with a common thread: the cyclical nature of violence, the consequence of accepting aggression *into* society and the question of assimilating combatants, who have engaged with violence foreign to the civilised establishment, back into the suburban. While this reading is dependent on some degree of allegory, these elements of socio-political mediation exist forthrightly in the thematic of each film. Tellingly, with *I Spit on Your Grave* aside, no major post-*Halloween* horror film would deal with the concept of rape again. It is hard to have 'fun' when sexual abuse is exploited, graphically, on the big screen (possibly another reason that rape became only briefly accepted into unsimulated sexploitation films).

Wood argues that the thematic of these films is 'deliberate if oblique'[27] – although a more suitable phrase is 'deliberate if cautious'. If the sexploitation film maintains that carnal utopia is dependent on either patriarchal approval or the flexibility of the feminine to masculinise itself (or to submit entirely to male fantasy à la *Behind the Green Door*), then the exploitation-horror film presents an America that encourages and harbours reactionary tendencies,

Figure 6.2   *The Texas Chain Saw Massacre*: few could have predicted the lasting impact of Tobe Hooper's 1974 classic. (Produced by Tobe Hooper and Kim Henkel)

leading to the cyclical nature of combat and intervention. It is tempting to sympathise with Wood's interpretation of this thematic as a desire to witness the fall of capitalism. However, the exploitation-horror film, as with sexploitation cinema and its own visual mediation of a promiscuous idealism, never indicates that a dissipation of the system is needed. Law and order may be frivolous to the narrative of these films but an anxiety about both the need for structured and humane leadership – as well as a desire to correlate the depiction of violence with inconsequentiality and desensitisation – maintains less an anti-capitalist agenda as it does an anti-war one. The America of the exploitation-horror film is one that is destroyed, from within, by an identity crisis: an expectancy of force and domination that delineates with a youth pacifism struggling to adapt to aggression.

The films do not present – or even suggest – answers to the questions being posited. If *Lorna*, *The Devil in Miss Jones* and *The Opening of Misty Beethoven* are films that present explicit sex while not necessarily condoning promiscuity then the titles of this chapter capitalise on gruesome corporeal destruction while retaining thematic disgust at the same elements that prove marketable. This conflict between what is being sold, and what is being said, is indicative of the cinematic imagination. The believable verisimilitude of violent acts can be achieved but, given that these moments will always be simulated, castigating a real-life equivalent causes fewer difficulties than the sexploitation film's presentation of, and critique of, sexual anarchy in, for instance, *The*

Devil in Miss Jones. The consummation of wealth – and the idealisation of social and labour equality – remains irrelevant to the politics that these titles draw upon and exploit. I will discuss this point next with a close reading of one of the most talked about horror films of all time: *Night of the Living Dead.*

NOTES

1. *I Spit on Your Grave*'s trailer and poster famously screams: 'This woman has just cut, chopped, broken and burned five men beyond recognition . . . but no jury in America would ever convict her!'
2. Crane, J, 'Come On-A My House: The Inescapable Legacy of Wes Craven's *The Last House on the Left*'. In Mendik, X (ed.), *Shocking Cinema of the Seventies* (Noir Publishing, London, 2002), p. 175.
3. Hallam, J and Marshment, M, *Realism and Popular Cinema* (Manchester University Press, Manchester, 2000), p. 124.
4. Ibid.
5. Kerekes, D and Slater, D, *Killing for Culture* (Creation Books, London, 1995), p. 18; emphasis in the original.
6. Ibid.
7. Ibid., p. 22.
8. The conclusion of Daniels' debut stage play *Masterpieces* features a woman retelling the plot of *Snuff* and confirming that the murder was genuine. Daniels, S, *Masterpieces*, Revised edition (Heinemann, London, 1984).
9. Kerekes, D and Slater, D, *See No Evil: Banned Films and Video Controversy* (Critical Vision, Manchester, 2001), pp. 249–54.
10. Kerekes, D and Slater, D, *Killing for Culture* (Creation Books, London, 1995), p. 23.
11. Jaworzyn, S, *The Texas Chain Saw Massacre Companion* (Titan Books, London, 2003), p. 100.
12. 'Review of *Night of the Living Dead*', *Variety* magazine (16 October 1968, Variety Media, California), p. 6.
13. McRoy, J, 'Parts is Parts'. In Conrich, I (ed.), *Horror Zone* (I. B. Tauris, London, 2010), p. 193.
14. Ibid., p. 194.
15. Ibid., p. 197.
16. Ibid., p. 193.
17. Ibid., p. 192.
18. Wood references 'the four most intense horror films of the 70s at exploitation level'. Cited in Wood, R, *From Vietnam to Reagan* (Columbia University Press, New York, 1986), p. 91.
19. Ward, G, 'Grinding out the Grind House: Exploitation, Myth and Memory'. In Fisher, A and Walker, J (eds), *Grindhouse (Global Exploitation Cinemas)* (Bloomsbury Academic, London, 2016), p. 27.
20. Wood, R, *From Vietnam to Reagan* (Columbia University Press, New York, 1986), p. 91.
21. Ibid.
22. Says Newman, 'In 1968, the year that popularised rebelliousness and nonconformity, *Night of the Living Dead* did its bit for the Age of Aquarius by ignoring decades of cinema convention.' Cited in Newman, K, *Nightmare Movies*

(Bloomsbury, London, 1988), p. 1. 23.   See Baxter, P, *Rhodesia: Last Outpost of the British Empire* (Galago Books, Cape Town, 2010), pp. 442–53.

24. Wes Craven would belatedly discuss this idea with more forthrightness, literally (he appears as himself), in 1994's tremendous and intelligent *Wes Craven's New Nightmare*.

25. Brottman, M, *Offensive Films* (Vaderbilt University Press, Nashville, 2005 [1997]), p. 149.

26. See Kerekes, D and Slater, D, *Killing for Culture* (Creation Books, London, 1995).

27. Wood, R, *From Vietnam to Reagan* (Columbia University Press, New York, 1986), p. 133.

7. CANNIBALISING TRADITION: ROMERO'S ZOMBIES AND A BLOOD FEAST

Just as *Lorna* is not is the first sexploitation film, *Night of the Living Dead* is not the first exploitation-horror film: this distinction belongs to *Blood Feast* (Herschell Gordon Lewis, 1963). *Blood Feast*, as with *The Immoral Mr. Teas* that instigated the sexploitation *cycle*, if not the sexploitation *style*, is shot in full colour – as opposed to the grainy 16 mm black and white of *Night of the Living Dead* – and exhibits the contemporary spectacle of mortality and mutilation that became the most recognisable and marketable *aesthetic* trait of the exploitation-horror form.[1] Beloved by fans of more left-field horror cinema (one suspects that when Sconce references paracinematic viewers who are tuned into the ineptness of 'trashy' low-budget excess he may have Lewis in mind), *Blood Feast* is an influential but technically amateurish film. For instance, Briggs comments that *Blood Feast* is almost entirely comprised of spectacle: 'the first movie in which people died with their eyes open, the first movie to show limbs hacked off on camera, the first movie to show brains and intestines and gaping wounds'.[2] Today, at least one academic has claimed *Blood Feast* as the film to inform 'the narrative themes and visual motifs' of so-called 'torture porn' movies such as *Hostel* (Eli Roth, 2005).[3]

As with *The Immoral Mr. Teas* – which presented loosely connected vignettes of corporeality in its imagery of nude women – *Blood Feast* permits an anarchic sense of bodily destruction but with minor regard for characterisation, narrative or even technical proficiency. Comments Briggs: 'a cultural artefact that was celebrated because it was forbidden, antisocial, sleazy, and bizarre'.[4] Miller concurs: 'the landmark *Blood Feast* (1963), which has the dubious distinction of being the first splatter film in the history of cinema'. It is this 'splatter' – slang term for the reveal of the gore 'money shot' – that permits *Blood Feast* to be influential but, much like the contemporary disregard for *Hostel* and its ilk, be dismissed as something almost too vile to be treated seriously. Released after the decline of American film censorship, *Blood Feast* takes the grubby and minimal locations of the sexploitation genre (the first scene of graphic death takes place in a rundown motel bathroom – it could just as easily be the visual cue for a sex sequence) and anticipates recurring moments of mortality. It *is* gruesome, but thanks to the nudge–nudge style of acting, which ramps up a sense of dramatic irony and farce, its tone is frequently comical. Indeed, not unlike *Hostel* itself – which has a strong sense of absurdity (in one gruesomely hilarious sequence a victim searches around a bloody floor for his missing fingers, while appearing to have suffered no evident pain) – *Blood Feast* is just as interested in inspiring laughs. This intent is even more apparent in director Herschell Gordon Lewis's later work, such as *The Gore Gore Girls* (1972), which features a female victim having her nipple sliced off and the resulting wound spurting chocolate milk (which is then drunk by the killer). It may not be politically correct, but these scenes – while in bad taste – belong almost unto a sub-genre of hitherto undefined 'exploitation comedy'.

Nevertheless, *Blood Feast* does introduce the concept of showing *everything* – of exposing the previously forbidden: full-colour carnage, intestines being yanked out of (mannequin) bodies, tongues torn from mouths. Even the grim actuality of the mondo spectacle – by way of the documentary camera being frequently positioned from the point of view of a bystander to the action – is virtually incomparable to the close-up depictions of innards and hacked asunder limbs offered by the simulations of *Blood Feast*. Camera space in sexploitation was initially consumed by the female torso before the sight of penetration and genitals took precedence in hardcore. In exploitation-horror, the screen is dominated by a similar insatiable consumption – the spilling of blood, the impact of bludgeoning or stabbing, the severing of limbs, the cannibalism of flesh: the camera refuses to turn away. If *The Immoral Mr. Teas* initiates the presentation of explicit nudity within a narrative structure, of showing us on-camera what Hollywood shied away from, *Blood Feast* is a calculated attempt at breaking the taboo of gore. As opposed to insinuating violent death or using montage, a technique that typifies the famous shower scene in *Psycho* (Alfred Hitchcock, 1960), *Blood Feast* lingers, in close-up, on its victims (almost always female) being eviscerated. It is not a coincidence that the first death of the film takes place in a motel bathroom – wherein a woman has her leg removed amidst a torrent of oozing blood. What *Psycho* only alluded to through sharp cuts, jarring music and montage is statically recreated in *Blood Feast* via colourful, uninhibited close-up: the spatial realm of the camera is, during scenes of murder, taken up entirely by limbs and bright red fluids.

In a sense, it does not matter that the special effects in *Blood Feast* are unconvincing – such as the scene where the oversized tongue of an animal is pulled from the mouth of a petite female.[5] It is the film's desire to progress horror cinema into a hitherto unthinkable verisimilitude of prolonged violence that makes *Blood Feast* – as a concept – influential. The challenge for subsequent horror filmmakers was to close the gap between the amateurism and comedic tone of *Blood Feast* and the attempted corporeal verisimilitude, documented in unflinching close-up, which the feature presented but failed to adequately simulate.[6] Lewis proved himself incapable of this task – as attested by the jokeshop special effects and heightened slapstick of his follow-up projects *Two Thousand Maniacs!* (1964) and *Gruesome Twosome* (1967) – and instead the proverbial baton was taken up by the more famous George Romero. As such, just as *Lorna* made the spectacle of nudity and intercourse a functional part of its narrative causality, *Night of the Living Dead* takes the graphic gore of *Blood Feast* and exhibits such repugnant imagery as a central part of moving its plot and story forward.

Figure 7.1 *Night of the Living Dead*: the film's fiery nihilism continues to inspire the horror genre. (Produced by Karl Hardman and Russell W. Streiner)

In *Night of the Living Dead* a brother, Johnny (Russ Streiner), and a sister, Barbra (Judith O'Dea), visit the resting place of their father. They become pursued by a mysterious ghoul – one of the 'living dead' – who kills Johnny. Barbra escapes into a farmhouse where she meets an African-American man called Ben (Duane Jones). In the basement of the house are two teenagers, Judy (Judith Ridley), and Tom (Keith Wayne), and a small family: father Harry (Karl Hardman), mother Helen (Marilyn Eastman) and their young, ill daughter Karen (Kyla Schon) – who has been bitten by one of the zombies outside. As tensions arise, and Ben and Harry fight over who should dominate the alpha-male position, the ghouls build up in number outside. Judy and Tom attempt to escape in a van outside but they fumble with a canister of fuel and instigate a detonation that immediately kills them. The marauders feast on their remains. Karen turns into one of zombies and stabs her mother to death, later devouring her. Ben and Harry engage in combat and Ben kills Harry with a rifle. Barbra, who fleetingly slips into hysteria, tries to board up the door to the farmhouse but is attacked by her brother Johnny, now also transformed, and pulled outside to her death. Retreating to the basement Ben survives until morning. An armed mob outside mistake the film's 'hero' for one of the dead and shoot him through the head. 'That's another one for the fire,' remarks the leader of the hunt.

Night of the Living Dead can be viewed as the *Lorna* of the exploitation-horror film: monochrome, disturbing, depictive of its spectacle but about more than just its title promises of saleable ghoulishness. *Night of the Living Dead* follows the graphic violence of *Blood Feast* by allowing gruesome special effects to centralise pivotal moments in the narrative, but it strips the narrative of any humour. *Lorna* followed *The Immoral Mr. Teas* by introducing the use of explicit sexual scenarios as contributory to the narrative rather than to act *as the narrative* and, likewise, it progressed the form by refusing to play its set pieces for comedic value. *Night of the Living Dead* presents its gruesome exhibitions within a more cinematic aesthetic that solidifies the style of the films that it inspired. For instance, Hoberman describes *Night of the Living Dead* as 'not bound by Hollywood decorum . . . closer to the raw immediacy of underground movies and cinema vérité than to any studio production'.[7] Expressionistic angles, handheld camera shots, long establishing sequences and even the presence of (simulated) news footage provide *Night of the Living Dead* with an amalgamation of disorientating film styles. Rarely does the film look like a Hollywood production: actual locations, jarring cuts, graphic close-ups on explicit violence and prolonged spectacle distinguish the aesthetic of *Night of the Living Dead*. The film notably lacks the studio expense of a Hollywood production. The cast is comprised of unknowns, the farmhouse looks lived-in, as opposed to a studio recreation, and when the film shows us news footage it looks and sounds *just like* news footage primarily because it has been staged as such: randomly shot, on the streets, with an amateur cast, no synthetic lighting, unaware passers-by and a handheld camera.

Moreover, when the ghouls in *Night of the Living Dead* consume human flesh they perform in an animalistic fashion – fighting over innards, chewing on bones and offal, scrambling for remains. This animalistic performance is captured by a distanced camera that only allows the close-up to function in order to highlight the verisimilitude of the special effects – doubtlessly butcher-shop carcasses ala Herschell Gordon Lewis but devoured by the cast in a means more degrading than a Hollywood production would reveal. And certainly more degrading than Lewis's splatter silliness ever evoked (actors typically fondling offal with their eyes piercing the camera). The film's rawness, including the dingy monochrome photography, immediates the same authenticity as Italian neorealism and arguably succeeds even more efficiently because it utilises additional documentary methods. The camera in *Night of the Living Dead* refuses to decline depiction – it frequently moves *with* the spectacle as opposed to making it apparent that it is consciously staging it: perhaps this is the key stylistic attribute that connects sexploitation and horror. That handheld desire among the two demarcations to contain the spectacle within the frame – to focus, zoom, fixate and even carefully choreograph the most heightened moments of physicality.

If we compare this approach to the famous sequence in *The Exorcist*, in which Regan (played by Linda Blair) slowly spins her head around – the camera remains fixed in one place. The 'trick' is to present the special effect, with minimal cutaway to reaction shots, in as static a form as possible, itself drawing attention to its intricate puppetry. By contrast, *Night of the Living Dead* – and subsequent exploitation-horror films – use documentary means to capture their spectacle ala the veracity of un-simulated intercourse in the sexploitation genre. The frequent technical inadequacy of this approach, for instance, the crudity of the illusion, actually adds to the raw aesthetic – a depiction of un-Hollywood glamour: be it unattractive performers and locations or seemingly haphazard locations and background activity. Perhaps all too aware of their inability to present the luxurious studio surroundings and/or Oscar-level special effects of a blockbuster title such as *The Exorcist*, the exploitation-horror film is inclined towards an impoverished stylisation. This handheld vérité approach, by necessity, is unavoidably reminiscent of the documentary lens. The camera in the exploitation-film attempts to mimic actuality: from sombre, low-key surroundings to the 'as-it-happens' spectre of protracted, violent death – usually implied or displayed by shaky, handheld camera work. By maintaining a static position and revealing an expensive special effect, these films would betray their low-budget origins (perversely this is why Lewis's work doesn't have much affect: he keeps his camera static). Without the financial resources to do this, the credible simulation of murder is what awards exploitation-horror films such as *Night of the Living Dead* their marketability: they are edgier, rougher and nastier than their Hollywood comparables. These aesthetic elements also make *Night of the Living Dead* sufficiently its own creation – too considered and serious to be a B-movie and too gruesome and experimental to be analogous to any horror film from Hollywood. The film has been written about in the past, certainly, but few actually have attempted to understand why it was so ground-breaking – the guts and gore, one may argue, are only one small element of its stylistic inventiveness.

Following this aesthetic, further exploitation-horror films would often confound the critical establishment. A common criticism was that these films went too far with their spectacle: *they became too convincing*. To return to Wood: the author answers a condemnation of the 'lowbrow' nature of independent horror cinema (or 'trash' as Sconce later suggests). Wood argues that there is a class bias within the critical establishment, one that fails to acknowledge that the gruesome commercial spectacle inherent in exploitation-horror films represents and allegorises socio-political reform.[8] In other words, some commentators fail to see *beyond* the spectacle. Even today scholars are quick to mention that, after decades of re-appraisal, *Night of the Living Dead* is about something more than just its horrors – 'about one generation cannibalising another in the grind mill of the Vietnam War'.[9] Given that, for instance, Sconce valorises marginal 'paracinematic' productions through their inability to rival the slick production values of Hollywood, this defensive status is understandable.[10] However the problem with, for instance, Wood's conclusion is that it does not permit the gritty simulation of death in these films to be seen as part of a wider attempt at subverting the normative visual procedures of Hollywood (that is, the unhiding what the mainstream refuses to show). Likewise, any metaphoric reading of *Night of the Living Dead* forgets that the undertones of Vietnam would, likely, have been lost on an audience of thrill-seeking genre viewers and, less this seem like an elitist or (heaven's forbid) smug comment, looking back at some of the reviews of the film indicate that few, if any, were engaged with the movie on this level.

What we should ask of exploitation-horror films, then, is what my previous chapter asked of sexploitation: what do titles such as *Night of the Living Dead* do *with* their spectacle? Corporeal destruction is inevitable to the marketability of an exploitation-horror release such as *Night of the Living Dead*, but the violence of the film arguably becomes more gratuitous, and less necessary, if one assumes Wood's reading of the text as a breakdown of capital/patriarchal relations. This is a thematic that does not require transgressive presentations of bodily destruction in order to purpose narrative intention. Accepting Wood's argument that the exploitation-horror film is a 'progressive' genre, itself bound to his discussion of the titles themselves as Marxist tracts that react against patriarchal hierarchy, is complicated by the spectacle that films such as *Night of the Living Dead* exploit. Aside from the inevitable problems of defending the commercial exploitation of generically popular violence for monetary return, Wood's argument belays the means of expression – always corporeal and with the intention of disgusting and/or shocking the audience – which these films confirm. In contrast, if we accept *Night of the Living Dead* and the subsequent key exploitation-horror titles as mimicking a deliberate documentary verisimilitude then these productions become not just of their time but *exploitative of their time*.

Indeed, *Night of the Living Dead* concludes with grainy still photographs – complementing the design of presenting increasingly more macabre simulations of combat: the Vietnam-era newsreels of the time are drawn upon to engage the viewer with a familiar atmosphere of gruesome presentation. This disorients the fictional presentation twofold: unlike the mondo genre, films such as *Night of the Living Dead* are presented as feature attractions. The incorporation of a style dissimilar to Hollywood, and reserved for 'grubby' sexploitation cinema, but also synonymous with television (shaky-documentary close-ups, unfocused zooms, handheld camera) permits a less predictable illusion of horror. Second, the *reveal* – the unhiding of what Hollywood cuts from – not just the cannibalism or arterial spillage but the indication that what is transpiring is within an actual location, heightens a danger that is missing from the gloss of Hollywood. Lewis could not present this because his plots still drew on some kind of oddball, otherworldly thread that was presented in an outlandish manner (that is, virgin sacrifice to the Gods in *Blood Feast*, resurrected ghosts of the civil wars in *Two Thousand Maniacs!*). Such stories are far removed from the sombre, serious tone of *Night of the Living Dead*.

Furthermore, exploitation-horror films simulate events, often happening in 'real time' (hence: *Night of the Living Dead*), to heighten the illusion of an actual documentation. Both *The Last House on the Left* and *The Texas Chain Saw Massacre* begin with on-screen titles that affirm the basis in reality for both stories. Carter mentions that the latter 'can be seen as a hyperreal representation' of an actual 'true life' crime scene: 'using the real event to create greater tension and transgression in the film. This transgression creates psychological terror in the viewer to complement the visceral reactions created by the film's graphic images.'[11] As with *Night of the Living Dead*, and its condemnation by at least one critic as 'the pornography of violence', the key to understanding the exploitation-horror film is through understanding its spectacle as reflexive: commercially aware of its own style. When the camera zooms into the close-up of a Manson Family-style slaughter in *The Last House on the Left*, or the writhing figure of a teenager impaled on a meat hook in *The Texas Chain Saw Massacre*, the 16 mm imagery mediates a grim association with televised reporting from a combat zone. The camera is unsteady, it captures the screams and writhing bodies, but it refuses to remain focused. As if mounted on the shoulder of a bystander, the exploitation-horror camera documents but, until the more fluid photography of *Martin*, refuses to remain in one place and to deliver multiple perspectives. The action feels, almost without interruption, as if it is emanating from one solitary camera lens.

To digress, slightly, and return to Bazin, it is worth noting the author's theory of pure cinema, something he recognises as subjective to the aesthetic and temporality of the cinematic image. The author speaks about the documentary *Kon Tiki* (Thor Heyerdahl, 1950), shot with a single 16 mm camera and capturing the famous journey of a raft expedition across the Atlantic Ocean. Bazin mentions the spectacle that is most memorable in this film – and, for the author, it is that that is most fleeting, such as when the filmmakers capture 'a whale hurling itself at the raft'.[12] However, the author concludes, 'Yet somehow *Kon Tiki* is an admirable and overwhelming film . . . the making of it is so totally identified with the action that it so imperfectly unfolds; because it in itself is an aspect of the adventure.'[13] The innate 'danger' of the expedition, alongside the natural wonders and their threat, move *with* the unfolding action of *Kon Tiki*: the 'documentary' can never replicate the actuality of the real thing – either in time duration or in the vastness of the environment – but its 'imperfection', its *rawness*, assembles footage of indelible power. The adventure becomes the spectacle of those rare moments of happening – the sudden appearance of a killer whale or the 'bouncing on the waves' of the raft.[14] The documentary style of the exploitation-horror film's spectacle, the sudden outbreak of violence captured in fleeting but gruesome detail, attempts to mimic this random outbreak of chaos that Bazin sees in such works as *Kon Tiki*. I think it is worth highlighting this because exploitation arguably works best when it mimics a similar aesthetic – the capturing of something that we realise is culturally ground-breaking: showing us things that catch us off guard and seem entirely accidental. *Our* reaction to this, perhaps, is why we continue to try to valorise these films within subjective terminology or ideas – they remain provocative.

If the exhibition of carnal relations in sexploitation, building to increasingly more surprising and subversive acts (the threesome of *The Devil in Miss Jones*, the female-on-male sodomy of *The Opening of Misty Beethoven*) indicates that the exploitation camera anticipates as well as shows, with a consistency of voyeuristic intrusion to what feels like chaotic, random happenings, then the violence of the movement's key horror titles further grounds this factor. We know that things are going to become nightmarish from the titles alone, but it is the suddenness, and protraction, of the violence that shocks and opposes the Hollywood 'way' of recreating scenarios of horror. 'In a thing (as opposed to a film) titled *Last House on the Left*, four slobbering fiends capture and torture two "groovy young girls" . . . It's for anyone interested in paying to see repulsive people and human agony' stated *The New York Times*.[15] That the bloody violence that the exploitation-horror film 'sells' is inseparable from what it condemns maintains a genre that is stylistically oppositional to its Hollywood other: any perceived allegory is synonymous with saleability – even down to the titles: 'Texas' and 'Massacre' in the same sentence mediating historic consequence; *The Last House on the Left*, indicating the anti-violent dichotomy of the violent images being commercialised.

Wood addresses his feelings on cinematic spectacle:

> Spectacle – the sense of reckless, prodigal extravagance, no expense spared – is essential: the unemployment lines in the world outside may get longer and longer, we may even have to go out and join them, but if capitalism can still throw out entertainments like *Star Wars* (the films' very uselessness an aspect of the prodigality), the system must be basically OK, right? Hence as capitalism approaches its ultimate breakdown, through that series of escalating economic crises prophesied by Marx well over a century ago, its entertainments must become more dazzling, more luxuriously unnecessary.[16]

Despite being financially incomparable to the extravagance of a Hollywood blockbuster, the exploitation-horror film maintains a spectacle that is unmistakably forthright. Titles such as *Night of the Living Dead* promise gruesome thrills and are consequently bound by their own capitalistic rules. The exploitation-horror film may not 'dazzle' or abide by 'luxury' but these titles are removed from any oppositional Marxist intent by their forthrightness in offering a form of transgressive corporeality that the more nuanced and 'luxuriously unnecessary' Hollywood product refuses. Ward calls exploitation cinema a 'nakedly market-driven economy'[17] and it is difficult to disagree but neither he nor Wood are arguing *how* this makes the form any different from its big-studio alternative. As mentioned, the rush for Hollywood to adapt the style of the exploitation movement into something *even more* commercial, and for the key filmmakers to respond by attempting to make their own low-budget projects slicker and more cinematic indicates how important the bottom line was. The idea, however, that exploitation can somehow be seen as a lesser form because of this 'nakedly market-driven economy' is unfair. Instead, what can be concluded is that each trend became quickly exhausted because B-exploitation cinema was, simply, not as interested in doing anything new outside of presenting the spectacle itself.

Certainly, just as the sexploitation film could – and did – provide audiences with a greater sense of erotic verisimilitude than its studio equivalent, the exploitation-horror genre removes the 'extravagance' and the consequent 'safety' that its Hollywood counterpart provides. It is as a result of lacking the monetary resources of the mainstream films that Wood critiques as cynical capitalist endeavours, that the exploitation-horror titles create a style synonymous with discomfort, persuasive spectacle and actualistic surroundings. These elements uniformly provide the exploitation-horror film with a style that can be commercially defined as dissident from its Hollywood 'other'. That this style is used to capitalise on audience apathy towards the 'excessively obvious' narratives (and spectacle) of Hollywood productions is, I would argue, more indicative of the exploitation-horror film's calculated opportunism rather than an imagined 'outlaw' alternative to the mainstream.

To criticise *Star Wars* for using its spectacle to sell tickets but to not criticise an exploitation film for its own binary of capital and transgressive corporeality indicates naivety on Wood's part: an argument based outside of any business considerations. The sole difference in the spectacle that Wood critiques is the expense invested and what the respective films *do* with the exhibition of such scenes. This point brings my own argument full circle: that the use of spectacle – especially in its relation to the wider thematic of the exploitation film – permits a wider reading of corporeal intention. This conclusion is dissimilar from Wood who argues that all screen spectacles must adhere to his own anti-patriarchal prism in order to be considered progressive – such as his reading of the ghouls in *Night of the Living Dead* as representative of 'psychic tensions that are the product of patriarchal male/ female or familial relationships'.[18] Wood negates a wider contextualisation of exploitation-horror films as presenting a similar wanton appeal to commercial excess via a style identifiably different enough to be commodified even insofar as their marketing. Films such as *Night of the Living Dead* and *The Last House on the Left* do not promote patriarchal collapse; they promote the threat of seeing something that Hollywood will not exhibit: 'To Avoid Fainting, Keep Repeating It's Only a Movie'.

At least one review of the era, however, anticipates the more modern reading of *Night of the Living Dead* as something that transcends its genre. Hence, Abagnato, writing in 1969, reasoned that *Night of the Living Dead* 'contains no nudity, but does contain gore, which made it eligible for 42nd Street. The fact is it should have been exposed as the work of art it really is.'[19] As with the arguments of Wood, the author feels a sense of disservice: that a film that exploits gruelling violence deserves better critical reception. There exists, in *Night of the Living Dead*, a more serious thematic intent yet it is *Night of the Living Dead*'s generic elements – the ghouls digesting human meat or the zombie-child stabbing her mother to death – that have ensured that its placement within the Academy is negated upon those who can and will stomach such visceral elements. Sconce and his 'paracinematic' labelling permits some notice of the film's marginal placement in scholarly discussion, but the saleable gruesomeness need not be considered so oppositional to *Night of the Living Dead*'s ground-breaking stylistic initiations within the exploitation movement. Bordwell maintains: 'in a capitalist society there is no opposition of business and art: most artists make art to make money'.[20] This statement is certainly true even if we were to use an auteurist argument in approaching the exploitation-horror film (which Wood does) – directors such as George Romero, Wes Craven and Tobe Hooper all gravitated towards making bigger budgeted films, often within the Hollywood studio system. The spectacle of their early work was assimilated within glossier productions even if the ultimate thematic of their films would occasionally remain.[21] The style of all key exploitation films is based upon selling an epoch-related depiction of some form of taboo back to the audience. This argument may muddy an idealistic assumption of the artist as one who promotes a singular voice outside of financial concern, but it should have no bearing on style. The 'excessively obvious' cinema of Hollywood is carefully, calculatedly destroyed in *Night of the Living Dead*. The characters fight among themselves while the ghouls function as an ideological army. When Ben is shot at the end of the film (by a good 'ol boy death squad whose fast decision to shoot a bullet at a black man, whom the gunman is convinced is a zombie, raises obvious questions) grainy still photographs, clearly indicative of a newspaper, document his being thrown on to makeshift crematoria. Prior to his death helicopters flutter by the besieged farmhouse. *Night of the Living Dead* is an aesthetic attempt to recapture the hazardous vérité of the newscaster.

As such, *Night of the Living Dead* effectively establishes the thematic rules of the exploitation-horror film, which I will now define:

1) *Nihilism*: The characters in exploitation-horror films are doomed to death, madness or entrapment. There is never a positive outcome for the characters. It is interesting that Freeland notes this of certain horror classics, too: 'a kind of uncanny threat' she maintains, 'escape may be impossible or only temporary or illusory'.[22] Freeland argues this with respect to *Night of the Living Dead* but also *The Birds* (Alfred Hitchcock, 1963) and *The Shining* (Stanley Kubrick, 1980). My main argument for why exploitation-horror films standout differently, insofar as nihilistic conclusions, is that these studio contemporaries still offer a rounded finality (in *The Birds* the heroes escape unscathed; in *The Shining* mother and child slay the 'beast' who is left, doomed to die).

2) *Inconclusive*: Whereas horror films previously finalised with the vanquishing of their antagonist, exploitation-horror films do not conquer their 'evil' and the threat continues to thrive after the plot concludes.

3) *Irrationality*: During crisis, chaos ensues – often in a top-down formation. Some form of trusted establishment (government, military, police, parents) struggle to react immediately to, and regain control over, violent events that itself causes more brutality.

4) *Misinformation*: Miscommunication and misplacement creates partition. This occasionally focuses on issues of social class, as in *The Last House on the Left*, but generally represents political division – the hippy versus the hawk, liberal versus conservative, demonstrator versus military. The exploitation-horror film has an 'us' versus 'them' thematic: the comfortable versus the war-torn – *Night of the Living Dead*'s zombies as symbolic of the Viet Cong who refused to die.

5) *Loss of property*: The primary threat in all the key exploitation-horror films is the loss of property and subsequently the loss of familiarity. This element of the exploitation-horror thematic claims sympathy with the overriding theme of invasion and war rather than any evidenced wish-fulfilment of patriarchal collapse (per Wood's suggestion). For instance, the thematic of home intrusion is not always perpetrated by forces of opposition: in *The Last House on the Left* two young girls looking to purchase marijuana find their way into a house in the 'bad side of town' whereupon they are preyed upon by a gang of murderers. *The Texas Chain Saw Massacre* has 'house invasion' committed by likeable American youths who are subjected to torture and cannibalism at the behest of the proprietors.

The loss of property affirms the combative nature inherent in these films: characters are literally displaced from home (that is, the

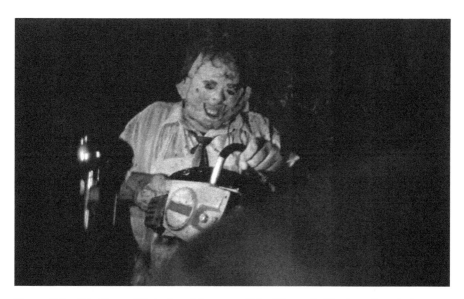

Figure 7.2   *The Texas Chain Saw Massacre*: Tobe Hooper's film introduced viewers to cross-dressing villain Leatherface. (Produced by Tobe Hooper and Kim Henkel)

war-torn), forced to protect their property against an irrational force (presented as either inhuman or *un*-human) or willingly enter property as a considered form of brutality (the combatant).

Having defined the genesis of the exploitation-horror style with *Blood Feast* and its evolution into *Night of the Living Dead*, I will now move on to discuss how this style evolves throughout further films. This will come with particular focus on another motion picture that has, over the years, gained a more serious approach to its various set pieces of splatter and slaughter: *The Last House on the Left*. By tracing the evolution of style from *Night of the Living Dead* to *The Last House on the Left*, and highlighting how the intervening years were also influenced by the growth in commercial sexploitation, the understanding of exploitation as a film movement will be further ascertained.

NOTES

1. Miller mentions that *Blood Feast* has 'the dubious distinction of being the first splatter film in the history of cinema'. Cited in Miller, C. 'Exploring Cinema's Sordid Side: The Films of Sonney and Friedman'. In Cline, J and Weiner, R (eds), *From the Arthouse to the Grindhouse* (Scarecrow Press, Blue Ridge Summit, 2010), p. 78. Brottman argues that it is 'the original narrative prototype' that led to the 'slasher' and 'cannibal' horror films that superceded it. Cited in Brottman, M, *Offensive Films* (Vanderbilt University Press, Nashville, 2005 [1997]), p.28. Clover also states that *Blood Feast* 'provides serial-murderer model' of subsequent horror releases. Cited in Clover, C, *Men, Women and Chainsaws: Gender in the Modern Horror Film* (BFI, London, 1996 [1992]), p. 32.
2. Briggs, J, *Profoundly Disturbing* (Plexus Publishing, London, 2003), p. 88.
3. Kerner, A, *Torture Porn in the Wake of 9/11: Horror, Exploitation, and the Cinema of Sensation* (Rutgers University Press, New Jersey, 2015), p. 60.
4. Briggs, J, *Profoundly Disturbing* (Plexus Publishing, London, 2003), p. 87.
5. Wrote a critic for *The Los Angeles Times*, 'a blot on the American film industry. In production, exhibition, and promotion it is an example of the independently made exploitation film at its very worst.' Cited in Briggs, J, *Profoundly Disturbing* (Plexus Publishing, London, 2003), p. 94.
6. States McDonough of Lewis in comparison to *Night of the Living Dead*: 'While *Night* is still disturbing today, Lewis' pictures are camp entertainment at best. Lewis was an isolated – though indicative – case; Romero defined a trend.' McDonough, M, *Broken Mirrors, Broken Minds* (The Guernsey Press, Guernsey, 2001), p. 154.
7. Hoberman, J, *The Dream Life, Movies, Media, and the Mythology of the Sixties* (The New Press, New York, 2003), p. 281.
8. Argues Wood in comparing *The Last House on the Left* with its foreign-language predecessor, *The Virgin Spring*, which it remakes: '*The Virgin Spring* is Art; *Last House* is Exploitation. One must return to that dichotomy because the difference between the two films in terms of the relationship set up between audience and action is inevitably bound up with it. I use the terms Art and Exploitation here not evaluatively, but to indicate two sets of signifiers – operating both within the films as "style" and outside them as publicity, distribution, etc – that define the audience–film relationship in general terms. As media for communication, both Art

and Exploitation have their limitations, defined in both cases, though in very different ways, by their inscriptions within the class system.' Cited in Wood, R, *From Vietnam to Reagan* (Columbia University Press, New York, 1986), p. 124. Wood takes *The Last House on the Left* out of the grindhouse and into the classroom. However, without contextualising that these films gained their initial fame from the fiercely capital-driven, urban theatrical circuit they played in, and maintaining them solely as products of academic worth, Wood can also be seen as dealing in a form of class naivety himself.

9. Kerner, A, *Torture Porn in the Wake of 9/11: Horror, Exploitation, and the Cinema of Sensation* (Rutgers University Press, New Brunswick, NJ, 2015), p. 78.

10. Mentions Weiner, speaking about Sconce and his term 'paracinema' 'his arguments rest ultimately on an evaluation of exploitation cinema that concludes with the assertion that these are "faulty narratives"'. Cited in Weiner, R, 'The Prince of Exploitation Dwain Esper'. In Cline, J and Weiner, R, *From the Arthouse to the Grindhouse: Highbrow and Lowbrow Transgression in Cinema's First Century* (Scarecrow Press, London, 2010), p. 52.

11. Carter, D, 'It's Only a Movie? Reality as Transgression in Exploitation Cinema'. In Cline, J and Weiner, R, *From the Arthouse to the Grindhouse: Highbrow and Lowbrow Transgression in Cinema's First Century* (Scarecrow Press, Blue Ridge Summit, 2010), p. 299.

12. Bazin, A, *What is Cinema? Vol 1* (University of California Press, Los Angeles, 1967), p. 161.

13. Ibid.

14. Ibid.

15. Wolf, W, '*The Last House on the Left* review', *Film Facts* magazine, 1972 compendium (vol. 15. 24, AFI, New York), p. 657.

16. Wood, R, *From Vietnam to Reagan* (Columbia University Press, New York, 1986), p. 166.

17. Ward, G, 'Grinding out the Grind House: Exploitation, Myth and Memory'. In Fisher, A and Walker, J (eds), *Grindhouse (Global Exploitation Cinemas)* (Bloomsbury Academic, London, 2016), p. 17.

18. This element of Wood's work has also been criticised from other scholars. For instance, Brottman argues that Wood's assumption that the 'horror house' in *The Texas Chain Saw Massacre* represents 'the dead weight of the past crushing the light of the younger generation' is 'an obliteration that has no redeeming or regenerative qualities whatsoever': Brottman, M, *Offensive Films* (Vanderbilt University Press, Nashville, 2005 [1997]), p. 118.

19. Abadnato, G, '*Night of the Living Dead*', *Interview* magazine (vo1. 4, 1969, New York), p. 23.

20. Bordwell, D, Staiger, J and Thompson, K, *The Classical Hollywood Cinema* (Routledge, London, 1991 [1985]), p. 367.

21. Wes Craven's most famous horror films typically involve some form of 'invasion' within the family unit – that is, *The Hills Have Eyes* (1977), *A Nightmare on Elm Street* (1984), *Wes Craven's New Nightmare* (1994) and *Scream* (1996). Romero and the collapse of/threat to social order would be explored further in *Dawn of the Dead* (1978), *Knightriders* (1981), *Day of the Dead* (1985) and *Land of the Dead* (2005). Hooper's later films have minimal consistency with his original *The Texas Chain Saw Massacre* but the 'threat' from an especially Southern/backwoods form of 'otherness' is presented in *Death Trap* (1977), *Salem's Lot* (1979) and *The Texas Chainsaw Massacre Part II* (1986).

22. Freeland, C, *The Naked and the Undead: Evil and the Appeal of Horror* (Westview Press, Boulder, 2002), p. 225.

8. SLASH AND BURN: THE EXPLOITATION-HORROR FILM IN TRANSITION

The late Wes Craven created one of the most notorious films of all time with *The Last House on the Left*, a loose remake of *The Virgin Spring* (Ingmar Bergman, 1960). In doing so, Craven took the horror spectacle of *Night of the Living Dead* and increased the verisimilitude of torture and death to agonisingly convincing heights (or depths, as some critics of the time concluded). As a consequence, the film was banned in Britain for decades – even, belatedly, becoming one of the famous 'video nasties' more than a decade after its conception. And, as with *Night of the Living Dead*, there has been a contemporary critical movement to rediscover and 'culturally reframe' the film as 'art'.[1] At least one thing I do want to conclude is that, 'art' or otherwise, *The Last House on the Left* – as with *The Devil in Miss Jones* – represents the most successful stylistic achievement of its genre.

The Last House on the Left certainly feels transgressive, even by today's standards of 'torture porn', splatter remakes and controversial direct-to-video schlock such as *Gutterballs* (Ryan Nicholson, 2008). For a start, the film humanises a quartet of murderous rapists – one of whom weeps following his torture and molestation of a 17-year-old female. This radical humanisation of 'evil' characters confuses our identification with the villains. One critic of the time commented: 'Lingering gore, senseless cruelty, sadism and fetishism shock and dismay viewers.'[2] Even some of the genre's most famous critics found themselves unsure of how to approach Craven's debut film. Celebrated *Fangoria* contributor Chas Balun would write that *The Last House on the Left* should be scorned for its 'explicit horror and mayhem ... one of the most repugnant "horror" films ever made'.[3] Similarly, Tobe Hooper's later *The Texas Chain Saw Massacre* would be banned in Britain for 'the limited encouragement of identification with the innocents'.[4] *The Texas Chain Saw Massacre*'s spectacle was also criticised for being 'very persuasive'.[5] The exploitation-horror film was successful in evolving its presentation of actuality to such an extent that censors and critics seemed conflicted as regards how to express their feelings about the obvious simulations on-screen in relation to the power (even if it was the power to offence) that they contained. For instance, *The Texas Chain Saw Massacre* becomes condemned, as opposed to praised, for being 'very persuasive' – although one may argue that this shows a very skilful manipulation of the cinematic form. Brottman approaches the film as a fairy tale but channels Bazin's discussion of 'pure cinema' by maintaining the invigorating spectacle of *The Texas Chain Saw Massacre* as 'one of the only stories of true horror that our culture has produced'.[6] The unrelenting grittiness and the raw actuality of unfolding terror and death of *Night of the Living Dead*, *The Last House on the Left* and *The Texas Chain Saw Massacre* invites commentary but frequently necessitates a 'defensive' position from the Academy – perhaps because of how overwhelming their horror spectacle is. Brottman's argument of *The Texas Chain Saw Massacre* as 'true horror' teases out a discussion of style that the author shies from: instead she maintains that the film should be reclaimed and reviewed as folk mythology – albeit one in which 'there is only evil'.[7]

With *Night of the Living Dead* and *The Last House on the Left* we see a consistent aesthetic and thematic within the exploitation-horror film. With the grainy, handheld, vérité approach to the on-screen events, and the use of the close-up to document corporeality, we have seen that the sexploitation film and the exploitation-horror film share a self-awareness of their spectacle and its presentation. On a thematic level, unlike the films of the neorealist movement, exploitation-horror films also share commonality. *Night of the Living Dead* and *The Last House on the Left* sell their era back to audiences via gruelling spectacle, mediating the gruesome images of Manson, My Lai and the Vietnam War within violent narratives that nonetheless question how a society that celebrates brute force intends to deal with its consequences.

Interestingly, *The Last House on the Left* was initially going to feature unsimulated sequences of sexual penetration to contribute additional verisimilitude to scenes of rape.[8] This element has previously been defended under the grounds of the film's financing: 'there were these backers from Boston who had told Wes [Craven] and Sean [Cunningham] something like, "We'll put in eighty thousand, or a hundred thousand, but we want the most violent script you could write"'.[9] This explicit merging of the era's sexploitation and horror spectacles would have been troublesome: an amalgamation of making violence more convincing through the actuality of rape. The act may be fictionalised, the performers consensual, but the penetration *is* taking place: a further opponent to Hollywood style.

Figure 8.1   *The Last House on the Left*: the Manson Family-inspired horror of this film also evolved the style of exploitation-horror. (Produced by Sean S. Cunningham)

In his own writing on *The Last House on the Left* Wood does not address the film's original basis as a violent hardcore sex feature – perhaps because his 'progressive' argument would be complicated by this revelation of (intended) unsimulated sexual violence and its accompanying monetary incentive. The author's own feelings on such imagery are indicated by his dismissal of the psycho-sexual horrors of Italian horror directors Dario Argento and Mario Bava: 'obsessively preoccupied with violence against women, dramatized in particularly grotesque images'.[10] Wood's 'progressive' argument of *The Last House on the Left* would thus become complicated had he addressed the film's genesis in sadomasochistic sexual explicitness. The motivation behind writing a scene detailing necrophilia with a mutilated corpse, and an opening sequence in which the film's teenaged character is shown 'masturbating in the shower', strongly indicate a greater box-office incentive – likely based on the success of *Deep Throat*[11] – behind the film's conceptualisation.[12] In discussing *The Last House on the Left*, it is important to mention these factors because, just as with *Night of the Living Dead*, the film exhibits a self-awareness that is both commercial and contextual. Had the hardcore sex, in other words, have indicated bigger box office it is doubtful that director Craven, or his producers, would not have included them.

As with *Night of the Living Dead*, *The Last House on the Left* introduces a considered thematic about the cyclical nature of violence and its manifestation into the everyday but does so within an understanding of the generic/commercial nature of horror and the subsequent need to deliver grue-some corporeality. Each pivotal exploitation-horror film that follows *The Last House on the Left* further explores a solitary event (as opposed to the nationwide tragedy depicted in *Night of the Living Dead*) with special focus on the human fallout from an aggression caused by remarkable inhumanity. In addition, each film would caution a socio-political thematic with a commercial self-awareness that necessitated the inclusion of increasingly grandstanding displays of corporeal destruction.

The Last House on the Left begins with a screen credit claiming that the events we are about to see are based on reality.[13] This title card establishes the feature's presence within the exploitation genre: claiming an 'educational/true life' basis even when none exists. It also refers back to my earlier point that *misinformation* is a pivotal element of the exploitation-horror film. Following the exploitative credit sequence of a nude girl taking a shower, her body fully exposed, the film takes us inside a bourgeois household belonging to 'The Collingswood family'.[14] The Collingswood father is a doctor and his wife is a liberal housewife. Their 17-year-old daughter Mari (Sandra Peabody) is going to be attending a rock concert from a band, Blood Lust, famed for their violent on-stage theatrics. She will be accompanied by a high-school friend, Phyllis (Lucy Grantham) from the 'wrong side of town'. They opt to buy some marijuana and are cajoled into visiting the hideout of three recently escaped convicts: Krug (David Hess), Weasel (Fred Lincoln) and Krug's girlfriend Sadie (Jeramie Rain). Krug also has a heroin-addicted son, Junior (Marc Shelffer). The two girls are beaten and raped (off-screen) and, in the morning, put in the boot of a car as the convicts make a race to the Canadian border. When their car breaks down the quartet take the girls into the woods and torture, rape and murder them. In one especially uncomfortable sequence the gang force the two to engage in lesbian sex. Both the duration and depiction of the girl's humiliation and eventual murder is difficult to endure. Meanwhile, two incompetent policemen, with a broken-down police car, fail to make inroads to the crime scene. The killers finally seek shelter in a nearby house – the house of Mari's parents. When mother and father find out who they are providing hospitality to, they kill each of the 'bad' family: Krug is bisected with a chainsaw, mother seduces Weasel and castrates him in mid-fellatio and Sadie has her throat slit. Junior attempts to stand up to Krug and is convinced to shoot himself through the head by his abusive but dominant father. *The Last House on the Left* comes to a close with the two policemen finally entering the Collingswood residence, helpless to stop the slaughter. The film ends on a still image, with the suggested apprehension of both parents. Jarring 'upbeat' comedy music closes the story and introduces the credits.

Wood was the first to see academic worth in *The Last House in the Left*, commenting that the film 'offers no easily identifiable parallels to Vietnam' but nevertheless:

> The domination of the family by the father, the domination of the nation by the bourgeois class and its norms, and the domination of other nations and other ideologies (more precisely, attempts at domination that inevitably fail and turn to mutual destruction) – the structures interlock, are basically a single structure. My Lai was not an unfortunate occurrence *out there*; it was created within the American home. No film is more expressive than *Last House* of a(n) (inter)national social sickness and no film is richer in Oedipal references – an extension, it its wildest implications, of the minutiae of human relations under patriarchal capitalist culture.[15]

Arguably even more so than *Night of the Living Dead*, *The Last House on the Left* is thematically suited to Wood's argument of 'patriarchal collapse' and its genesis in a division between class and gender (a factor Craven would explore further in his sophomore film *The Hills Have Eyes*). As well as paying lip service to Freud with the graphic depiction of castration-avowal, and a brief dream sequence of teeth removal, the film presents two divisive family portraits – one of a bourgeois family and the other of a family from a roughshod area of the city.[16] As one of the 'bad' family proclaims after eating at the dinner table of the 'good' family: 'Goddamn high class tight ass freakos. All that goddamn silverware. Who do they think they are anyway? People in China are eating with sticks and these creeps got 16 utensils for every pea on the plate.'[17] The statement also represents the confusion of the political spectrum of the era – China, of course, was still being ravaged by the brutality of Mao's Cultural Revolution and its impoverished people and famines had been government created. On the other hand, the American bourgeois were products of capitalism – the same system that, on the surface, promoted democracy and equal opportunity. Yet, by 'sympathising' with a peasant in China, the 'bad' family of *The Last House on the Left* are only indicating their misunderstanding of the outside world and its politics. It is this similar inability to comprehend international situations that led America into Vietnam (which had long fought to be an independent nation) – at the expense of indigenous politics including the betterment of the working classes. But there is moral ambiguity to the dialogue that I have quoted here: is Craven indicating his own solidarity with the 'poor' in China and (in turn) his own confusion about the horror of Mao? Or is he inviting us to recognise that his family of criminals are ignorant about the potential for capitalism to provide a way out of poverty (that Mao's command economy never allowed)? Either conclusion indicates that the morality of *The Last House on the Left* is not quite as 'liberal' as Wood, and more recent academics, would wish us to believe. This factor, in turn, brings me back to my recurring point – that the exploitation movement frequently dealt in conservative narratives because the spectacle being promoted was unavoidably concurrent with appealing to audience expectancies of scandal.

The 'domination of the father' is also depicted in *The Last House on the Left* – most notably in the sequence where Krug forces his young son, whom he has hooked on heroin in order to control him, to commit suicide. Unlike *Night of the Living Dead*, *The Last House on the Left* gives clear commentary – or at least satire – on class division and patriarchal supremacy. However, Wood's comment that the film mediates a wider thematic of 'the domination of the nation by the bourgeois class and its norms' (and thus the consequent wish-fulfilment breakdown of its rule) is unconvincing. This is because, although *The Last House on the Left* family are depicted as 'hiding out' in the 'bad area' of town, their social class is never explicitly mentioned or referred to. The gang's disparity at the wealth of the Collingswood family, who live in a countryside retreat that is removed from both suburb and town, does not necessarily indicate evidence of pauperism. The (arguable) heroine of *The Last House on the Left* is not Mari, the rich girl, or her parents, but Phyllis: the working-class female who urges an escape plan from her violators while under duress and threat. Phyllis seeks to find solace by attempting to run from capture and find refuge and assistance in the 'good' part of town where Mari and her parents come from. *The Last House on the Left* deals with the integration of uncivilised behaviour into a society that itself promotes conflict and violence, however passively.

However, Wood's mention of the notorious massacre of civilians at My Lai is not inconsiderable: *The Last House on the Left* approaches violence as something that, once it enacts itself on society, is impossible to repair or simply 'hide' from. By indicating the actual challenges, effort and agonising pain that involves the taking of human life, under any circumstances, *The Last House on the Left*, however perversely, does convince as an anti-violence film (not that this factor should necessarily be the bulwark of the left). It is reflexive to the extent of selling the horrors of war back to the American public. As with *The Devil in Miss Jones* and its conflicted approach to capitalising upon graphic sex, while presenting a narrative that critiques the very spectacle being sold, *The Last House on the Left* represents the peak of the exploitation-horror style because it is both corporeally aggressive and evidently aware of the contradictions of promoting violence within a capitalist product. Tender music accompanies harrowing scenes of violence, comedic asides jar with brutal rape and torture and both 'good' family and 'bad' family become engaged in hideous acts of violence. *The Last House on the Left* sensationally presents this, but its style objectifies the very obscenity of violence: the audience, in accepting and anticipating contemporary horror, must endure prolonged and agonising simulations of graphic death.

Prior to their capture, Mari and Phyllis are on their way to see a band called

Bloodlust – a rock group famed for their on-stage brutality, including the sacrifice of a live chicken. Mari's parents are confused about their daughter's interest in such horrors but do not wish to intrude on her own path of youthful self-discovery. They encourage her friendship with Phyllis, make playful jibes about her exposed breasts and even joke, 'I thought you were the peace generation.' *The Last House on the Left* indicates that the two girls wish to *view* violence but instead end up *experiencing* violence. This factor is important: the suggestion that violence must be contained within entertainment or else it will surface in a more damaging guise.[18] The Bloodlust concert is introduced to indicate that the voyeurism of acts of violence, while potentially disturbing, permit us to satiate our curiosity around gruesome spectacle (in the same way watching a horror film such as *The Last House on the Left* may). The Vietnam War was televised and permitted a distanced disassociation with a foreign conflict that involved such intrusions and barbarities as My Lai. Spectacle and involvement are two different things and *The Last House on the Left* makes a concerted attempt to document and implicate the viewer in the drawn-out horrors that the foreignness of My Lai permitted exclusion from. The contemporaneous style of the film is vital to the exhibition of two young people being tortured and killed: *it brings the war home.*

As maintained by the film's producer, Sean Cunningham:

> Wes and I came out of the '60s as sort of 'flower children' ... we were both graduates of that peace-and-love generation. And one day we were watching a Clint Eastwood movie ... We noticed that there were something like five hundred and twelve dead bodies in the movie, but the nature of the violence was like, 'Bang! Bang! You're Dead!' That led to a conversation about how if ever saw a movie in which it looked like you really killed one person, that it would be a real mind-fuck ... It would be really disturbing. We thought it might be worth doing as a way to turn violence around on itself, to make people re-evaluate that which they call entertainment. 'You want to watch a movie where people are dying? Watch this!'[19]

Given the grainy 16 mm stock that *The Last House on the Left* is filmed on, the absence of studio lighting, the use of actual locations and the unsteady handheld camera work, simulating the vérité style of news photography, the film is both familiar and unfamiliar. It shares an identifiable aesthetic style with *Night of the Living Dead*, and also such sexploitation titles as *Lorna*, but its refusal to look away – instead moving into, and focusing upon, gruelling scenes of brutality as they unfold and, in unflinching close-up, recording Mari's rape and torture, furthers an unfamiliar atmosphere to the proceedings. Whereas the impact of *Night of the Living Dead* was minimised by its black-

and-white photography, *The Last House on the Left* channels the washed-out, and occasionally unfocused, 16 mm newsreel footage of the era to produce an actuality that complements its low-budget production values. The unfamiliarity comes with the film's ability to force its audience to unlearn everything that Hollywood has taught them: the 'good' characters will not escape; they will instead be subjected to extensive horror and humiliation (Phyllis is made to urinate herself and then have lesbian sex with her friend Mari). The villains will be destroyed but the consequence is not cathartic. Their deaths are soul-destroying; the 'revenge' the audience anticipates is presented as a hopeless culmination of bloodlust. Both parents, after murdering the 'bad' family, are shown collapsing in their living room, disgusted and disorientated at the very acts they have carried out.

Notes Crane:

> There can be no innocent return to earlier modes of spooky torment post *Last House*. Whenever discrete violence is preferred, whenever the camera looks shyly away, whenever the body is not torn, a conscious choice is made between turning back or savouring the once unimaginable. Now, even when ultra violence is eschewed, we know what could have been. Prior to *Last House*, the audience was not at liberty to envision the impossible.[20]

The extent of *The Last House on the Left*'s horrors, and the narrative basis in a faux-reality, alongside the skid-row production values and the unknown but persuasive actors, lends *The Last House on the Left* a verisimilitude that is palpably disturbing.[21] *The Last House on the Left* builds upon *Night of the Living Dead*'s gritty illusion of death and dismemberment by giving the horror a more recognisable, human face. *The Last House on the Left* functions as a journey *through* the era that it comes from. It is no coincidence that the film's sole female murderer is named Sadie and, in one horrific and effusive moment, guts Phyllis. Sadie was the pseudonym used by Susan Atkins, a leading member of the Charles Manson family, who slaughtered Sharon Tate.[22] Lowenstein mentions that Krug and his gang 'stand in for the era's most terrifying counterculture "family," the Mansons'.[23] This connection provides the film with a perverse, but commercially recognisable, image of the counterculture gone bad: *The Last House on the Left* 'family' ironically captured, post-rape and murder, under the 'peace' sign in Mari's room is perhaps the foremost attempt to indicate this. The theme song to *The Last House on the Left* maintains that 'the road leads to nowhere'. The film asks whether we can justify dehumanising and destroying our human monsters when violence is something that needs to be controlled rather than enacted. The film's style, including the grainy re-enactment of handheld death, presents a mimesis of agony and chaos that even *Night of the Living Dead* shied from. Exploiting Manson, Vietnam and delivering a death spectacle that convinces, *The Last House on the Left* popularised the exploitation-horror film's refusal to shy away from anything. Its genesis as a sex production *with* violence may have provided the exploitation movement with a conclusive verisimilitude of the obscenities that Bazin feared the camera lens could sell audiences in the name of 'entertainment'.

AN EVOLVING STYLE

Following *The Last House on the Left*, the exploitation-horror spectacle would become more refined. *The Texas Chain Saw Massacre* retains the documentary-style approach of its two predecessors and also a sense of exploitation carnival: in an opening narration, viewers are promised exposure to 'one of the most bizarre crimes in the annals of American history'. In *The Texas Chain Saw Massacre* five 'hippy' youths meet a family in the backwoods of Austin who have been put out of work due to technical advancement in the farming industry. They now run a small gas station that is suffering due to a nationwide oil shortage. The family murder some intruders on their spacious but dilapidated estate so that their flesh can be served as barbeque. The American wilderness, with its imagery of cowboys, Great Plains and the gold rush, is now depleted: unemployment looms, its inhabitants are mentally and physically fractured and murderous activity is a commonality that is either ignored or concealed. As one character states while the film's youthful victims travel to their eventual destiny with the cannibal clan: 'Things happen here about, they don't tell about. I see things. You see, they say that it's just an old man talking. You laugh at an old man, it's them that laughs and knows better.' As with *The Last House on the Left* (and *Night of the Living Dead* to some extent – as well as *Behind the Green Door* and *The Devil in Miss Jones*) there is the sense that if a society does not speak about what it represses, the repression will inevitably need to be expressed in a more excessive form than ever before.

Denial is evident throughout *The Texas Chain Saw Massacre*: the mountain of abandoned cars at the clan's house has gone un-investigated, the state-wide grave robbing has gone unsolved and the warnings given to the youths about trespassing go ignored.[24] The young victims of *The Texas Chain Saw Massacre* must combat against their armed protagonists – whose property they have invaded – in conditions of extraneous heat and unfamiliarity. *The Texas Chain Saw Massacre* initiates its horrors by explaining that something in the immediate cosmos has been broken. One young character, reading her horoscope, mentions: 'Travel in the country, long-range plans, and upsetting persons around you, could make this a disturbing and unpredictable day. The events in the world are not doing much either to cheer one up.' As with *The Last House on the Left* and its road that 'leads to nowhere' *The Texas Chain*

Saw Massacre gives its wayward youth no escape. The escalation of violence permeates the film: its antagonists both drawn to the macabre and disgusted by it ('I get no pleasure from killing . . . just some things you gotta do' states the head of the cannibal family). Their bloodlust has become a part of life. The normalisation of conflict and horror is contextualised and commercialised: the on-screen transgressions acting as a proponent of cinematic nightmare. The frequent zooms, jump cuts, handheld tracking shots and the camera's willingness to provide evidence to the 'crime' promised to spectators, convinces of a documentary actuality. Also similar to *Night of the Living Dead* and *The Last House on the Left*, *The Texas Chain Saw Massacre* 'feels' like an ambiguous camera person is recording the violent terrors as they unfold.

Extreme close-ups of eyes, faces, chainsaws and the 'bad' family's house cut together to validate a sense of madness. If the close-up in the sexploitation film is designed for titillation and character progression, from virginal to insatiable, the close-up in *The Texas Chain Saw Massacre* – with its increasing use as the spectacle becomes grittier and nastier – simulates a growing madness of both 'good' and 'bad' characters. Oppositional to Hollywood, the frequent focus on eyes and screaming mouths, which typify a prolonged sequence in which the final survivor is tied to a dinner table and tormented, intrudes the privacy of both scenario and performer and permits a voyeurism more suited to televised news.

Wood comments, 'On the other hand, to empathise exclusively with the violators is to adopt the position of the sadist, seeing the victims as mere objects; it is a position to which *The Texas Chain Saw Massacre* comes perilously close, in its failure to endow its victims with any vivid, personalised aliveness.'[25] Wood fails to appreciate the allegory of the human as 'meat' in *The Texas Chain Saw Massacre*. The film's power lies in its ability to treat its young cast as expendable. As with the personalities in *Night of the Living Dead* or Mari and Phyllis in The *Last House on the Left*, the simulation of brutal conflict need not channel accepted notions of 'good' and 'bad'. The morbidity of *The Texas Chain Saw Massacre* is so powerful that any thematic attempt to ground the young personalities as anything other than proverbial cannon fodder would only damage the distance that the film takes to its portrayal of the haphazard and faceless nature of victimisation.

Romero's later *Martin* arguably gives us the exploitation-horror film's final commentary on the era that birthed its existence. The war now concluded, Martin (John Amplas) symbolises the returnee: a young drifter who stays with his superstitious grandfather in a small, dilapidated Pittsburgh suburb while attempting to settle into normalcy. However, his bloodlust is unavoidable: convinced he is a vampire by his abusive family, Martin takes to the streets at night to kill and drain his bourgeois female victims of their blood. And as with all the films discussed so far (and also sexploitation such as *Lorna* and *The Devil in Miss Jones*) it is the left-behind that is once again the focus: Martin is virginal, sexually frustrated, confused. His family life involves his verbal degradation. Any attempt to assimilate back into the ruinous society that surrounds him, either through a failed relationship or via employment as a delivery boy, proves fruitless: he remains attracted to violence even when the 'war' is over. The victims may feel 'safe' in their suburban inhabitancy but the cycle of brutality, and especially the brutal sacrifice of youth, remains present. Hence, what began with the ghouls of *Night of the Living Dead* became a more human monster: the murderous quartet of *The Last House on the Left*, the childish denial, regression and frustration of *The Texas Chain Saw Massacre* and, finally, the inability to deplete violence, in the wake of a conflict that has defined an entire nation, in *Martin*.

Wood comments on *Martin*: 'The problem . . . is that it evades the dilemma rather than resolving it: Its eponymous hero isn't really a monster but a social misfit who has been led to believe he is a monster.'[26] Wood also maintains that the film would have worked better as a '"realist drama"'.[27]

Wood teases at my own argument here. Contextualised within a movement, these films draw inspiration from a style grounded by what this book has defined as 'realist' cinema and, thematically, build upon one another. That *Martin* has been led to believe he is a monster, and allegorised as a returning veteran, completes the exploitation-horror film's 'journey' from the gritty

Figure 8.2 *Martin*: George Romero's film developed the exploitation-horror style into more ambitious visual landscapes. (Produced by Richard P. Rubestein)

aesthetics of *Night of the Living Dead*, in which the outbreak of violence forced otherwise rational human beings to commit increasingly greater acts of inhumanity. As generic as these films undoubtedly are (that is, they are *horror productions*: designed to scare/disgust) their style *is* comparable to the 'realist dramas' of foreign cinema that Wood believes *Martin* could, and should, function as. My own argument is that all the key exploitation films take from aspects of 'realist drama' and that Wood's belief that *Martin* would be better without its generic attributes (gory murders and so on) indicates the style's evolution into a more forthright depiction of the grainy 'reality' that began with *Night of the Living Dead*.

Was *Martin* – which made a figure of 'old' period cinema (the vampire) contemporary and undoubtedly inspired the later *Let the Right One In* (Tomas Alfredson, 2010) – the last exploitation-horror film? I would certainly argue that it is the last film of its genre to represent the *exploitation movement*. With Craven's *The Hills Have Eyes* and Romero's own *Dawn of the Dead*, what we can see is the inevitability of where the style would go. If *Martin* hinted at surrealist experimentation and the lure of carefully staged, believable special effects, Romero's later *Dawn of the Dead* – with its endless spectacle of zombie munchings and (literal) skull-crushing gore – ushers in the *Fangoria* magazine era, where horror, much like sex films, could be all about the set piece (regardless of any narrative satire or 'message'). With *The Hills Have Eyes*, meanwhile, Craven takes the low-fi style of *The Last House on the Left* but offers more stylish cinematography, a professional cast (including Dee Wallace Stone) and stunt and special-effects work that showcases an ambition towards the multiplex. Both *The Hills Have Eyes* and *Dawn of the Dead* repeat the thematic of their original templates, *The Last House on the Left* and *Night of the Living Dead*. Craven continues to explore the nature of savagery with a portrait of a civilised family in battle against an unrefined 'wild' one and Romero argues that, ironically on the brink of the Reagan years, a 'liberal' America will continue to repeat its interventionist ideas, and concept of exceptionalism, so long as no one can learn from the past.

Throughout this chapter I have ascertained that to understand the key exploitation-horror films they need to be viewed as part of a greater movement while understood in generic terms: aesthetically and thematically building upon one another and expressing a similarly virulent approach to the verisimilitude of bodily destruction. I have concentrated on *Night of the Living Dead* and *The Last House of the Left* and, through a summary of two other key films, *The Texas Chain Saw Massacre* and *Martin*, indicated how the exploitation-horror style grew and concluded with a concept of era that both grounded and commercialised its existence. If the spectre of violent social events was an unavoidable stylistic influence for a genre built upon the verisimilitude of corporeal agony then the next part of this book, focused on the blaxploitation film, will present a similar context. Once again, the exploitation of spectacle is synonymous with the commercialisation of contemporaneous concerns. In the sexploitation film the central thematic of female sexuality evolved from duress and demonisation to insatiability, expurgation and masculinisation while the centre point of each title remained focused on gender and environment. The evolution of the sexploitation thematic emerged by mediating the challenges of the sexual utopia that, on the surface, these films seek to exploit against the conservative wills of American society. The mediation of a relatable contemporaneous environment in the exploitation-horror film interrelates with a growth in character and a greater illusion of spectacle. This factor is especially relevant as each title moves further into the Vietnam-era and the eventual conclusion of the war: the newsreel style becomes gradually superseded by a more technically intricate and accessible approach that brings the movement to a logical conclusion.

No longer seeking to mimic the 'real' time events of a short, night-long happening, for instance, *Martin* or *Dawn of the Dead* permit a greater gravity of narrative ambition and, with more complex technical wizardry (courtesy of make-up superstar Tom Savini) these are films that provide the viewer with prolonged glimpses of arteries being struck open or innards torn asunder. The style has evolved to the extent of providing a greater illusion – but the illusion also becomes the star attraction. In *Martin*, veins open, blood flows, a chest is caved in: we want to know *how* this magic was created, as opposed to reminding ourselves, faced with what looks like grainy documentary footage, that 'it's only a movie'. In other words: the exploitation-horror style had gravitated into something else – anticipating the VHS boom where attention spans could be shorter and films rented solely so that the audience could 'zip forward' to the 'good bits'. Does this mean, for instance, that Troma is not exploitation? Stylistically, not at all – films such as *The Toxic Avenger* (Lloyd Kaufman and Michael Herz, 1984), for instance, bear far more scrutiny to the B-movies of Ed Wood or Samuel Arkoff than they do *The Last House on the Left*. The fact that sex and violence are prevalent does not, I would still maintain, make a horror film also an 'exploitation film' unless we subscribe to the very loose (and ironic) 'paracinematic' idea of the term.

Towards the end of the 1970s, the exploitation-horror film – removed from the vérité approach of its predecessors – would, as with sexploitation in the wake of the ambitious *The Opening of Misty Beethoven*, attempt to merge with the more linear and visually 'acceptable' generic attributes of the mainstream. While occasional titles, which also include *I Spit on Your Grave* and *The Driller Killer* (Abel Ferrera, 1979), would claim the documentary/minimalist style of previous films, they failed to build upon it. The handheld recording of New York crowds and streets, interspersed with the occasional sight of grisly death in *The Driller Killer*, for instance, mimics the same aesthetic approach of *Night of the Living Dead* and *The Last House on the Left* but – outside of its epoch-defining punk-rock soundtrack – does little to advance this exploitation style further. Following *Martin*, the gore-spectacle that these films built themselves upon, and the reflexive use of taboo and transgression to draw attention to the 'real life' horrors of Vietnam or Manson, were generally concluded. With the success of *Halloween* and *Friday the 13th* a slicker horror film would emerge: based upon providing the cartoon thrills of 'jump-scares' set within the contemporaneous 'home invasion' premises established by the exploitation-horror of the past. Symbolising the merger of past and present, exploitation and mainstream, *Friday the 13th* would be purchased for distribution by Paramount Pictures, who would also finance and exhibit seven subsequent hit sequels.

In my next chapter I will discuss the final genre of this book: the blaxploitation film. As with sexploitation and exploitation-horror I will define what the term 'blaxploitation' means, with particular reference to a style of independent filmmaking that should be seen as distinct from the mainstream and also from copycat productions that arose in the wake of initial successful productions. As with sexploitation and exploitation-horror cinema, blaxploitation films mediate a merging of handheld camera work, explicit sex and gruelling violence, but interracial urban existence is also confronted, sensationalised and capitalised upon for maximum sensationalism.

NOTES

1. Egan, K, *Trash or Treasure: Censorship and the Changing Meanings of the Video Nasties* (Manchester University Press, Manchester, 2008), p. 245.
2. Szulkin, D, *Wes Craven's* Last House on the Left (FAB Press, London, 1997), p. 129.
3. Balun, C, *The Connoisseur's Guide to the Contemporary Horror Film* (Fantaco Books, New York, 1992), p. 39.
4. Phelps, G, 'Family Business', *Sight and Sound* (vol. 45. 2, spring 1976, BFI, London), p. 84.
5. The former head British censor, James Ferman, speaking about *The Texas Chain Saw Massacre* – refers to 'how good it is. It's very persuasive all the way through, and you do feel you are watching reality.' Cited in Matthews, T, *Censored* (Chatto & Windus, London, 1994), p. 228.
6. Brottman, M, *Offensive Films* (Vanderbilt University Press, Nashville, 2005 [1997]), p. 112.
7. Ibid.
8. Szulkin, D, The Last House on the Left: *The Making of a Cult Classic* (FAB Press, London, 1997), pp. 35–6.
9. Ibid., p. 43.
10. Wood, R, 'What Lies Beneath?' In Schneider, S (ed.), *Horror Film and Psychoanalysis* (Cambridge University Press, Cambridge, 2004), p. xvii.
11. Much of the celebratory documentation of *Deep Throat*, including the hit documentary *Inside Deep Throat* (Fenton Bailey, Randy Barbato, 2005), conveniently

ignores the fact that the film ends with a break-in during which the robber attempts to rape the actress Linda Lovelace. While the two go on to have consensual sex – the scene does indicate that hardcore was willing to utilise a similar sense of threat to sustain some kind of narrative tension.

12. Szulkin maintains the commercial considerations behind these scenes: 'Money and marketing were undoubtedly the factors that motivated the raunchy aspect of the script. At the time the project was conceived, X-rated films were on the cusp of their emergence as an immensely profitable genre; at the same time the market for bloody horror pictures was also booming.' Cited in Szulkin, David, The Last House on the Left: *The Making of a Cult Classic* (FAB Press, London, 1997), p. 35.

13. 'The events you are about to witness are true. Names and locations have been changed to protect those individuals still living.'

14. Interestingly, and attesting to the exploitation movement's general unpredictability, just as *The Last House on the Left* begins more like a sexploitation film so does *The Devil in Miss Jones* begin more like a horror film.

15. Wood, R, *From Vietnam to Reagan* (Columbia University Press, New York, 1986), p. 128; emphasis in the original.

16. Drawing upon Freud's conclusion of dental stimulus dreams with masturbatory urges, Wood attributes this dream sequence in *The Last House on the Left* as a 'castration nightmare' allegorical of 'Oedipal guilt'. Cited in Wood, R, *From Vietnam to Reagan* (Columbia University Press, New York, 1986), p. 127. Given that the character is then castrated during fellatio following his nightmare, having hours earlier committed an act of rape, necessitates my earlier argument that exploitation cinema frequently deals with its allegories *on the surface*: the castration-fear and consequent realisation in *The Last House on the Left* is made blatant – especially since masculine dominance and invasion (both of the body and the home) is perverted into insecurity and murder.

17. Szulkin, D, The Last House on the Left: *The Making of a Cult Classic* (FAB Press, London, 1997), p. 124.

18. With his later film *New Nightmare* (1994), Craven further explores the concept of 'nightmares' becoming unleashed because society no longer has the ability to control them through fictitious means: 'Well the idea actually goes all the way back to Greek theatre. They said that if you did not tell stories about horrific things, which were invisible, then the horrific things themselves, if they were not given name and shape and something we could grapple with, would have more power.' 'Wes Craven: The Last Word on *Last House*' by Waddell, Calum, April 2009, Total Sci-Fi (Titan, London) – website since dismantled.

19. Szulkin, D, The Last House on the Left: *The Making of a Cult Classic* (FAB Press, London, 1997), p. 34.

20. Crane, J, 'Come On-A My House: The Inescapable Legacy of Wes Craven's *The Last House on the Left*'. In Mendik, X, *Shocking Cinema of the Seventies* (Noir Publishing, London, 2002), p. 175.

21. One violent sequence from the feature was deemed so convincingly simulated as to later be used as 'evidence' of 'snuff film' footage for a pseudo-documentary released in Europe entitled *Confessions of a Blue Movie Star: The Evolution of Snuff* (Andrzej Kostenko, Karl Martine, 1976). Cited in Szulkin, D, The Last House on the Left: *The Making of a Cult Classic* (FAB Press, London, 1997), p. 81.

22. According to Sanders, Sadie and two accomplices stabbed the pregnant Sharon Tate sixteen times. Just as her *Last House on the Left* namesake shows no mercy, nor did the 'real' Sadie: '"It felt so good, the first time I stabbed her"' she said of the Manson murders and the killing of Sharon Tate. Cited in Sanders E, *The Family* (Thunder's Mouth Press, New York, 2002 [1971]), p. 216.

23. Lowenstein, A, *Shocking Representations* (Columbia University Press, New York, 2005), p. 118.
24. 'You don't want to go fooling around other folks' property. If some folks don't like it . . . they don't mind showing you', states the character of the gas shop owner.
25. Wood, R, *From Vietnam to Reagan* (Columbia University Press, New York, 1986), p. 126.
26. Ibid.
27. Ibid.

9. BLAXPLOITATION CINEMA: RACE AND REBELLION

Blaxploitation may seem like a very self-explanatory term: it was Richard Roundtree as John Shaft and African-American actors firing weapons, talking 'street' lingo, seducing beautiful women and acting 'badass'. Indeed, Koven offers the (seemingly) clearest of definitions – 'Blaxploitation films are, by definition, "black exploitation" films.'[1] However, if we have come to realise that exploitation may refer to something more than just a vague sense of 'excess', then can we also perhaps identify a 'blaxploitation' style and a number of key films? Furthermore, may this style indicate something more than a trend in movies that shared something more than just the race of the leading actors and actresses? In addition, could that style fit into what this book has, so far, identified as the 'exploitation movement'? My answer to all of these questions is yes – predominantly because the key blaxploitation films share more stylistic similarity with the concurrent sexploitation and exploitation-horror productions than they do so-called big studio 'black' movies such as the *Shaft* series.

Consequently, while the term *blaxploitation* has been widely discussed within the Academy[2] as a reference to 'the formulaic cycle of black-centred action films produced in the early to mid-1970s', there is more groundwork to be done.[3] Indeed, such blanket categorisation fails to comprehend the amount of divergent titles that found themselves typified as 'blaxploitation'. Moreover, what began as 'blaxploitation' is certainly not – at least in terms of style – how the genre concluded. By the time of late-in-the-day films such as *J.D.'s Revenge* (Arthur Marks, 1976) and *Black Samurai* (Al Adamson, 1977), the genre had metamorphosed into something very different – the former introduces supernatural horror elements and the latter is indebted to Japanese swordplay cinema. As such, any stylistic link that these films have to such genre trendsetters as *Sweet Sweetback's Baadasssss Song* (Melvin Van Peebles, 1971) and *Super Fly* (Gordon Parks, Jr, 1972) is identifiably minimal – they do not look the same and they certainly do not share a similar thematic. Most recently, Fisher admits that a generally unheralded cycle of 'blaxploitation western' be given more scrutiny[4] – even while Koven, a contemporary documenter of the form, insists that these are 'not blaxploitation films'.[5] He also wonders if blaxploitation, given how widely dissimilar most of the texts are from one another, is even a genre.[6] As such, debate about the term 'blaxploitation', and its common usage, does occasionally surface – a factor that should not be ignored. Nonetheless, as blaxploitation – the term – is unlikely to ever fade, I want to distinguish *blaxploitation*, as it relates to the wider exploitation movement, from *blaxploitation* as a referent to the brief commercial demand for black-led, generally low-budget, films.

In this chapter, therefore, I will define blaxploitation as a style that was introduced by the ground-breaking and confrontational 'race uprising' film *Sweet Sweetback's Baadasssss Song*. I will argue that this style was built upon by two further productions: *Super Fly* (Gordon Parks Jr, 1972) and *Coffy* (Jack Hill, 1973). While the agitprop style of *Sweet Sweetback* would reappear in some later blaxploitation films, such as *Penitentiary*, by then blaxploitation had largely come to embrace the more colourful studio aesthetic of *Shaft* and, especially, the hit indies *Coffy* and *Foxy Brown* (Jack Hill, 1974). As such, any idea that blaxploitation movies were 'street' films really fades as the genre begins to embrace glitzier production values and a more bombastic sense of action spectacle. By the close of the 1970s, blaxploitation films had faded from theatres and possibly become synonymous with the *Shaft*-style private-detective narrative. But this is not how the demarcation began.

Interestingly, the term 'blaxploitation' was coined in 1972, as a derogatory reference to race-exploitation films by the National Association for the Advancement of Colored People (NAACP).

This group catalogued the genre as one that glorifies 'black males as pimps, dope pushers, gangsters and super males with vast physical prowess but no cognitive skills'.[7] These stereotypes are commonplace in many of the films produced in the 1970s that featured a black cast and exploitable sound-alike titles (*Black Shampoo* (Greydon Clark, 1976)/*Black Snake* (Russ Meyer, 1973)/ *Black Fist* (Timothy Galfas and Richard Kaye, 1974)), but the key films in the genre have a more complex relationship with their era than this summation may indicate.

For instance, I have previously stated the problems that arise through the use of vaguely defined blanket terms such as 'paracinema' or 'trash'. Such terminology consequents in the homogenisation of filmmaking that exists on

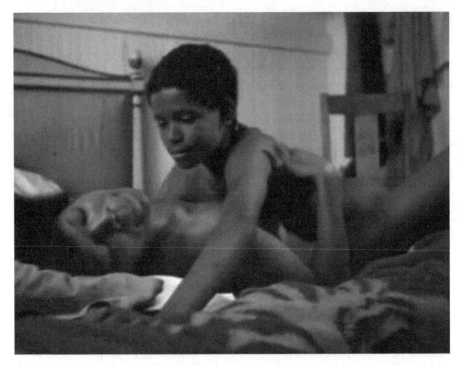

Figure 9.1   *Sweet Sweetback's Baadasssss Song*: Melvin Van Peebles' film faced
controversy for its opening scene where a child – played by the director's
son – is coerced into having sex with a prostitute. (Produced by Jerry
Gross and Melvin Van Peebles)

the fringes of the mainstream and allows little flexibility for the recognition
of particular titles that introduce, or progress upon, an identifiable and even
influential cinematic style or trend.

The broad use of the term *blaxploitation* – to loosely refer to films that
'exploited' some form of racial disintegration arguably carries similar problems. A large amount of productions, featuring prominent African-American
actors, were released during this era including westerns,[8] horror,[9] kung fu,[10]
major studio detective features,[11] a small number of foreign productions[12]
and even an animated variant.[13] Blaxploitation, as an umbrella term, fails to
sufficiently acknowledge this diversity of activity across identifiably divergent
genres let alone any stylistic link between films. I don't, however, want to argue
that 'black exploitation' is a misleading term. Taken as a historical clump of
celluloid history, there is little doubting that these movies, which branch genres
and even national identities (with some being shot in the Philippines and, later,
South Africa instigating its own strain of race-action films), present a provocative form of eugenics: black as heroic avenger against either corrupt villains of

the same race, usually seduced by power or money, or some dastardly white antagonist. Nevertheless, lumping these films together as anything other than this – namely, a label that refers to skin colour – feels like a remarkable brick wall when the demarcation itself has a lot more complexity.

DEFINING A BLAXPLOITATION STYLE

Within the Academy and popular critical studies, contextualisation of blax-ploitation cinema has frequently been associated with the American civil rights movement or, as Yearwood affirms: 'themes of black militancy, black revolt, and black consciousness'.[14] While these elements are thematically fundamental in structuring the forward causality of the film narratives discussed in this chapter, the foremost titles in the blaxploitation pantheon commercialise their sensational content alongside an aspirational presentation of grassroots rebel-lion. It is this urban opposition to (typically) government or police authority that exploits any anti-establishment rhetoric. This rebellious thematic is fur-thered by explicit instances of interracial coupling, frequently with a physically statuesque black male or female seducing a white character whose relevance to plot and story is minimal. The relationship between the racial subjugation of an African-American character, their rise to the status of heroic avenger and a triumphant conclusion (either against legal authority, urban despot or illicit trade) is the thread that inspires the narrative causality of *Sweetback*, *Super Fly* and *Coffy*. Most notably, as with the final victim or decision-maker in exploitation-horror (be it Ben in *Night of the Living Dead* or Martin the fake-vampire) or the insatiable sexploitation heroine, blaxploitation is focused on strong, driven and physically imposing *individuals*. The blaxploitation hero or heroine is just as fierce-minded as Vixen or Miss Jones: their narrative prominence even involves using sex to obtain their end goals.

Meanwhile, the explicit wish-fulfilment of these films involves a desire to escape from some form of threat and intrusion: be it law (*Sweetback*), urban Mafioso (*Super Fly*) or criminal tutelage (*Coffy*). Within these symbolic 'call to arms', in which the on-screen African-American leads are forced to prevail against seemingly insurmountable circumstances, it is possible to see 'themes of black militancy, black revolt and black consciousness' but these elements are inseparable from the exploitable corporeality that progress each story. In *Sweetback* and *Super Fly* the black protagonist is hypersexual, promiscuous and misogynistic. The former film features the 'hero' raping a woman at knife-point; the latter involves a pimp who views women solely as objects of leisure. *Coffy* begins with the 'insatiable' Pam Grier seducing a drug pusher and then shooting him in the face with a shotgun. We witness the gory explosion in gruesome close-up: the spectacle delivers a chaotic presentation of mortality that shares as much commonality with the exploitation-horror film as it does the blaxploitation titles that preceded it. Blaxploitation, in these three produc-tions, is as much about the exploitation of buxom or muscular bodies *ala* sexploitation, and shocking violence, ala horror films such as *The Last House on the Left*, as it is merely provoking a sense of racial superiority. Indeed, the racial hierarchy – the 'black avenger' who is every bit as morally pure (at least insofar as doing things by the law) as he or she is radicalised, really only took off with *Shaft* and later *Cleopatra Jones* (Jack Starrett, 1973).

Williams mentions that the blaxploitation genre is 'every bit as exploitative of sex as the sexploitation films it followed'.[15] The author avoids further stylistic comparisons between the two demarcations but her evaluation of the similarities between the two genres teases at my aforementioned insist-ence of discussing blaxploitation *as* exploitation. This discussion also involves contextualising the contentious, but commercially popular, elements that these films present. The most enduring element of all exploitation genres is, of course, the spectacle that registers with audiences: the graphic reproduction of sex in sexploitation or the gruelling simulation of torture and gore in the exploitation-horror film. This element of identification via spectacle is probably why blaxploitation has been used as a blanket term as opposed to a stylistic reference: the most marketable elements of the genre maintain a distinct presence in the most famous titles. Williams describes blaxploitation as 'the overt exploitation of racialised sex and violence'.[16] The financial success of *Sweetback* – which has plenty of 'racialised sex and violence' – resulted in the film being accepted as the instigator of a 'new' kind of black cinema, defined by its 'resistance to classical Hollywood cinema form'.[17] Bordwell also refers to how *Sweetback* 'exploited a variety of New Wave techniques'.[18] As I will discuss, *Sweetback*'s non-linear editing and agitprop style indicate some influ-ence from the French avant-garde films most associated with Jean Luc Godard, such as *À bout de soufflé* (1960) and *Week-end* (1967).[19] However, the use of real locations, gritty, grimy atmospherics and claustrophobic trappings, as well as a jarring and consistent close-up fixation on images of sex and threat, make *Sweetback* very much of the same style and movement as *Night of the Living Dead* and *Behind the Green Door*.

It is also important to point out that Williams' identification of blaxploita-tion as the commodification of 'racialised sex and violence' does not describe every film that gained commercial traction and also featured the recurring post-*Sweetback* staple of a leading black avenger. The major studio release *Cleopatra Jones* (Jack Starrett, 1973) was rated 'PG' and marketed to family audiences. *The Spook Who Sat By the Door* (Ivan Dixon, 1973), although discussed by Dunn as part of the blaxploitation pantheon, is another PG-rated release, featuring no exploitable sex and minimal violence (the style, however, draws more on the low-key documentary-like aesthetics of *Sweetback* and *Super Fly* than on *Shaft*).[20] The key titles in the blaxploitation trend singled out for discussion in this chapter *do*, however, appeal to Williams' description: inspiring a small cottage industry of films that formatted the imagery of *Sweetback*, the macho, promiscuous avenger. The fact that other productions *do not* follow the formula of *Sweetback* further necessitates the need to view blaxploitation, within a wider exploitation movement, as something a little more complex rather than a loose term that indicates the presentation of African-American characters on-screen. Furthermore, to disregard the blatantly commercial elements that successfully led to the launch of popular black filmmaking, in the wake of Sweetback, and instead celebrate a more idealistic vision of perceived cinematic 'black militancy, black revolt, and black consciousness' is to ignore the monetary reality of the explicit moments of sex and violence that many of these films capitalise upon. The very idea of exploitation – the selling of marketable taboo and provocative imagery – was perhaps never more forthright than it is in the Melvin Van Peebles film. I will address this next with a more detailed discussion of *Sweetback*.

BLAXPLOITION *AS* EXPLOITATION

Director Melvin Van Peebles portrays his own creation in *Sweet Sweetback*: a silent, handsome, muscular loner. The moniker of 'Sweetback' itself is '70's black slang for a large penis'.[21] The title of the film indicates a consequent self-awareness of exploitation marketability to its astute target audience: 'Sweetback' merits acknowledgement of sexual domination and the consequent exhibition of salacious entertainment. This *is* sexploitation, best placed somewhere between the more comical buxom misogyny of *Vixen* (which, via its conservative narrative, refused its buxom white heroine sex with a 'radicalised' black man) and the graduation to hardcore with *Deep Throat* (which has no interracial sex). *Sweet Sweetback* begins with a prologue in which a young black orphan is adopted by the owner of a Los Angeles brothel. We view the character, played by the director's own 14-year-old son, lose his virginity to a prostitute. She forces the boy to have sex with her – partly by challenging his manhood. The woman in this sequence is fuller in stature than would ever be seen in a Hollywood sex scene (but *not*, notably, as per *The Devil in Miss Jones*, a sexploitation movie). Her breasts are large, natural and wilt over her body. The exploitation lens, as established, refuses to hide anything: her exposure is graphic but naturalistic; her weight and imperfections are shown in close-up. The sex scene she participates in is captured by handheld means, grainy 16 mm photography, with minimal lighting and bare set decoration. As with other exploitation spectacles, the camera moves *into* the corporeal act as the sexual act begins to unhide itself. The woman loudly compliments the teenager on the size of his penis. Celebratory gospel music plays over the soundtrack – a Russ Meyer-like 'jokey' punchline.

The story then moves forward to showing us Sweetback as an adult: a male prostitute who performs in live evening sex shows. Two white policemen arrive to pressure the brothel owner into allowing them to arrest Sweetback on suspicion of a murder he is not connected with. They promise to release him in a few days, just long enough to show that they have done some investigation. The plot is agreed upon and Sweetback is taken into their car. He never speaks or refuses. On the way to the station the two men pick up a young Black Panther and handcuff him to Sweetback. They take the two into a deserted area. The sounds of a construction mill fill the soundtrack. There is no music score. The officers proceed to bludgeon the Black Panther. The scene is shot documentary-style: haphazard handheld shots, the camera kept at a 'safe' medium distance: it is a moment that, colour filming aside, could sit comfortably in *Night of the Living Dead*. A break from the violence is provided by zooms into Sweetback's face. As he becomes more agitated, the camera uses close-ups – both on his face and in capturing the increasingly brutal attack on the Black Panther. Again, the camera closes in on the spectacle as it begins to unhide itself. Sweetback finally intervenes and knocks the two officials unconscious. From here, the story follows Sweetback's attempt to escape over the Mexican border – with the help of the city's black community who sympathise with his plight.

Yearwood argues that *Sweet Sweetback* represents a stylistic evolution for black filmmaking because it disregards the form of casual reality and visual glamour that Bordwell details in his famous definition of Classical Hollywood cinema. Yearwood comments: 'As a cinematic document, Van Peebles' creative use of film language immediately set him up in opposition to the dominant ideologies of the cinema. *Sweetback* represents a significant formulation of the political uses of non-documentary cinema.'[22] This statement may indicate that *Sweet Sweetback* is unique from the exploitation pantheon, but Van Peebles utilises filmmaking practices that were introduced by several independently made sex and horror productions. Titles such as *Lorna* and *Night of the Living Dead* initiated the use of natural locations, non-actors, crash-zooms, travelogue footage (frequently shot from the window of a moving car), handheld camera techniques, minimal lighting and a lack of sets. *Sweet Sweetback* also disturbs the Classical Hollywood form by showing imagery that is oppositional to studio filmmaking: full-frontal (black) male nudity, graphic interracial sex, a child being coerced into intercourse, extracted scenes of white-on-black violence and unglamorous female bodies. This element of physically unhiding sexual transgression owes its lineage to sexploitation cinema – and without Sweet Sweetback's prolonged spectacle of interracial sex it is debatable that we would have seen a similar – and equally extended – sequence of intercourse between a black man and a white woman take place in *Behind the Green Door* the following year. Van Peebles' use of the close-up to heighten the orgasmic spasms of his female performers while they are engaged in carnal activity is evidently inspired by *Lorna* and *Vixen* – this is before *Deep Throat*. Unwilling to show 'hardcore' inserts, Van Peebles simulates sex via a tight focus on faces/hands/legs/breasts. The style of *Sweetback* is less synonymous with calculated political filmmaking and more akin to the veracity of the documentary-style approach of other exploitation productions. Van Peebles' prominent use of spectacle, and the capturing of sex and violence in firm close-up, singularises *Sweetback* as an exploitation film.

Discussing *Sweetback*'s possible lineage to other exploitation films, Hartmann mentions:

> For its target audience the film may not have presented a novel treatment of sex, violence or bodily functions. One early 1970s' survey found that urban, working-class Black film viewers saw more low-budget cinematic productions, such as zombie movies and pornography, than its other demographic groups. Those viewers who were used to the roller-coaster rides of exploitation film might not have found *Sweetback* as much of a breakthrough as did nearly every member of my press sample, in one way or another.[23]

Hartmann's point is an important one: it is worth establishing the audience that *Sweetback* will have initially connected with. Yearwood's attempt to reclaim the film outside of the exploitation pantheon indicates a reflexive approach to a production that is extremely savvy in playing to the commercial expectancies and interests of its audience – in particular the stylistic tropes of sexploitation. In fact, *Sweetback* sells the very revolution it instigates on the screen via the capital appeal of sex and violence: both factors allow Van Peebles' character to escape to freedom. For the exploitation audience, who may have witnessed black heroics in *Night of the Living Dead* and the graphic interracial sex in *Behind the Green Door*, these elements would doubtlessly have been expected from a low budget, independent release playing in urban cinemas. The 'political' elements in *Sweetback* are, like other exploitation films, progressed by set pieces of corporeal sensationalism. Sweetback, on the run, hides from the police by raping a woman at knife point – her breasts exposed in close-up. The police mistake them for two lovers and ignore them. Still in handcuffs, Sweetback is 'freed' by a black female acquaintance but only after he agrees to sleep with her (providing the film with another graphic love-making sequence). The story will only continue after Sweetback has sexually satisfied her. The narrative comes to a brief conclusion so the spectacle can take precedence. Again: this *is* sexploitation. Sweetback escapes from a potential beating from a motorcycle gang by impressing them with his sexual prowess and dominating a white woman (who performs a random striptease before submitting to

Van Peebles). The sex takes place, again, in close-up. As the film reaches its conclusion, Sweetback's muscular frame is captured by the camera. His body, perfectly formed, is exploited as an irresistible, sweat-encrusted image of black power: the film ends with a slogan stating, 'A Baaad Assss Nigger is coming back to collect some dues.'

The politics of the Sweetback character are dichotomous to the saleability of his sexual allure – he *wants* to escape from American soil but to do so he must exploit his own body. His 'irresistible' masculine prowess offers the film repeated opportunity for the very sequences that provide it with audience appeal. While the political thematic of *Sweetback* is apparent insofar as white hierarchy is shown to abuse freedom of movement for African-American men (and the police are shown to be corrupt), it is Van Peebles' reliance on sex and shock that proved vital in making his film controversial.[24] A recent retrospective critique on *Sweetback* affirmed that 'present-day audiences might be taken aback by the seedy, steamy sex show performed by male hustler Sweetback and his in-house family of black hookers for the delectation of white thrill-seekers'.[25] Note that the author mentions the surprised reaction that 'present-day audiences' may have to *Sweetback*'s forthright presentation of sex and sexuality. The low-budget 'seedy' and 'steamy' nature of *Sweetback* would be unlikely to receive a cinema release today – the spectacle, and its presentation, share little common ground with what would be deemed contemporarily 'commercial'.

As with the other key titles of the exploitation movement, the topicality mediated via the narrative of the central blaxploitation films remains inseparable to the graphic sensationalism that the movement promotes. For instance, the scene where *Sweetback* is chased by overhead helicopters mediates a similar sight to that shown during the closing moments of *Night of the Living Dead*. In both cases, the presence of a helicopter reminds one of newsreel footage from Vietnam. This spectacle of *Sweetback* – inseparable from the modernity of the era – is exhibited in a style that maximises its relationship with era. The seedy sex club where Van Peebles is exhibited to paying white customers is almost indistinguishable from that shown in *Behind the Green Door*: the latter film appropriating the voyeurism but with additional verisimilitude (that is, some cuts indicate unsimulated intercourse, although both films use the female face, and evolving expressions of gratitude, to indicate the pleasure of the interracial 'taboo'). This association with epoch assists with topical subversion: the footage of Sweetback, chased by helicopter, may not bear obvious allegory with Vietnam but, as with the documentary-style of other exploitation films, it channels a potential audience connection to immediate concerns. The topicality of a concurrent happening: the conflict in Indochina is documented by 'real' news crews. By initiating this style, including filming from a helicopter, *Sweetback* instigates its own exploitation of socio-political affairs in order to establish its own actualistic simulations.

Figure 9.2   *Super Fly*: blaxploitation began to depict glamorous gangsters as with *Super Fly*. (Produced by Sig Shore)

In continuing his discussion of *Sweetback*, Yearwood stresses the difference between narratives that present 'an accurate picture of black life' as opposed to 'stereotyped depictions'.[26] The author maintains a dislike of the term 'blaxploitation' because, he argues, this is 'unable to adequately differentiate between exploitation films and other films'.[27]

In terms of style, the author argues that positive black cinema would initiate narratives 'that empower the black community' and 'refuse to reproduce Hollywood's cinematic grammar and syntax'.[28] With the depiction of Sweetback on the run from the law, and one of his black friends bludgeoned and tortured but still refusing to release details of the fugitive's whereabouts, it is possible to see why Yearwood believes that *Sweetback* contains a narrative of empowerment. The film's style also includes the use of montage, split-screen and intrusive cutaways to minimally related inserts. These techniques further establish the agitprop tendencies of the narrative and occasionally disconcert the documentary approach that the bulk of *Sweetback* adheres to. A brutal funk-rock also repeats itself on the soundtrack, finally collapsing into a ragged and repetitive gospel hymn: 'You Bled My Mother, You Bled My Father, *But You Won't Bleed Me*'.

However, Yearwood's argument for *Sweetback* as 'an instrument for transforming social existence through its own expressive modes' is confused by the film's afore-discussed reliance on the salacious visualisation of exploitation spectacle to maintain the forward causality of the plot and story.[29] *Sweetback* may present white rule as detrimental to black empowerment, but its thematic consistently supports patriarchal dominance. The film *exploits*, rather than expresses, desire for racial revolution: Sweetback, as a cinematic black superhero, only 'succeeds' in the bedroom. His 'revolution' is maintained *through* the explicit, raw and protracted sexual imagery of the exploitation style. The focus on female sexuality, uncontrolled but finally satiated in the presence of the 'irresistible' Sweetback, led one author at the time of the film's success to critique Van Peebles with the words: 'man is not my liberator, nor can he be his own if he lays those chains on me'.[30] It is certainly difficult to deny that Sweetback is a far more understandable commercial proposition if one places it within the sexploitation demarcation, bridging the move from softcore to 'rougher' hardcore and, in doing so, giving us an idea of 'blaxploitation'. By the same token, *Behind the Green Door* could be argued to fit within blaxploitation – the length of its graphic interracial coupling offers an audience of 1972 an even more provocative spectacle than *Sweet Sweetback* – an evolution of taboo. If the Sweetback character was white it would probably be seen as an experimental initiation of the exploitation style but identifiable and contextual as a film that fits within the sexploitation cycle. Indeed, it is interesting that Koven, writer of *Blaxploitation Films*, would address his own negative review of Sweetback in the reprint edition of his book: 'Since the first edition of Blaxploitation Films was produced, I have studied a variety of exploitation cinemas, and the maturity I have gained . . . means that some re-evaluation of this film is required. In other words, I was *totally wrong*.'[31]

Was Koven really so wrong to see such little worth in a film as groundbreaking as *Sweetback*? Perhaps – but what his admission reveals is that this is a movie that makes far more sense in the grand pantheon of other exploitation cinema. And I would suggest that style is everything in understanding this. Nonetheless, Van Peebles' use of occasional non-linear editing disorients the more accessible storytelling of even the most ambitious exploitation films. Concluding titles in the key exploitation genres, such as *The Opening of Misty Beethoven* or *Martin*, introduced montage and flashback into the previously linear, raw and minimalist stylistic and generic approach – perhaps indicating the influence of Peebles' style. *Sweet Sweetback* also instigates this scope of ambition by marrying the grittiness of its action and spectacle with elements that confound the exploitation style: the breaking of the fourth wall or random inserts of simulated documentary interviews. Such visually confounding techniques confirm blaxploitation as its own genre, although such experimentation maintains itself through a substantiation of the established exploitation approach to location and spectacle. To further clarify: *Sweet Sweetback* evokes not just a neorealist-inspired approach to surrounding but occasional avant-garde techniques as well – brief sequences appear out of focus due to their being filmed, at speed, from moving transport. In this amateurish evocation of documentary-style travelogue footage, Van Peebles heightens the racialised socio-political aspects of the narrative. The fast-movement of the visuals consequent the speed at which the story of *Sweet Sweetback* unfolds. The extensive use of handheld camerawork, including the filming of entire sequences while literally *on the move*, deliberately fragment the linear nature of the feature's narrative (that is, Sweetback's escape to the Mexican border) for the purpose of exploiting the need for oligarchical reform.

Sweet Sweetback also presents a fierce surface ideology that reminds the viewer of the racial nature of its exploitative elements. The film maintains a stark simulation of its surroundings: the sex is grubby and actualistic and the bodies (except for Sweetback himself) are notably flawed and 'everyday'. And with its explicit display of black uprising, *Sweet Sweetback* maintains its radicalism *through* the exploitation style: ultimately selling and sexualising the very revolt it pertains to treat with upright seriousness. The result is possibly to succeed on both levels – critically and scholarly as a story of 'revolution' but commercially through the presentation of brutal sex and violence that crosses racial boundaries. *Sweetback* harbours awareness of the demands of the exploitation market but also of the flexible approach to capturing and exhibiting fictional presentations of sex and violence – and the potential for both acts to succeed as allegory. Van Peebles may be faithful in harbouring desire for urban uprising, but this 'uprising' is necessitated to an audience via physical transgressions that are paid for and presented with explicit carnal enthusiasm and brutal racial horror.

The presence of exploitation films set within obvious unreality (that is, the zombies of *Night of the Living Dead* or the fantasy scenario of *Behind the Green Door*), indicate that the movement retains and maintains its actualistic style *through* a raw and gritty approach rather than an applicable thematic of immediate pertinence. Whereas the key sexploitation and exploitation-horror films symbolise or vocalise their own transgressions – demonstrated by the assassinated black hero of *Night of the Living Dead* or the religious subjugation of women in *The Devil in Miss Jones* – *Sweet Sweetback* explicitly *invades* its own gruelling exhibition with images and sounds of revolt. This aspect is evident, for instance, in such sequences as Van Peebles' dehydrating in the California desert and struggling on foot towards the freedom of Mexico – which is interspersed with a white man having his shoes shined by a black man in the city. The black man turns and, breaking the fourth wall (another brief indication of avant-garde technique), rubs his backside on the white man's shoes while looking at the audience.[32] During another scene we cut to an impoverished woman and her children in a small room. The woman bemoans how her children, when they grow up, are taken away from her (that is, imprisoned) by the state. Sequences in a police room, with officers investigating Sweetback's whereabouts, are designed to look like a fly-on-the-wall investigation. A moment in which a police car is vandalised and engulfed with flames courtesy of a young black mob interrupts Sweetback's journey. The image may or may not indicate the character's own fantasies or experienced past. The exploitation style is further fragmented by the use of split-screen and montage. *Sweetback* outwardly exploits a symbolic representation of black persecution via filmmaking techniques that are its own (and play out as documentary propaganda) and thus initiate what could be seen – and argued – as *blaxploitation*.

Sweetback is the first exploitation film that is explicitly devised for an African-American viewership. Van Peebles presents black sexual proficiency and gruelling shock-scenarios for an audience already familiar with the sensationalistic tendencies of exploitation cinema (the grindhouse cinemas that exhibited many key films were based in urban multicultural environments). The film's graphic portrayal of sex, and such bodily grotesquery as the taking of a child's virginity, as well as the depiction of defecation (which is immediately intrusive) and a scene in which Van Peebles digests a live lizard, indicate little doubt about *Sweet Sweetback*'s desire to shock. Moreover, *Sweet Sweetback* indicates that the exploitation form can be adapted to serve a forthright manifesto via the same approach that previously capitalised on the topical treatment of sex and shock-horror. This sensationalism also provides *Sweet Sweetback* with its message of 'revolt'. Just as the sex of sexploitation assisted in developing the character arc of Lorna, Miss Jones, Misty and so on the carnal and violent actions of the characters in *Sweet Sweetback* function as narrative causality. The image of the empowered African American domineering on the streets, and in the bedroom, is elicited to evoke applause by the very nature of its taboo.

Sweetback was also produced, marketed and styled as an *exploitation* film: Van Peebles abridged union laws by pretending he was making a sex film.[33] His distributor, Cinemation Industries, 'specialised in low budget exploitation films'.[34] The film opened in inner-city grindhouse theatres that exhibited sex and horror.[35] Van Peebles also marketed *Sweetback* with an X-rating.[36] This rating is representative of sexploitation: the 'X' indicating, and promising, carnal sensationalism. To further the link between the two genres, *Sweet Sweetback* features four sequences of explicit carnality that are captured in vérité close-up, utilising handheld camera techniques. The narrative of *Sweet Sweetback* does not demand these lengthy copulation sequences, one of which documents the image of Van Peebles' penis, a sight hitherto exclusive of the sexploitation film. These sequences may define the Sweetback character as sexually adept and domineering but this physical trait is only central to the saleable masculinity of the film itself. Van Peebles himself would refer to the sensational nature of his work by advising aspiring black directors, hoping to make an independent film: 'Put a couple of chicks on the block, raise the money and make a film.'[37] To encourage this sensationalistic aspect further, the director claimed that unsimulated contact between himself and his female stars during the filming of sex scenes resulted in him obtaining gonorrhoea.[38] Such revelations succeed in making the production of *Sweetback* appear as oppositional to Hollywood as the final product. Van Peebles is alert to the marketing of exploitation cinema outside of the barriers of mainstream acceptability.

Commenting on *Sweet Sweetback*'s sexually explicit scenes, Yearwood argues that the sex act is presented 'more in terms of shock than titillation' (mirroring similar critical discussion about *The Devil in Miss Jones*).[39] He adds:

> *Sweetback* is no simple pornographic film. Pornography in the cinema is constructed upon the economic and voyeuristic exploitation of the female body – and its control of the male. Pornographic film is a celebration of unequal relations in society through its exploitation of the body strictly in sexual and economic terms within the system of patriarchy characteristic of society.[40]

As my discussion of sexploitation evidences, this is an incorrect assumption of the sexually provocative cinema that was dominant at the time of *Sweetback*'s release (presuming this is what Yearwood is referring to by his blanket term use of 'pornography'). *The Devil in Miss Jones* introduces a reflexive commentary on the subjugation of women and the binary between female sexuality, and the exploitation of such, within a society of patriarchal suppression. *Behind the Green Door* indicates that only within the realms of fantasy can a female truly succumb to the 'unequal relations' supposed of them by a society that harbours interest in the pornographic image but consequents the popular repression of it. The 'control of the male' is deliberately transgressed in *The Opening of Misty Beethoven*, which concludes with Misty taking on the role of penetrator and sodomising the bourgeois sexist male, collapsing his masculinity. Further, the use of 'shock' – which Yearwood mentions is dichotomous to the female bodies that he considers to lack glamour, and that engage in sexual conduct with Van Peebles and his Sweetback character – does not immediately prohibit the exploitation of corporeality. The lack of 'perfectly formed, luscious, erotic sexual creatures' that Yearwood identifies in *Sweet Sweetback* can also be seen in the orgy sequences of *Behind the Green Door*, in which obese and middle-aged women copulate with their partners.[41] The ageing physique of Georgina Spelvin in *The Devil in Miss Jones* may also be removed from the 'exotic' image that many viewers will associate with titillation. The presentation of sex in these films transgresses the physical expectancies of Hollywood performers because the raw exhibition that *is* the exploitation style demands a convincing actuality. Whether or not the presence of atypical cinematic bodies is arousing would be dependent on the individual watching.[42]

According to the biography on the making of *Sweet Sweetback*, entitled *Baadasssss!* (Mario Van Peebles, 2003), which was authored by the director's son – sexual arousal *was* intended by the film's many moments of nude female flesh.[43] *Sweet Sweetback* exhibits black physicality but does so removed from the style of Hollywood. The bodies are not only imperfect but presented in grubby surroundings and – because of the use of close-up – forego the restraint of the mainstream. But can such shameless sexploitation also be politically liberating? I will look at this question next.

NOTES

1. Koven, M, *Blaxploitation Films* (Kamera Books, London, 2010), p. 9.
2. See Dunn, S, *Baad Bitches and Sassy Supermamas: Black Power Action Films* (University of Illinois Press, Chicago, 2008); Guerrero, E, *Framing Blackness: The African American Image in Film* (Temple University Press, Philadelphia, 1993); Sims, Y, *Women of Blaxploitation: How the Black Action Film Heroine Changed American Popular Culture*, (McFarland Publishing, Jefferson, 2006); Yearwood, G, *Black Film as a Signifying Practice: Cinema, Narration and the African-American Aesthetic Experience* (Africa World Press, Trenton, 2000).
3. Dunn, S, *Baad Bitches and Sassy Supermamas: Black Power Action Films* (University of Illinois Press, Chicago, 2008), p. 46.
4. Fisher, A, ' Go West, Brother: The Politics of Landscape in the Blaxpoitation Western'. In Fisher, A and Walker, J (eds), *Grindhouse (Global Exploitation Cinemas)* (Bloomsbury Academic, London, 2016), p. 184.
5. Koven, M, *Blaxploitation Films* (Kamera Books, London, 2010), p. 114.
6. Ibid.
7. Cited in Howard, J, *Blaxploitation Cinema: The Essential Reference Guide* (FAB Press, London, 2008), p. 12.
8. *The Legend of Nigger Charley* (Martin Goldman, 1972), *The Soul of Nigger Charley* (Larry G. Spangler, 1973), *Adios Amigo* (Fred Williamson, 1975), *Kid Vengeance* (Joe Maduke, 1976).
9. *Blacula* (William Crain, 1972), *Blackenstein* (William Levey, 1972), *Scream Blacula Scream* (Bob Kelljan, 1973), *Abby* (William Girdler, 1974), *Sugar Hill* (Paul Maslansky, 1974), *The Devil's Express* (Barry Rosen, 1975).
10. *Force Four* (Michael Fink, 1974), *Black Belt Jones* (Robert Clouse, 1974), *Black Samurai* (Al Adamson, 1976).
11. Of which *Shaft* (Gordon Parks, 1971) and *Across 110th Street* (Barry Shear, 1972) are the most famous.
12. *Crazy Joe* (Carlo Lizzani, 1974) and *Take a Hard Ride* (Antonio Margheriti, 1975) from Italy, *The Black Dragon* (Tony Liu Jun Guk, 1974) and *The Black Dragon's Revenge* (Tony Liu Jun Guk, 1975) from Hong Kong, *Mister Deathman* (Michael Moore, 1977) from South Africa and *Ebony, Ivory and Jade* (Cirio H. Santiago) from the Philippines.

13. *Coonskin* (Ralph Bakshi, 1974).
14. Yearwood, G, *Black Film as a Signifying Practice: Cinema, Narration and the African-American Aesthetic Experience* (Africa World Press, Trenton, 2000), p. 89.
15. Williams, *Screening Sex* (Duke University Press, Durham, NC and London, 2009), p. 93.
16. Ibid.
17. Dunn, S, *Baad Bitches and Sassy Supermamas: Black Power Action Films* (University of Illinois Press, Chicago, 2008), p. 57.
18. Bordwell, D and Thompson, J, *Film History: An Introduction* (McGraw-Hill, New York, 1994), p. 708.
19. *Sweetback*'s director, Melvin Van Peebles, spent years writing poetry in Paris and also made the short film *Cinq cent balles* (1965).
20. Dunn, S, *Baad Bitches and Sassy Supermamas: Black Power Action Films* (University of Illinois Press, Chicago, 2008), pp. 56–84.
21. Williams, L, *Screening Sex* (Duke University Press, Durham, NC and London, 2009), p. 96.
22. Yearwood, G, *Black Film as a Signifying Practice: Cinema, Narration and the African-American Aesthetic Experience* (Africa World Press, Trenton, 2000), p. 187.
23. Hartmann, J, 'The Trope of Blaxploitation in Critical Responses to "Sweetback"', *Film History* (vol. 6. 3, autumn 1994, Indiana University Press, Bloomington), p. 394.
24. In the February 1973 issue of the UK's *Monthly Film Bulletin*, Strick mentions that the explicit sexual nature of *Sweetback* resulted in it being 'so far rejected by the British censor'. Cited in Strick, P, '*Superfly* Review', *Monthly Film Bulletin* (vol. 40. 469, February 1973), p. 37.
25. Eshun, K, 'Escaping the Genre Ghetto', *Sight and Sound* (vol. 15. 6, June 2005, BFI, London), p. 8.
26. Yearwood, G., *Black Film as a Signifying Practice: Cinema, Narration and the African-American Aesthetic Experience* (Africa World Press, Trenton, 2000), p. 126.
27. Ibid., p. 89.
28. Ibid., p. 109.
29. Ibid., p. 216.
30. Hartmann, J, *Film History* (vol. 6. 3, autumn 1994, Indiana University Press, Bloomington), p. 387.
31. Koven, M, *Blaxploitation Films* (Kamera Books, London, 2010), p. 20; emphasis in the original.
32. For instance, in Godard's avant-garde classic *À bout de souffle*, actor Jean-Paul Belmondo breaks the fourth wall.
33. Dunn, S, *Baad Bitches and Sassy Supermamas: Black Power Action Films* (University of Illinois Press, Chicago, 2008), p. 66.
34. Guerrero, E, *Framing Blackness: The African American Image in Film* (Temple University Press, Philadelphia, 1993), p. 86.
35. Eshun, K, 'Escaping the Genre Ghetto, *Sight and Sound* (vol. 15. 6, June 2005, BFI, London), p. 8.
36. 'Rated X by an all-white jury' declared the film's theatrical posters.
37. Guerrero, E, *Framing Blackness: The African American Image in Film* (Temple University Press, Philadelphia, 1993), p. 91.
38. Wiggins, B, 'You Talkin' Revolution, Sweetback: On *Sweet Sweetback's Baadasssss Song* and Revolutionary Filmmaking', *Black Camera* (vol. 4. 1, winter 2012, Indiana University Press, Bloomington), p. 29.

39. Yearwood, G., *Black Film as a Signifying Practice: Cinema, Narration and the African-American Aesthetic Experience* (Africa World Press, Trenton, 2000), p. 199.
40. Ibid., p. 216.
41. Yearwood, G., *Black Film as a Signifying Practice: Cinema, Narration and the African-American Aesthetic Experience* (Africa World Press, Trenton, 2000), p. 215.
42. According to a recent study the market for amateur pornography remains popular. See Weitzer, R, *Sex for Sale: Prostitution, Pornography, and the Sex Industry* (Routledge, New York, 2010).
43. In *Baadasssss!* (Mario Van Peebles, 2003), the film that Melvin Van Peebles' son directed about the making of *Sweetback*, Mario Van Peebles – portraying his own father – tells one African-American woman that her explicit nudity will allow her to become 'our Mae West or Marilyn Monroe'.

10. SEX, VIOLENCE AND URBAN ESCAPE: BLAXPLOITATION TROPES AND TALES

The famous African-American theorist, Cornel West, mentions how 'Americans are obsessed with sex and fearful of black sexuality. The obsession has to do with a search for stimulation and meaning in a fast-paced, market-driven culture; the fear is rotted in visceral feelings about black bodies and fuelled by sexual myths of black women and men.'[1] Even today when one travels across the Far East the influence of Western beautification is apparent – darker skinned models are almost entirely eliminated from advertising in favour of the American idealism of the pale-faced, pale-eyed clothes-horse. Black bodies are still so taboo in East Asia that in China a recent advertisement had a black man literally 'washed clean'.[2] In light of this modern conflict between black as somehow 'inferior' to both Asian and white beautification, it is worth drawing on blaxploitation as something that, for all of its exploitative motifs, at least drew audiences into a cinema to view the 'myths' of African-American sexuality in a forthright '*How do you like that?*' manner. Blaxploitation was as much a force for not only affirming the worst of the non-black audience's fears but subverting such expectancies by showing the black man (or woman) in a recreated world in which *their* sexuality was more in demand than any other. In this regard, as exploitative as blaxploitation cinema undoubtedly is of African-American sexuality, it is difficult to accuse the form as being demeaning when so few films, even now, are willing to offer *any* kind of black sexuality to audiences.

With this said – West propositions a familiar Marxist argument: the limitation of leisure time, and the surplus of labour time, initiates a desire for 'stimulation and meaning'. This search is temporarily satiated via the commodification of escapism and the saleability of images that stimulate some form of fantasy (and usually male fantasy). Media-entertainment industries manipulate sex into a product for capital gain: exploitation cinema as an obvious example – including that age-old taboo of interracial coupling. West's description of a 'search for meaning and stimulation' certainly found an outlet in the popularity of *Sweet Sweetback*: despite a slow start, playing in grindhouse theatres, it would become the number one film on American release less than two months after its premiere.[3] This popularity indicates that African-American sexuality was proving curious to a wider audience than 'just' black cinemagoers. The obsession with sex that West sees expressed in a leisure-time search for 'stimulation and meaning' was perhaps satiated by the taboo of viewing black sexuality in the presence of other spectators. *Sweetback* features sex scenes that take place in a brothel, in front of paying onlookers, and adheres to the reflexive approach typical of the exploitation style. Van Peebles exploits the *very* idea of looking at African-American sexuality, initiating the normalisation of this indulgence as a commodification (ala its X-rated sexploitation contemporaries) rather than as an exotic 'mystery'. In lieu of this, the bodies in *Sweet Sweetback* have to be oppositional to the beautification of Hollywood. West's critique of 'the devastating effect of persuasive European ideals of beauty on the self-image of young black women' is subverted by the blaxploitation lens.[4] As with the key sexploitation films, physicality in blaxploitation is *exploited* but the on-screen bodies do not represent any sort of homogenous commonality. They represent the ordinary: what may even be labelled a neorealist approach to a sexuality that was hitherto hidden from the American and international cinema screen.

West also mentions a fear of 'black sexuality' – a factor that, given its use to drive the narrative causality of *Birth of a Nation* (D. W. Griffiths, 1915), is nearly as old as cinema itself. *Sweetback*, and subsequent blaxploitation films, attempt to transgress this theory by demystifying the image of African-American coupling. *Sweet Sweetback* succeeds in shocking only insofar as society wants to be shocked: the penis of the white male is replaced with the penis of the black male and the concept of paying to see non-Caucasian presentations of intercourse is introduced. This taboo consequents another argument that surrounds *Sweet Sweetback* and the blaxploitation films that it inspired – namely that the presentation of African-American heroes become interrelated to their sexual versatility.

For instance, West refers to the stereotype of 'Jack Johnson . . . the super performer – be it in athletics, entertainment, or sex'.[5] The author further maintains that 'fearful sexual activities are deemed disgusting, dirty, or funky and considered less acceptable'.[6] The black seduction of a white woman is presented in the opening scene in *Super Fly* and also features in *Sweet Sweetback*.

In an early scene in *Sweet Sweetback*, for example, a white female onlooker shows interest in Van Peebles, during one of his live sex shows. Two Caucasian police officers in the small crowd indicate that this is prohibited *on their watch*. In this moment Van Peebles builds up anticipation to the eventual sequence in which he will be permitted a sexual liaison with a white woman. By initially denying the audience this spectacle he exploits and anticipates his own on-screen taboo that is later shattered. While the character's eventual coupling with a white woman could be interpreted to symbolise a literal dominance over the white establishment, it is also oppositional to the asexual manner in which black men were presented in popular Hollywood films. Van Peebles defies the Uncle Tom caricature: Sweetback is insolent of white authority, literally mounting his 'enemy' (the woman and her gang, only moments earlier, threatened violent engagement) and sexualising a racial 'victory' in the film's interracial love-making sequence. With this scene, *Sweet Sweetback* comes perilously close to confirming to West's Jack Johnson stereotype – the revolution begins and ends with Van Peebles' hypersexuality and appeasement of women in the bedroom.

However, in his defence, Van Peebles never presents his character's carnal relations as 'dirty' or 'funky' or 'less acceptable' – rather, in line with the actualistic style of exploitation cinema, *it just is*. Sweetback utilises his sexuality to further his own cause. Initially, this is for capital in a brothel; later it is to satisfy those who can assist his struggle. The sex in the film (much like in similar softcore texts such as *Lorna* or *Vixen*) functions as narrative: it presents a consistent hurdle to the hero who needs to carnally pleasure others in order to gain assistance with his cause to reach the Mexican border. With the various sexual encounters, *Sweet Sweetback* permits Van Peebles to deliver something more than political tract. In other words, it delivers *exploitation* and, of course, *black*-exploitation. Let's also put the character, and the launch of the blaxploitation 'hypersexual' thematic, into some further context. Sieving mentions the adaptable, apolitical character of Dr John Prentice (Sidney Poitier) in *Guess Who's Coming to Dinner?* (Stanley Kramer, 1967): 'wholly defined within the context of white America'.[7] Given the short space of time between *Guess Who's Coming to Dinner?* and *Sweet Sweetback*, a concession needs to be made for the latter as a reaction to the former – and to the history of demeaning roles given to black actors.[8] Yearwood's insistence on *Sweet Sweetback* as a ground-breaking film is correct, but his failure is to try to argue this point outside of the wider spectrum of the exploitation style that Van Peebles works within.

Sweet Sweetback exploits the fears and curiosities that white people may have inhibited about black sexuality while confirming the dominance of such (a 'worst nightmare' scenario of sorts) for the commercial pleasure of the African-American audience. West's statement that African-American sexuality has been deemed 'fearful . . . disgusting, dirty, or funky and considered less acceptable' is answered by the presentation of the sex act in *Sweet Sweetback*. Possibly aware of the potential criticism of presenting black physicality within an aspirant glamour – that is, that this may be seen as a deliberate reaction *to* the notion of 'fearful, disgusting, dirty' sex, *Sweet Sweetback* also details an exposure of flawed and ordinary bodies. Van Peebles provides sexual voyeurism but also demystifies something previously hidden from the cinema screen. Although criticised for 'the historic white supremacist construct of black male hypersexuality' that 'taps into the political revision of black male sexuality as a sign of black masculine power' *Sweet Sweetback*'s chauvinistic portrayal of the libidinous African-American would change the race relations of cinema. [9] Exploitation cinema would now and *could now*, finally, illustrate black sexuality without any connotations of the 'disgusting' and 'dirty'. *Vixen*, released just three years prior to *Sweet Sweetback*, would refuse its insatiable female lead a liaison with an African-American character. This was one taboo too far. *Sweet Sweetback*'s success indicated that there was an audience for this presentation – that African-American sexuality *could be* exploited.

And how important was this provocation?

Prior to the success of *Sweet Sweetback*, Hollywood and independent studios such as American World Pictures (who made *Coffy*) were facing bankruptcy (this is also why I have included *Coffy* in this book; while AIP were certainly a B-movie house, their sudden and brief turn to exploitation was out of necessity).[10] The concept of exploiting the African-American body, however, undoubtedly inspired the production of other blaxploitation films – while the demystification of naked black flesh crossed over to other demarcations. As discussed, the African-American lover, played by Johnny Keyes, who copulates with Marilyn Chambers in *Behind the Green Door*, is the most obvious example. Prior to *Sweet Sweetback*, race was only occasionally used to drive causality, narrative and spectacle in the exploitation film – in other words, these exploitation films spoke to one another; they continually pushed boundaries of what could be exhibited. In the case of *Vixen*, for instance, the sole black cast member has to define himself against a physically idealised white sexuality. *Night of the Living Dead* refused to touch upon its leading actor's skin colour: the African-American character proves disinterested in his white female co-star and is presented as a dishevelled, unwilling, everyman hero. His sexuality is never exploited: he is just the right man, in the wrong situation, with one goal – to stay alive. *Sweet Sweetback*'s direct and most immediate influence, then, is surely on the unsimulated interracial sex that takes place in *Behind the Green Door*. As with the various love-making sequences in *Sweet Sweetback* this scene is also displayed in front of an audience of voyeurs within a brothel. The style involves cross-cutting between spectator fixation/reaction and the close-up of skin and sweat. In both films the audience can be seen as metaphor: they watch – much as the paying audience do – and, through doing so, become uninhibited by the taboo of miscegenation. In *Behind the Green Door* this involves the onlookers, themselves of various ages, shapes and sizes, engaging in sexual conduct. *They* are ultimately aroused by the 'sexual myth' of the Jack Johnstone figure come to life. Keyes is the first male that Gloria encounters in *Behind the Green Door* and he is also the one who commands her first orgasm. While the voyeurs of *Sweet Sweetback*'s many sexual engagements keep their desires private, there is no doubting the inhibitions that are shattered – as seen in the sequence where a white woman offers to become Van Peebles' next 'conquest' only to be refused by the police. The black man has become topical and the figure of curiosity and sexual temptation. Certainly, both *Sweet Sweetback* and *Behind the Green Door* relate a more progressive aesthetic display of interracial activity than the solitary, brief kiss that is shown in *Guess Who's Coming to Dinner?* Even with an adherence to the Jack Johnston stereotype, both exploitation films indicate that the African-American figure does not surrender to an Uncle Tom identity.

SELLING THE REVOLUTION

Also of note is the use of the 'square up' in *Sweet Sweetback*. An opening crawl of words maintains: 'Dedicated to all the Brothers and Sisters who had enough of the Man' while the film concludes with the aforementioned sloganeering – 'A Baaad Assss Nigger is coming back to collect some dues'. At least one critic mentioned that *Sweet Sweetback* fails as revolution because it never indicates what 'dues' the character played by Van Peebles hopes to accumulate: 'When? And what's he going to do? I don't pretend to know the answer and I don't think Peeples [*sic*] does either. Offing pigs is the only thing the movie hints at.'[11] I have already argued that the square up, which evolved as part of the classical exploitation film as a pseudo-educational framing device, was repositioned in the contemporary form to denote a self-awareness of topicality and to heighten the presentation of physical taboo. In the sexploitation film *Behind the Green Door*, the visual 'square up' maintains to the audience that the on-screen fantasies are masculine *and* permissible being that they exist 'within the narrator's mind'. Removed from this 'square up', the unsimulated sex spectacle, based upon a gradually willing kidnapped female, would assume a position of force and consequent a loss of titillation to many viewers. Exploitation-horror films such as *The Last House on the Left* and *The Texas Chain Saw Massacre* utilise opening statements or narration to create unease: this story *actually happened* . . . the horror on-screen is mediating a documented and now recreated reality. The use of on-screen proclamations in *Sweet Sweetback* similarly offer claim to the exploitation film's simulation of a gritty actuality: its sloganeering insists contemporaneous aggression and concern. However, it does not matter what 'dues' *Sweet Sweetback* plans to collect. Once such a cinematic spectacle has been exhibited, and claimed box-office receipts, one can presume it will be displayed again. With Sweetback, graphic interracial carnality was here to stay. The 'dues' being collected are those from the audience's pocket – they *will* respond to this most shocking of corporeal presentations (and, in turn, 'blaxploitation' will be born). Reflexive ideas, such as this, are as much part of the exploitation movement as that well-repeated mantra of visual excess.

BLAXPLOITATION AFTER *SWEET SWEETBACK* – THE 'SHAFT' FACTOR

Whenever anyone talks about the *idea* of what blaxploitation is, the main film that is raised is not *Sweet Sweetback* but rather *Shaft*. Guerrero describes *Shaft* as 'an industry-backed, moneymaking venture'.[12] The producers of *Shaft* are even rumoured to have decided to change the skin colour of their hero from white to black in order to capitalise on the popularity of *Sweet Sweetback*.[13] Regardless of *Shaft* being a Hollywood film, it is no less reflexive of its own race-exploitation than *Sweet Sweetback* – but the two are very different texts even if John Shaft (Richard Roundtree) is still a Jack Johnston figure: hyper-sexual and irresistible to both black and white women. *Shaft* centres its narrative on a 'badass' private detective but conforms to the style of the Classical Hollywood gangster movie: the hero is hired to rescue a kidnapped girl and, come the conclusion, does so (with no narrative surprises, minor spectacle or 'twists'). *Sweet Sweetback*, *Shaft* and *Super Fly* all arrived in cinemas within a year of one another. *Shaft* and *Super Fly* are linked by their directors: *Super Fly*'s Gordon Parks, Jr is the son of *Shaft* director Gordon Parks – but, stylistically, *Super Fly* owes its gritty aesthetic approach, and thematic of escape, to *Sweet Sweetback*.

Indeed, *Sweet Sweetback* and *Shaft* exhibit different styles of filmmaking. Where the former features handheld camera work, the latter has lavish crane, dolly and tracking shots. Where the former is inconclusive and expresses disdain for (a frigid and repressed) white authority, the latter ridicules the bureaucracy of white law-makers but maintains their usefulness. Judged on its style, *Shaft* is not an exploitation film – rather, it belongs to a trend of violent Hollywood detective features that also include *Bullitt* (Peter Yates, 1968) and *Dirty Harry* (Don Siegel, 1971). In writing about *Dirty Harry*, Jeffords mentions that the famous detective Harry Callahan, played by Clint Eastwood, although successful in assassinating the film's villain, fails to change the wider social order. The author comments, 'though Callahan "solves" the crimes by killing the culprits, the institutions that enabled these criminals to operate in the first place retain power, and the incompetent individuals who run them remain in charge'.[14] Jeffords does not touch upon the blaxploitation era but *Shaft* – and its two sequels – follows a similar narrative to the *Dirty Harry* films.[15] John Shaft may despair at his expectancy to work *within* the system, but he never transgresses the establishment by adequately rebelling against it. Both the black man and the white man are treated with the same level of benevolence by Roundtree's street-smart John Shaft – he is neither above demanding extortionate wages to investigate the kidnapping of a distraught African-American mobster's daughter or withholding valuable information to the local white police chief. Where Sweetback defies the law, and is forced to run from it, Shaft works within the mainstream establishment. Shaft's interest is his private-eye business, his penthouse apartment, his earnings and the beautiful women who are, almost without exception, attracted to his rugged charisma. He is even, in this regard, less radical than Dirty Harry – who, at least, offers a right-wing alternative to the accepted liberal bureaucracy of the San Francisco police and courts.

The director of *Shaft*, Gordon Parks, quoted at the time of the film's release, mentioned, 'It's just a Saturday night fun picture which people go to see because they want to see the black guy winning.'[16] In a later interview, Parks would insist that to 'mix it [*Shaft*] up with black exploitation . . . just breaks me to my heart'.[17] Presumably, the seedy squalor and sex of *Sweet Sweetback* was not something Parks wanted his more glitzy gangster thriller to be placed alongside – even under the blanket term of 'blaxploitation'. As such, the influence of *Sweet Sweetback* only occasionally, and very briefly, surfaces in *Shaft*: primarily in the film's opening travelogue footage of New York's famous 42nd Street and its surrounding areas of grimy urban disentrancement. Where an exhausted Van Peebles was shown navigating the sprawling roads, streets and neon lights of Hollywood Boulevard in *Sweet Sweetback*, albeit shot by a handheld camera or from a car window, in *Shaft* we find the handsome, healthy figure of actor Richard Roundtree *displaced* within a similar environment of sex, squalor and criminal activity. Sweetback, as a male prostitute, *belongs* in the seedy sex and hustle of Hollywood Boulevard, whereas Shaft is presented as displaced in 42nd Street: too cool and tough to be entertaining the pimps and hustlers. To capture the hustle of 42nd Street, Parks 'put the camera on top of a Times Square building and shot without clearing the street'.[18] This attempt to mediate the actuality of exploitation's use of real locations is notable but the aggressive anti-white thematic of *Sweet Sweetback* is largely eradicated by *Shaft* along with Van Peebles' use of documentary-style aesthetics, avant-garde agitprop storytelling, non-linear editing and the spectacle of graphic nudity and sex.

Briggs notes that '*Shaft* is such a conventional Hollywood movie that you could have made the character white – or Chinese, for that matter – with very little alterations'.[19] While the presence of Roundtree as John Shaft, and the occasional sharp line in which the actor conscribes his ethnic presence, gives the film more edge than *Guess Who's Coming to Dinner?* the aesthetic and thematic transgressions of *Sweet Sweetback* remain decidedly non-existent. *Shaft* is colourful, lavish and *stylised* where *Sweet Sweetback* is awash with montage, jump cuts, extensive handheld tracking shots and grimy depictions of squalor and desperation. John Shaft is vocal, comedic and charming – *cinematic* – where Sweetback is silent, exhausted and threatening. In *Shaft* the hero wins and there is the set-up for a sequel (indicating the forthright commercial intentions of the film) whereas *Sweetback* is inconclusive, finalising with a freeze-frame. The advertising for *Shaft* confirms its deviance from the low-budget 'black exploitation' of *Sweet Sweetback*. The film's tagline screams 'Hotter than Bond, Cooler than Bullitt' – indicating a mainstream ambition and familiarity that figures blockbuster cinema as its comparison. In contrast, *Sweetback*'s iconic one sheet claims to be 'Rated X by an all White Jury' – images of revolution and violence, captured in grainy black and white, anticipates the sensationalistic, voyeuristic nature of the film. Aside from both *Shaft* and *Super Fly* featuring African-American leading men, there are few intertextual similarities between them.

Robinson mentions that blaxploitation films 'transmuted liberation into vengeance, the pursuit of a social justice which embraced race, class, and gender into Black racism, and the politics of armed struggle into systematic assassination'. [20] This idea of false liberation is perhaps best evidenced by the form's post-*Sweetback* focus on Van Peebles' enduring image of the hypersexual 'badass' black male. The complaint about the 'vast physical prowess' of the blaxploitation hero (and heroine) is important to consider: especially since critics of blaxploitation have focused on the misogyny within the genre.

For example, Dunn comments on the opening sequence of *Sweet Sweetback* – in which the title character, at just twelve years of age, is forced into sex with a prostitute and impresses her with his manhood: '*Sweetback*'s initial sex scene sets its focus on the historic white supremacist construct of black male hypersexuality and taps into the political revision of black male sexuality as a sign of black masculine power.'[21] This 'black male hypersexuality' may be exploitative but there is also an unmistakable aspiration in its exhibition. Sweetback's role as a pawn to capital (he is literally a prostitute) is subtly initiated as something he also wants to escape from – quite literally as the film's narrative progresses. From the prologue we are aware that the Sweetback character has been forced into this 'supremacist construct', hence he uses his sexual prowess to benefit his cross-border escape rather than for actual personal satisfaction (Sweetback never verbalises or indicates enjoyment at intercourse – he is as silent as Gloria in *Behind the Green Door*. Again, the sex *just is*). The most obvious recurring thematic in blaxploitation cinema, which no study to date has focused upon, is that each character – regardless of how sexually provocative they are presented – is *unsatisfied* with the very presentation given to them. And this ultimately contradicts such readings as Dunn's and also complicates a more straightforward acceptance that the films are misogynistic. John Shaft, in opposition to the male characters of both *Sweet Sweetback* and *Super Fly*, does not wish to escape: his penthouse apartment and the women who want to sleep with him are embraced. As we have seen, though, in exploitation films, the characters need to escape.

Dunn mentions that '*Shaft* and *Super Fly* embody the key formal and thematic features that came to define the aesthetic style of the developing blaxploitation genre, taking the model of *Sweetback*'s black male hero up against white male power into the crime or underworld action drama genre'.[22] While *Super Fly*, like *Shaft*, transplants the anarchic and convoluted roadways and side-streets of *Sweet Sweetback*'s Los Angeles for Manhattan, the similarities between the two films are slim. Aesthetically, *Super Fly*, not unlike *Sweet Sweetback*, utilises its low budget to its strength, creating a gritty reproduction of urban dishevelment by using actual inner-city locations. Almost the entire opening sequence, in which a character is chased through Harlem, is shot handheld or via the inside of a moving vehicle (interestingly, much like the opening of *Sweet Sweetback*, it is unclear whose side we, the audience, are even supposed to be on). The use of crash zooms, montage and lengthy, interrupted sequences of actuality (that is, a car travelling through the crowded Manhattan roads) presents an avant-garde aesthetic that – as with *Sweet Sweetback* – works within a reality of the immediate: everything in *Super Fly* is captured as it happens. The photographing of local people and actual street life, captured unaware by the feature's documentary camera, is even more immediate in *Super Fly* than in *Sweet Sweetback*. The use of the close-up is further evident – especially in a lengthy sex scene, provide a visual intertextuality between *Super Fly* and *Sweet Sweetback*, rather than the more polished, and less corporeally explicit, *Shaft*.

John Shaft is engaged in a profession that demands positive engagement with white authority and that exists lawfully. His respect in the immediate community is derived from his position as a Private Eye: he may be violent and hypersexual, but his status maintains deference. He earns a high, legal wage *within* the capitalist system. Thematically, *Super Fly* continues the same anti-authoritarian mythos of *Sweet Sweetback* even if, on the surface, the film glamorises an unfathomable and morally regressive ghetto existence. *Super Fly* replaces the *silent*, hypersexual, individualistic character of Sweetback with the *outspoken*, hypersexual, individualistic character of Youngblood Priest (played by Ron O'Neal). Where Sweetback defies the law to escape to safety and flee to Mexico, Priest defies the law by working as a drug dealer, but the characters are, to a great extent, interchangeable. Both Sweetback and Priest want to work against white authority but where the former was criticised for using his penis as a symbol of freedom, the latter gained controversy for its depiction of an illicit African-American Mafioso whose sole intention is to obtain lavish capital gain.[23] Nevertheless, each is hypersexual and each is integrated into an underground network of African-American friends who exist as a support mechanism against the corruption and discrimination of white lawmen.

Guerrero states that such glamorous pimps as 'Super Fly' were imperative to 'stunting the development of a black political voice'.[24] In *Super Fly*, black revolutionaries, women, gangsters and also the white police department are certainly met with scorn by Priest. His sole interest is in himself and capital gain. After an introductory sequence in which we see Priest sniffing cocaine while in bed with a white woman, we witness him chase a man across the streets of Harlem. He eventually catches him, and the man is revealed to be one of Priest's street workers. 'I got 50 men on the street and if they all have bitch problems, I starve,' he shouts at the pusher who is behind on his payments (the man explains that he has had personal issues at home). As the man vomits from being repeatedly kicked in the stomach by Priest (as with *Sweet Sweetback*'s use of defecation, body-horror is used to derive an actualistic impact in *Super Fly*) he is given an ultimatum. If he does not find the capital immediately, Priest will force his wife out on 'whore's row' because 'someone's gotta work tonight'. Priest is not a sympathetic character but then neither is Sweetback. Furthermore, neither is Vixen or even, perhaps, Gloria or Miss Jones. And, of course, the juxtapositions of the exploitation-horror films exist to show us alternative propositions of family, class or youth rebellion. What Priest and Sweetback channel is the concept of individualism: both care only about themselves and the outcome of their immediate goals. Numerous follow-up films to *Super Fly* revisited the concept of an African-American outlaw who exploits others, either drug mules or prostitutes, for monetary gain – attesting to the popular appeal of the Priest character.[25] In approaching a film such as *Super Fly*, then, it is possible to suggest that critical and scholarly derision has arisen from both a lack of understanding of what exploitation *is* (both these blaxploitation films exploit topical fears of blackness – including sexuality and criminality) and the disappointment that the initial run of 'black' films do not exist as a homogenous entity of progressive and 'politically correct' themes. Guerrero comments that *Super Fly* represents 'the cinematic inscription and glorification of the parasitic, hustling milieu of the black urban underworld'.[26] A review in the *Monthly Film Bulletin* argued that 'one could find more black power in a coffee bean'.[27] *Super Fly*, as with *Sweet Sweetback*, is blaxploitation in that the spectacle exploited is a foremost depiction of racialised sex and violence – designed to provoke blackness as 'Other' but not necessarily as a political 'Other'. Most notable about both films is that Sweetback and Priest are goal-orientated and empowered by their fierce ambition to meet their respective goals. Thus, the style of both films only represents 'black power' insofar as exploitation cinema seeks commodity in what Hollywood refuses to exhibit. The leading men of blaxploitation do not need to be 'heroes' any more than the white leading men of Hollywood.

Figure 10.1   *Super Fly*: the film raised controversy for its taboo mixture of sex, violence and heightened racial conflict – a recurring thematic of the blaxploitation film. (Produced by Sig Shore)

For example, thematically *Super Fly*'s presentation of an African-American gangster, determined to achieve the 'American Dream' on his own illicit terms, is comparable to that of the Corleone Family in *The Godfather* (Francis Ford Coppola, 1972). The transgression in *Super Fly* is the colour of the hero's skin and the forthrightness of the thematic ('He's got a plan to stick it to the man' stated the original theatrical poster) – the *exploitable* elements, in other words. Of course, Al Pacino's Michael Corleone is given an epic story arc evolving from teenage soldier to mobster whereas Priest in *Super Fly* is shown to be ethically corrupt from the initialisation of the film.

Nevertheless, one of these portrayals was considered more acceptable than the other (*The Godfather* was awarded with Oscars; *Super Fly* was so controversial that Warner Bros. – who picked the independent film up for distribution – would not handle the sequel).[28] This separation of what may be perceived as art/exploitation is itself open to accusations of racial subjuga-tion. Ultimately, such an attitude presumes that a fictional white gangster is acceptable to audiences – capable of comprehending the fantasy of the cinema screen – whereas a black gangster, synonymous with a wider reality of urban crime, is not. Guerrero comments, '*Superfly* [*sic*] was widely recognised for making fashionable the gold necklace with attached coke spoon, and, as critics have noted, for contributing to the dramatic increase in cocaine use among inner-city black youth.'[29] The author's presumed 'connection' between film and audience (stating that something is 'widely recognised' is hardly conclusive evidence) may also indicate implied, if unintentional, racism. Guerrero's comments assume that the exploitation audience is more driven to assimilate the simulations on-screen into their own lives. This is a factor that may also have affected the censorship of the key exploitation films of this study: the assumption that an inner-city 'grindhouse' viewership is more likely to respond with titillation or celebration to the spectacles of sex and violence that are central to these productions. Perhaps noting this hypocrisy, the following year's theatrical poster for *Coffy* would emphasise the character as '*the Godmother of them all*'. This reflexivity invites audiences to make a more informed comparison between characters in blaxploitation cinema and their Hollywood 'gangster' counterparts.

Arguably, the appeal in an African-American gangster defying their own environment is born from the very urban racial segregation that *Super Fly* presents. The valid criticism that *Super Fly* glamorises a criminal existence indicates that the ghetto class of Priest was more problematic to critics than that of *The Godfather*'s wealthy Corleone Family. Blaxploitation presents class as something that has enslaved the African-American community: Sweetback is helpless to take legal means against the corrupt police officers who chase him and cuff and beat a helpless Black Panther. Priest realises the urgency of folding his business and escaping from Harlem (and thus the threat of arrest) and Pam Grier's Coffy, as I will later discuss, explores armed revolution as a method to eradicate criminal elements from exploiting the black community. While *Super Fly* glamorises a life of excess, *sex, drugs* and *urban hymns*, just as *Sweet Sweetback* panders to a distinctly masculine fantasy of male sexual domination, the film also maintains a greater sense of comprehension about the relationship between race and capital.

West mentions:

> Post-modern culture is more and more a market culture dominated by gangster mentalities and self-destructive wantonness . . . Sexual violence against women and homicidal assaults by young black men on one another are only the most obvious signs of this empty quest for pleasure, property and power.[30]

West presupposes this argument to maintain his theory that *nihilism* is the dominant factor in the disillusionment, sexism and violence found in poor black neighbourhoods – that is, the expectance of the African-American minority to integrate into, and accept, a culture that is built upon white exclusivity (Steve Biko, famously, would argue the same about the black South African and his 'imposed' colonial identity politics). The author argues that this 'pleasure, property and power' is an invention of the American market-economy establishment that in its current design excludes the majority of the country's non-white people. West continues: 'How people act and live are shaped – though in no way dictated or determined – by the larger circumstances in which they find themselves.'[31] To solve this social issue, West calls on the expansion of the public sphere in order to further equality and combat poverty but also affirms a dogmatic swing from extreme market capitalism to full-scale nationalisation (which African-American militants concurrent to the blaxploitation era, such as Angela Davis, suggested) is unwise.[32] The author instead argues for an entire rethink of what the American population *consume*: from images of racial beautification to the leaders and popular culture that they follow and aspire towards. He insists that white America is inexorably linked to a 'cultural conservatism' that 'takes the form of an inchoate xenophobia (e.g. against whites, Jews, and Asians), systemic sexism, and homophobia'.[33] These conclusions bear relevance to the blaxploitation style that works *against* the beautification and racism of Hollywood while embracing images of sexism and, in the case of *Super Fly*, presenting a character in lieu to the 'pleasure, property and power' of American capitalism. The blaxploitation style exploits the muscular hyper-sexuality of African-American avengers as the most succinct image of opposition to Hollywood's avoidance of black heroes. This is interlinked to the very 'dirty' and 'funky' societal attitude towards young African-American males that existed during the blaxploitation period – that is, there is immediate taboo (and resulting commercial allure) in the transgressive sight of interracial sex. However, the presentation of blaxploitation *as* sexploitation, including multiple partners for a single male, also initiates a depiction of African-American individualism and greed. This egoism, in the examples of *Super Fly* and *Sweet Sweetback*, is dichotomous to criminality: white authority is being deliberately transgressed by, respectively, the pimp and the prostitute. Furthermore, the white women are being *taken* from the white establishment and pleasured beyond what their same-race partners can provide – scenes in both films make this factor clear. Therefore, the blaxploitation style complicates accusations of either liberation or regression.

To explain further: *Super Fly*, like *Sweet Sweetback*, can be seen as an attempt to define black aspiration. Priest does not want to operate on the streets but his success in narcotics/prostitution is interrelated to the capital opportunities afforded to the African-American community. When he explains to a friend that he intends to leave the urban lifestyle, he is faced with the following retort: 'You're gunna give all this up? Eight Track Stereo, colour T.V. in every room, and can snort a half a piece of dope every day? That's the

American Dream, nigga!' But Priest *does* want to leave this behind and *Super Fly* is careful to not condemn what it exploits. Given the sale of illegal drugs within the film's racially segregated urban environment this can be viewed as an obvious moral failing but Priest's aspiration of obtaining enough wealth to retire also highlights the dead-end of the system he partakes in. He is wise to the system of white patriarchy that will not offer him a path to legitimacy. Priest understands that his own position in the African-American community, as a drug pusher and gangster, is cumbersome and troublesome. His wealth, and status, is a stigma born from West's analogy of black nihilism. Priest is a successful illegitimate businessman because the wealth that American society asks him to acquire is difficult to achieve via legitimate means. His final escape indicates a derision of both urban nihilism and white patriarchy. And *Super Fly*, much like *Sweet Sweetback*, dictates that the black community is no longer subservient to what white authority *asks* or *expects*. Priest sleeps with white and black women and intermingles with white and black society. His ultimate monetary goal defines an ambition of individualism comparable to Sweetback's escape to the Mexican Border. In both cases, the desire is to *disappear*. To suggest that the blaxploitation style glamorises these characters is to misinterpret their ultimate intention. Contradictory to the hedonistic pleasure experienced by John Shaft as he guns down criminals, both *Super Fly* and *Sweet Sweetback* present black men who do not need to, *or wish to*, engage in labour that favours any form of racial supremacy. Shaft, lest we forget, is defined as the 'black private dick' – he is who is because of the *uniqueness* of his race – whereas Priest and Sweetback work in illegitimate and illegal trades. Inherent both within, and *outside of*, the on-screen thematic of both *Sweetback* and *Super Fly* is the proposition of African-American personalities engaging with monetary and social relationships without the influence of white society. Finances are exchanged in their respective underground industries of drugs and sex for services dominated by black men. The thematic acceptance of black power, albeit on the criminal or salacious fringes of 'acceptable' society, is thematically opposite to the more 'homely' presentation of Hollywood's Sidney Poitier.

Films such as *Super Fly* and *Sweet Sweetback* could not exist except as part of the exploitation underground. *Sweet Sweetback*, made under the guise of a pornographic film, even avoided union conscription because it was shot under the radar of Hollywood. *Super Fly* defied predictions of audience disinterest by obtaining distribution from a major studio.[34] In *Super Fly* and *Sweet Sweetback* we see the exploitation of race-relations and of African-American sexuality: both factors that are represented in stories of black individualism. The blaxploitation style should thus be considered synonymous with an aspirational thematic of urban escape – a reflexive criticism, and exploitation, of the nihilism that West advocates tackling through cultural imagery and the delineation of capital longing. The aesthetic of these films is central to breaking the white domination of Hollywood sexuality: lingering close-ups of African-American bodies engaged in coitus destabilise the normalcy of American screen carnality. Viewers are offered lengthy, actualistic sex scenes. Environments of ghetto disrepair, or street spectacle, provide the blaxploitation style with a visual honesty – the whorehouse of *Sweet Sweetback* and the cold, concrete capitalism of *Super Fly*'s New York complement the wish of each character to renounce their surroundings. The actualistic presentation of an environment foreign to Hollywood persuades the immediate necessity of upheaval and/or escape. The neorealist approach of capturing the dilapidation, and even the emptiness, of the ghetto, or the urban hopelessness of illicit industry, permits both *Sweetback* and *Superfly* to argue, without explicitly condoning, an any-means-necessary position as regards individual rebellion against the existing labour system. Such aspiration is placed alongside graphic sex and violence, itself shattering the Hollywood illusion of black characters as Uncle Remus or Sidney Poitier personalities, who seek acceptance into middle-class white environments.

The blaxploitation genre may also have launched black filmmakers but, after the success of *Sweet Sweetback*, *Shaft* and *Super Fly*, white producers and directors began to dominate the form. American International Pictures, the B-movie company that had produced many of Roger Corman's directorial films, began a line of blaxploitation features directed by white males.[35] Criticism was subsequently forthcoming about the role of black people in the actualisation of these productions – and a group entitled Coalition Against Blaxploitation was formed.[36] In discussing American International Pictures' *Coffy*, it should be noted that the film was written and directed by Jack Hill, a journeyman white director. And, once more, we are presented with a thematic of escape and an aesthetic of urban disposition, interlinked with a focus on gregarious nudity and brutal violence.

As with other exploitation genres, the blaxploitation style also shows evidence of evolution and an aspiration to integrate its spectacle with a more ambitious narrative scope. This is evidenced in *Coffy* through the presentation of a hypersexual *female*. *Sweetback* and *Super Fly* sexualise revolution and masculinise black power, while affirming that capital opportunity for African Americans is often available but not as part of the accepted channels of the white establishment. *Coffy* engages with this thematic but does so through a female perspective. This launched a second kind of blaxploitation feature – what Dunn calls the 'Baad Bitches and Sassy Supermamas' film.[37] I will discuss this short-lived phenomenon next.

NOTES

1. West, C, *Race Matters* (Vintage Books, New York, 2001 [1993]), p. 119.
2. https://www.theguardian.com/world/2016/may/28/china-racist-detergent-advert-outrage, accessed 20/08/2017
3. Eshun, K, 'Escaping the Genre Ghetto', *Sight and Sound* (vol. 15. 6, June 2005, BFI, London), p. 8.
4. West, C, *Race Matters* (Vintage Books, New York, 2001 [1993]), p. 28.
5. Ibid., p. 119.
6. Ibid., p. 120.
7. Sieving, C, *Soul Searching* (Wesleyan University Press, Middletown, 2011), p. 93.
8. Referencing *Birth of a Nation*, Williams speaks about 'the exaggerated suffering of the white woman at the hands of the hypersexual black man'. Cited in Williams, L, *Playing the Race Card: Melodramas of Black and White from Uncle Tom to O.J. Simpson* (Princeton University Press, Princeton, 2001), p. 111.
9. Dunn, S, *Baad Bitches and Sassy Supermamas: Black Power Action Films* (University of Illinois Press, Chicago, 2008), p. 63.
10. Howard comments that MGM 'held an infamous yard sale of celebrity props and costumes', such was the studio's dire financial situation. Furthermore, after the success of Sweetback, the script to Shaft was rumoured to have been quickly re-written by MGM to change the title character from white to black – including an increased hypersexuality. Howard, J, *Blaxploitation Cinema: The Essential Reference Guide* (FAB Press, London, 2008) p. 10.
11. Hartmann, J, 'The Trope of Blaxploitation in Critical Responses to "Sweetback"', *Film History* (vol. 6. 3, autumn 1994, Indiana University Press, Bloomington), p. 385.
12. Guerrero, E, *Framing Blackness: The African American Image in Film* (Temple University Press, Philadelphia, 1993), p. 92.
13. Ibid., p. 91.
14. Jeffords, S, *Hard Bodies: Hollywood Masculinity in the Reagan Era* (Rutgers University Press, Princeton, 1994), p. 18.
15. *Shaft's Big Score* (Gordon Parks, 1972), *Shaft in Africa* (John Guillermin, 1973).
16. Andrews, N, '*Shaft* Review', *Monthly Film Bulletin* (vol. 39. 456, January 1972), p. 15.
17. Sims, Y, *Women of Blaxploitation: How the Black Action Film Heroine Changed American Popular Culture* (McFarland Publishing, Jefferson, 2006), p. 133.
18. Briggs, J, *Profoundly Disturbing* (Plexus Publishing, London, 2003), p. 114.
19. Ibid., p. 117.
20. Robinson, C, 'Blaxploitation and the Misrepresentation of Liberation', *Race & Class* (vol. 40. 1, 1998), http://journals.sagepub.com/doi/pdf/10.1177/030639689804000101, accessed 8 August 2017.
21. Dunn, S, *Baad Bitches and Sassy Supermamas: Black Power Action Films* (University of Illinois Press, Chicago, 2008), p. 63.
22. Ibid., p. 49.
23. Lerone Bennett, Jr – a writer for the African-American digest *Ebony*, maintained of *Sweetback* at the time, 'If fucking freed, black people would have celebrated the millennium 400 years ago.' Cited in Guerrero, E, *Framing Blackness: The African American Image in Film* (Temple University Press, Philadelphia, 1993), p. 100.
24. Ibid., p. 97.
25. Examples include *The Mack* (Michael Campus, 1973), *The Candy Tangerine Man* (Matt Cimber, 1975) and *The Human Tornado* (Cliff Roquemore, 1976).

26. Guerrero, E, *Framing Blackness: The African American Image in Film* (Temple University Press, Philadelphia, 1993), p. 96.
27. Strick, P, '*Superfly* Review', *Monthly Film Bulletin* (vol. 40. 469, February 1973), p. 37.
28. *Superfly T.N.T.* 'was to have been released by Warner Bros. but at the last moment the distributor backed away from the pic in presumed fear of black-press opposition'. Cited in 'Review of *Superfly T.N.T.*', *Variety* magazine (20 June 1973, Variety Media, California), p. 28.
29. Guerrero, E, *Framing Blackness: The African American Image in Film* (Temple University Press, Philadelphia, 1993), p. 97.
30. West, C, *Race Matters* (Vintage Books, New York, 2001 [1993]), p. 10.
31. Ibid., p. 18/
32. 'After a period in which the private sphere has been sacralised and the public square gutted, the temptation is to make a fetish of the public square. We need to resist such dogmatic swings.' Ibid., p. 20.
33. Ibid., p. 42.
34. The *Variety* review of *Super Fly* maintained, 'with all the available black slanted product now out, some of fairly high quality, it's doubtful whether the intended market will buy this entry with no cast names to lure and word of mouth certain to hurt'. 'Review of *Super Fly*', *Variety* magazine, (2 August 1972, Variety Media, California), p. 99.
35. American International Pictures milked the success of *Shaft* with such 'badass' tough guy action films as *Slaughter* (Jack Starrett, 1972), *Black Caesar* (Larry Cohen, 1973) and *Hell Comes to Harlem* (Larry Cohen, 1973). Their production of *Coffy* (Jack Hill, 1973) is singled out by this chapter, because it evidences influence from the style of *Sweetback* and *Super Fly* rather than *Shaft*.
36. Howard, J, *Blaxploitation Cinema: The Essential Reference Guide* (FAB Press, London, 2008), p. 13.
37. See Dunn, S, *Baad Bitches and Sassy Supermamas: Black Power Action Films* (University of Illinois Press, Chicago, 2008).

11. THE BLAXPLOITATION FEMALE

My chapters on sexploitation and on exploitation-horror concluded that these controversial but profitable genres fatigued their commercial profile because of two things: *1)* the novelty of what they are exploiting becomes embraced and remade in the form of numerous 'B-exploitation' take-offs, usually which are *all spectacle*. This factor quickly exhausts the market and *2)* the major studios, or an aspirant independent filmmaker (such as Sean Cunningham or John Carpenter) popularise a more accessible version of the style that is contingent to the presentation of taboo. Blaxploitation is no exception to this and *Coffy* indicates a conclusive attempt to evolve the genre and its style. This evolution, most obviously, comes through characterisation – the female figure of Pam Grier removes the genre from its masculine genesis: something that probably had to be done given the criticism of *Sweet Sweetback* and *Super Fly*. The consequence, in *Coffy*, is of a more glitzy and lavish appropriation of the cinematic style that made *Sweet Sweetback* and *Super Fly* unique from other 'black avenger' films. As with *The Opening of Misty Beethoven*, or the special-effects horror and surrealist flashbacks of *Martin*, a style that had begun as a gritty, vérité, low-fi style graduates into an ambition of special effects, set dressings, costumes, stunts and an even more grandstanding spectacle.

When *Coffy* emerged, blaxploitation had become typified as a 'macho' genre.[1] This assumption became even more evident when a wave of cash-in features began to appear, each following the formula of a hypersexual, tough, African-American male battling against (usually) a white adversary. Described by the National Association for the Advancement of Colored

People (NAACP) as 'Super Nigger' films and equated to 'cultural geno-cide' the blaxploitation genre encountered boycotts, controversy and critical disdain.[2] As I have indicated, both *Sweet Sweetback* and *Super Fly* exist *within* the exploitation movement. Their consequent commercialisation of, and stylistic approach to, graphic sex, violence and themes of fractured race relationships would perhaps have been more acceptable to the audience of *Night of the Living Dead*, *Behind the Green Door* and other key exploitation texts. However, because *Sweet Sweetback* and *Super Fly* represent the arrival of commercial black filmmaking they were faced with even more scrutiny than the more monetarily blatant gore and sex of comparable exploitation releases. The genesis of *Coffy* indicates how producers answered the criticism of blaxploitation as a male-dominated medium while maintaining appeal to the genre's core audience. *Coffy* is the first film to present a female action hero but, in preserving the sexploitation aspect of blaxploitation, Pam Grier's character is eroticised, exposed and sexually humiliated. This humiliation has led to discussion about whether or not Coffy (the character) can be seen as a feminist personality or one who replaces 'the mammy, the exotic other, Aunt Jemima and Sapphire with alternate sexual stereotypes of African-American women'.[3]

To answer this point, I want to initiate the theory that the collapse of the blaxploitation film can be attributed to *Coffy*'s glamorisation of armed revolution. This thematic factor brings a finality to the genre on the basis that what *Sweetback* only suggests (the 'Baaad Assss Nigger' who 'is coming back to collect some dues') is finally, and *conclusively*, introduced to the forefront. Through maintaining this, it will become evident that the Coffy character walks a thin line between female sacrifice and strength, and a sexualised, fantasy Angela Davis figure, solving problems at gunpoint while dressed in revealing outfits. It also, to some extent, robs Davis of her actual real political threat – instead she is re-imagined as a figure for male erections. It is to Pam Grier's credit that any of the revolutionary zeal of Davis still lives in Coffy – beyond the explicit demand for the actress to undress.

Certainly, the sexual exploitation of Grier is essential to *Coffy*'s commercial-ity but less relevant to the film's wider presentation of grassroots rebellion. Dunn, for instance, criticises the narrative's replacement of black power with 'pussy power'.[4] Engaging with such criticism would force a de-contextualising of not only *Coffy* as exploitation but as an action film and, one could argue, Dunn's criticism is misogynistic in its own right – arguing, as she seems to do, that sex as a weapon is inherently immoral. However, the character's gun-fetishism makes her a cinematic replacement for the *Dirty Harry* or *Shaft* action hero: within the generic tropes of action cinema, the Pam Grier character – as sexualised as she undoubtedly is – remains the first of a 'new wave' of aggres-sive female heroines. This is a point that I will now discuss in more detail, with reference to how *Coffy* evolves and concludes the blaxploitation style initiated by *Sweetback*.

In *Coffy*, the actress Pam Grier is cast as 'Miss Coffin', a nurse. The name works as doubly self-referential: not only do we witness Coffy at work in emergency wards, struggling to assist in saving human life, but by night she takes to the street to slaughter drug dealers by masquerading as an upmarket prostitute. Again: the black character can only function and 'succeed' at their goals by performing in industry removed from the 'legal' and accepted capitalist establishment. Coffy's 11-year-old sister is a recovering heroin addict. Her ex-boyfriend, Carter, a handsome African-American policeman (William Elliot), explains to Coffy that the drug syndicate in Los Angeles goes further than just the streets. He is soon killed in a brutal attack orchestrated by his own department. A local dealer and pimp called King George (Robert DoQui) shows interest in Coffy as a potential escort for his illicit firm. Coffy turns the mob against him by informing them that King George is trying to take over their turf. He is lynched and dragged to his death by white gangsters ('this is how we lynch niggers'). Coffy's current boyfriend, a potential African-American senator called Brunswick (Booker Bradshaw), accepts sponsorship from the drug mafia for his political campaign. When Coffy discovers this, he arranges her assassination at the hands of two white henchmen. She survives and returns to Brunswick. She finds him making love to a white woman in his lavish beachside apartment and fires at his crotch, killing him.

The release of *Coffy* demonstrates how quickly the blaxploitation trend had become depleted. American International Pictures had already premiered a blaxploitation horror variant, *Blacula* (William Crain, 1972), as well as *Slaughter* (Jack Starrett, 1972), an action film based along similar grounds as that of *Shaft*. Less than two months after *Coffy* opened at theatres in May 1973, a PG-rated black action film with a female lead, *Cleopatra Jones* (Jack Starrett, 1973), was released by a major studio – Warner Bros. – diluting the sex and violence of the former in favour of a more family-friendly espionage narrative. After several months on release, positive word of mouth had boosted *Coffy*'s reputation and the film reached number one at the American box office.[5] Subsequent blaxploitation productions, highlighting a female avenger, appeared until the popularity of the form fatigued – largely within just two years.[6]

Symbolically, death surrounds Miss Coffin: her work in an emergency ward, her slain friends and her own murder spree.

Growing aware of the futility of outside assistance, she seeks escape from an urban environment of drug abuse and prostitution – factors that are presented as synonymous with a white establishment seeking to keep the black minority segregated and despondent. The protagonist African Americans, such as the corrupt politician Brunswick, are presented as having 'cheated' on their own

Figure 11.1   *Coffy*: Pam Grier undoubtedly changed the way that African-American
            actresses were depicted with her ground-breaking role as Coffy.
            (Produced by Robert A. Papazian)

race – literally, in the film's climax, when the character is shown to be sleeping
with a white, blonde-haired woman. This anonymous female is the symbol of
capitalist beautification criticised by West: 'The ideal of female beauty in this
country puts a premium on lightness and softness mythically associated with
white women and downplays the rich stylistic manners associated with black
women.'[7] The presentation of the white female in *Sweet Sweetback* – who Van
Peebles has to sexually dominate in order to avoid being mugged – or of the
anonymous Caucasian woman whom Priest is pictured in bed with (before
disregarding) in *Super Fly*, is dismantled in *Coffy*. The blonde haired, blue-eyed,
pale-skinned female as a symbol of perfection (and male sexual achievement
– including black male sexual achievement) is at least made to look physically
inferior to the statuesque Grier, whose gun-wielding dominatrix is presented
throughout *Coffy* as rugged, strong and sexually insatiable/aggressive. As with
Sweetback and *Super Fly*, the stylisation of *Coffy*, city landscapes and street grit
permits Grier's character to standout in a veritable 'concrete jungle'. The film's
camerawork may be more fluid, and provoke less of a vérité approach, but the
use of actual LA locations allows Coffy (the character) to be presented as a rare
beacon of hope in a corrupt city. Indeed, throughout the film, Coffy's LA is
revealed to be hiding drugs, vice and rackets: from the alleyways to the interior
penthouses that Grier's character is displaced within. The film's use of genuine
locations is consequently pivotal: it is difficult to imagine *Coffy* with studio sets.

NAKED AMBITION

Grier's nurse/avenger is displayed fully nude throughout *Coffy*. She utilises her sexuality to satisfy her own goals (in this case assassinating narcotics dealers). Commenting on this, Dunn argues that *Coffy* offers a 'pornographic vision of the black female body through a racist, patriarchal narrative structure'.[8] While the author muddles the release date of *Coffy*, incorrectly approaching the film 'as a result of Warner Brothers' success with *Cleopatra Jones*' – her argument centres upon a masculinisation of the feminine.[9] She maintains: 'Coffy is completely marginalized by white patriarchal institutional power; she is a working class black woman, a nurse, who uses sex to infiltrate her enemies' power structure.'[10] Continues the author: 'The film is replete with phallic symbolism, most importantly the shotgun that Coffy uses.'[11] Dunn's discussion of *Coffy* indicates a film that replaces the testosterone-fuelled brutality of *Sweetback* and *Super Fly* with a female who acts as a male sex object and replicates the behaviour of the masculine action-film hero. In opposing this argument, I maintain that it is also possible to see Grier's heroine as a character that deliberately subverts and evolves the blaxploitation style by offering audiences the commercial expectancy of the genre while symbolically opposing its most vital ingredients. For instance, commenting upon the film in the July 1974 issue of Britain's *Monthly Film Bulletin*, Glaesnner identified *Coffy* as part of 'the black sexploitation mill'.[12] The use of the term *sexploitation* is important to note because it complements Williams' assertion of the blaxploitation film as 'every bit as exploitative of sex as the sexploitation films it followed' and indicates how the stylistic links between genres has, over time, become less acknowledged (that is, blaxploitation is treated as separate from sexploitation). Glaesnner's comment also indicates that, upon *Coffy*'s initial theatrical release, audiences and critics were aware of the connection between blaxploitation and sexploitation: a commercial expectance of nudity and interracial coupling. The sexualisation of the Coffy personality needs to be taken as essential to this market and even stylistic insistence. Criticism of Grier's repeated nudity, or her character portrayal of sex as a weapon, as representing the 'Sapphire-jezebel mythology', ignores the film's attempt to feminise communal uprising while desexualising the iconography of male dominance in *Sweet Sweetback* and *Super Fly*.[13]

Sweet Sweetback and *Super Fly* initialise the concept of black liberation via grassroots opposition to both Caucasian industry and patriarchy but neither suggests that such ideology is anything *but* individualistic. Sweetback and Priest are employed outside of the accepted, and legally acceptable, industries of white society. The ability of these characters to outwit the authorities leads to their eventual renegade victory. Coffy is represented by a dual personality that is emblematic of these factors. In the first instance she is a nurse: she contributes to a multi-ethnic society and works within the system of legal, taxable work that Sweetback and Priest repel. Alternatively, she moonlights as an escort, exploiting the illicit capital-return of the underground industry of sex and drugs that Sweetback and Priest embrace. Coffy does this in order to annihilate those she sees as responsible for the subjugation of the black working class. When we see her executing drug dealers or, in the case of King George, men involved with prostitution, she is – symbolically – destroying the very concept that men like Sweetback or Priest could be seen as liberators. In this sense, Dunn's argument that Coffy 'is completely marginalized by white patriarchal institutional power' makes little sense.

Speaking about the Coffy character, Glaesnner adds:

> Coffy is shown to inhabit a world where exploitation, both sexual and political, is simply the norm; and just as the film seems about to incorporate a serious discussion of a way out of the appalling heroin impasse, it quite casually reveals the one person in a position to give voice to the radical policies the situation demands, and to implement them, to be totally corrupt herself.[14]

This corruption also functions as commentary. It is the concept, as suggested by *Sweetback* and *Super Fly*, that Coffy must pander to promiscuity or narcotics in order to ground herself as a progressive figure for the black community that Grier's heroine opposes. She is the figure of *healer* (nurse) and *protector* (her vigilante actions to prohibit narcotics in her inner-city community). The Coffy character is thus twofold: she is the fictional persona placed within an action/sexploitation narrative and also representative of an attempt to destroy, and rebuild, the facets of the blaxploitation genre in a less masculine, and more politically explicit, form. *Coffy* exists as part of the exploitation style: with obvious crossover to sexploitation and an urban link to both *Sweet Sweetback* and *Super Fly*. However, the film's narrative opposes the previous two blaxploitation landmarks: indeed, the Coffy personality is deliberately set up to be placed within the stylistic tropes of the very genre she succeeds in infiltrating. Grier's character is exploited by the generic expectancy for her to be a black avenger who must still 'sell' an image of sexual insatiability. And she is exploited by the masculine insistence that blaxploitation characters be 'successful' drug lords (Priest) or prostitutes (Sweetback). Her assassination of this imagery is as much a comment on the conclusion of the blaxploitation style as it is a cynical adherence to misogyny or the stereotype of the 'Jezebel'.

Dunn's description of Coffy, armed with a shotgun, is as a figure who represents a transformation into a 'ghettoised black female sexuality'[15]. As with Sweetback and Priest, the character played by Pam Grier still turns to murder to upset the balance of power. Blaxploitation was initiated with an outsider figure, Sweetback, who is framed by white authority after saving the life of an African-American man from the police force. *Super Fly* took this renegade personality and presented it in the context of an isolationist narcotics dealer whose rise to financial security is obtained within criminal, but still capitalist, entrepreneurship. *Coffy*, with its suggestion of armed revolution, takes the fringe African-American character even further into an alienation from white authority. Coffy is a murderer but also an antithesis to the politically confused ideology of Sweetback and the selfish monetary pragmatism of Priest in *Super Fly*. Both Dunn and Sims mention the character played by Pam Grier as exploitative of the African-American communist Angela Davis: from the afro hairstyle and the fugitive lifestyle to the close association with firearms and the thwarting of legal authorities.[16] It is this exploitation of thematic that has perhaps confused blaxploitation critics the most. Dunn mentions the 'extreme sexual objectification of black women'[17] in films such as *Coffy*, but also maintains Grier's characters as 'the antithesis of the extreme capitalistic ethos that privileges money over humanity'.[18] As established, the exploitation style often critiques the very things that it visualises for financial gain: sex, violence and – in the example of *Coffy* – the call to armed revolution. Grier's presence with an armed weapon, conflicting with her 'legal' role as a nurse, permits her to subvert the action iconographic rather than to masculinise herself while also making Davis (whom she is clearly meant to be drawing upon) a more sexualised avenger – ironically less troublesome than the real, fiercely intelligent, communist revolutionary. This factor may give us a profound comment on the nature of patriarchy, but it also provides us with an insight into how the exploitation movement would sexualise *any* live socio-political issue of figure if it meant box-office returns.

Grier herself notes:

> These films liberated women. It was the conservatives that saw them as exploitation. The black conservatives, especially, wanted me to be less of a dominant woman in these films – you know, with the guns and the violence. They just didn't want me to walk in a man's shoes. Up until then that genre was focused on the men and their masculinity. But my movies featured the strong woman – who would use herself as bait and then turn the tables on her enemies. I think people were just left scratching their heads – they didn't know if they could say it was exploitation or not because it was the first time this had been done. It was about the power of women and the power of their sexuality.[19]

The dominance of Grier's 'strong' Coffy character is dependent on the very 'men' and 'masculinity' that surround her in the story. Her power is consequent upon her ability to lure a succession of gullible men into thinking that they have an opportunity to bed her. Her vengeance initiates the concept of a female being just as vengeful, and homicidal, as Harry Callahan or John Shaft (Sweetback and Priest are amoral but never indicative of assassinations and cold-blooded murder). Grier's comment that audiences were 'left scratching their heads' indicates the evolution of the blaxploitation style itself. By the time that *Coffy* arrived, the movement of the genre was dictated less by *Sweetback* and *Super Fly* and more by *Shaft*, probably because the disparate avant-garde visuals, including the shaky photography of location and action (dictated by shooting whatever happens by), was more difficult to successfully duplicate than a Classical Hollywood detective film.

The Coffy character operates within a genre in a transformative stage, albeit one that still presents subservience to masculine authority. Her gun fetishism, however phallic in appearance, is therefore emblematic of the attempt to present an African-American leading lady as a figure of vengeance rather than 'the mammy' or 'the exotic other'. Grier's ability to appeal to both the cinematic iconography of masculine heroics (James Bond, John Shaft), while maintaining a character that is oppositional to the stereotype of cinematic black females of the past (Coffy is a hardworking nurse), allows the *Coffy* film to be both exploitative and progressive. Grier's persona rebels in the fiction of the cinema screen and also the 'real world' marketing of previous blaxploitation films and the marketing of African-American women as theatrical personas. Furthermore, at least some tropes are inarguable: prior to *Coffy*, black actresses were *not* permitted to sell a film. Grier's avenger is an amalgamation of *Sweet Sweetback*, *Super Fly* and *Shaft* but endeavours to progress what makes each character a failure of intention: a hesitance to *act* on the very promise of an alternative 'blaxploitation' race-rebellion. Unlike *Dirty Harry*, *Shaft* and other American action films of the time, Coffy is given humanity and doubts: '*I feel like I am in a dream*' she softly confides to Carter, trying to reveal her actions to him (and thus warranting her arrest).

At the end of the film, after shooting and killing Brunswick, she is pictured walking alone, in an apparent state of shock, along an empty beach. *Coffy* certainly exploits sex, violence and racial tensions, but the film is more thematically complex than Dunn credits. Rather than Dunn's belief that 'pussy power' proves Coffy's 'ultimate resource' – the film, with its sombre ending, presents her with a very human, and even motherly, face. [20] Her true resource is in her fleeting but nonetheless expressed doubts about what she is doing and the ease with which she is able to do it, a factor that Dunn fails to identify. The bold machismo, the individualism and the body-capital of the illicit underground are used by Grier to destroy the film's antagonists. While Dunn reads this as a perpetration of the actress's sexual form, and a subsequent misogyny when this form is threatened with rape and torture, the character's sexuality is instead developed to expose the futility of the 'rebel without a cause': the very concept that revolution can be defined at the end of a penis rather than a gun. Hence, *Coffy* explicitly presents what *Sweet Sweetback* and *Super Fly* only suggest: a literal call to arms. In doing so, it gives this violence a conflicted face. Coffy ends the film, unlike Sweetback and Priest in their respective stories, without any sign of jubilation or victory. Her body has been demeaned by both black and white characters and her attempt to stage a revolution has failed. However, by criticising the renegade mentality of the blaxploitation genre itself, especially given its white writer-director and producers, *Coffy* may also be seen to harbour racial anxieties of its own. The Sweetback and Priest characters are slaughtered in *Coffy*: the hypersexual black male and African-American Mafioso, combined into the figure of King George, is shown lynched by two white men. The suggestion may be seen that these stereotypes play into the hands of racist white critics.

Interestingly, a *Variety* review of *Coffy* praised the film as being 'realistic'.[21] This conclusion is perhaps based on the film's evident stylistic lineage to *Sweet Sweetback* and *Super Fly*: the use of real locations, urban cityscapes, handheld camera work, chaotic and random (close-up) acts of sex and violence and jarring editing techniques indicate a lineage to these earlier films. *Coffy* also boasts an evolution towards Hollywood visualisation: interior set dressing, extensive and colourful costumes and a recognisable 'B' actor in Pam Grier. The film's transgressive thematic prevents *Coffy* from successfully marrying the exploitation style with its studio 'other' and the result of this is stylistically redundant to the exploitation form, regardless of its progressive elements. Post-*Coffy* blaxploitation films would adhere to a more linear narrative and replace the documentary style of *Sweetback* and *Super Fly* with the more professional 'Hollywood' approach of *Shaft*. Further, the use of non-actors, non-linear editing, montage, agitprop techniques or explicit sexual spectacle was also replaced by home-grown blaxploitation celebrities. Grier would make several films in the genre, although her star power would wane when successive titles failed to repeat the financial gains of *Coffy*.[22]

Ultimately, blaxploitation – despite a number of films that would further exploit both male and female 'badass' gangsters or detectives – turned out to be a short-lived style. *Sweet Sweetback* and *Super Fly* introduced an aesthetic and thematic that was adapted and subverted by *Coffy* into a conclusion that answered critics of the form while playing to the same sex, violence and urban decay (albeit with more technical sophistication) that audiences expected. After the success of *Coffy*, white producers and directors continued to control the most prominent productions, with a focus on adapting the 'black avenger' further into the Classical Hollywood style and with increasingly less explicit corporeal spectacle. Grier would return, with *Foxy Brown*, and an even more heightened sense of spectacle and absurdity (concluding in a sequence where she gives her female adversary her lover's penis in a pickle jar). As the blaxploitation films became every bit as cartoonish as Grier's castration-happy heroine, the style of *Sweet Sweetback* and *Super Fly*, including the travelogue 'direct cinema' approach, would fade almost entirely. Similarly, the garish gruesome violence of *Coffy*, which with its exploding heads prefigures the likes of *Dawn of the Dead* and even *Martin* in its horror-film sensibilities, would also be toned down. Only *Foxy Brown* would offer a similar spectacle of blood and guts – making these films concurrent with the growth in special-effects nastiness that George Romero, in particular, would make mainstream with his later zombie horrors. Nevertheless, the influence of blaxploitation remains a part of popular culture – and when Halle Berry was unveiled as Catwoman in 2004, there was no question that, even as critics scowled at the comic-book lunacy of the motion picture, it was Grier's equally larger-than-life Coffy or Foxy Brown that she was drawing upon.

NOTES

1. Described as 'violent expressions of black manhood' by author Ed Guerrero. Cited in *Framing Blackness: The African American Image in Film* (Temple University Press, Philadelphia, 1993) p. 101.
2. Ibid.
3. Sims, Y, *Women of Blaxploitation: How the Black Action Film Heroine Changed American Popular Culture* (McFarland Publishing, Jefferson, 2006), p. 22.
4. Dunn, S, *Baad Bitches and Sassy Supermamas: Black Power Action Films* (University of Illinois Press, Chicago, 2008), p. 108.
5. Sieving, C, 'Pam Grier as Star Text', *Screening Noir* (autumn/winter 2005, University of California, Santa Barbara), p. 16.
6. Examples include *TNT Jackson* (Cirio H. Santiago, 1974), *Get Christie Love!* (William A. Graham, 1974) and *Lady Cocoa* (Matt Cimber, 1975).
7. West, C, *Race Matters* (Vintage Books, New York, 2001 [1993]), p. 130.
8. Dunn, S, *Baad Bitches and Sassy Supermamas: Black Power Action Films* (University of Illinois Press, Chicago, 2008), p. 17.
9. Ibid., p. 16.
10. Ibid., p. 116.
11. Ibid., p. 21.
12. Glaessner, V, '*Coffy* Review', *Monthly Film Bulletin* (vol. 41. 486, July 1974), p. 145.
13. Dunn, S, *Baad Bitches and Sassy Supermamas: Black Power Action Films* (University of Illinois Press, Chicago, 2008),p. 116.
14. Glaessner, V, '*Coffy* Review', *Monthly Film Bulletin* (vol. 41. 486, July 1974), p. 145.
15. Dunn, S, *Baad Bitches and Sassy Supermamas: Black Power Action Films* (University of Illinois Press, Chicago, 2008), p. 115.
16. Dunn also mentions that the tribulations faced by Coffy exploit the very racism that Davis would speak about. In one sequence in *Coffy*, Grier is threatened by rape – a form of punishment that Davis maintained was used by white slave owners. Cited in Dunn, S, *Baad Bitches and Sassy Supermamas: Black Power Action Films* (University of Illinois Press, Chicago, 2008), p. 21.
17. Ibid., p. 24.
18. Ibid., p. 31.

19. 'Grier, P, Interview' by Waddell, C, Conducted by phone, 6 November 2012. Available on Arrow Video *Foxy Brown* Blu-ray (2012) as part of booklet 'The Foxiest Femme' (Calum Waddell, 2013).
20. Dunn, S, *Baad Bitches and Sassy Supermamas: Black Power Action Films* (University of Illinois Press, Chicago, 2008), p. 108.
21. 'Jack Hill, who wrote and directs with an action-atuned hand, inserts plenty of realism in footage in which Pam Grier in title role ably acquits herself.' Cited in *Variety* magazine, 'Review of *Coffy*', (16 May 1973, Variety Media, California).
22. See: Sieving, C, 'Pam Grier as Star Text', *Screening Noir* (autumn/winter 2005, University of California, Santa Barbara).

12. EXPLOITATION AS A MOVEMENT

As detailed in my introduction, in 2007 American director Quentin Tarantino teamed up with Mexican filmmaker Robert Rodriguez for a major Hollywood production entitled *Grindhouse* (2007). The film cost in the region of $53 million to produce[1] and ran for more than three hours. *Grindhouse* exhibited two movies in the style of old double-bill programming: Rodriguez's *Planet Terror*, a throwback to the horror of *Night of the Living Dead* and the zombie genre that it inspired (including, in particular, the Italian splatter epic *Nightmare City* (Umberto Lenzi, 1980)), and Tarantino's *Death Proof*, a psycho-sexual 'mad maniac' movie about a serial killer who drives an ominous black Dodge Charger car. As two of America's most famous directors, Rodriguez and Tarantino probably introduced the term 'grindhouse' to a new generation but their multi-million-dollar homage was in the style of a major Hollywood blockbuster and bore little similarity to the films it drew inspiration from. In *Planet Terror* and *Death Proof* the minimal locations, unknown actors, genuine surroundings and prolonged, raw documentary-style depictions of agony and horror (detailed in close-up and real-time) that typify films such as *Night of the Living Dead*, *The Last House on the Left* and *Martin* were replaced by special-effects extravagance, lavish production values and A-list performers such as Bruce Willis and Kurt Russell. Nudity, meanwhile, was teased at but not exhibited, and ethnic portrayals were wisely shorn of any stereotypes from exploitation past. Yet, in avoiding such tropes, *Grindhouse* could never really be a love-letter to 'exploitation'. Indeed, such a thing in today's world would simply not suffice.

Nonetheless, the popular awareness of *Grindhouse* – even if the box office was less than thrilling – resulted in the term 'exploitation' being discussed in the mainstream press, albeit in the same vague terms of Sconce's discussion of paracinema. Referencing the Rodriguez/Tarantino double bill, Atkinson acknowledges 'the grindhouse "tradition" of exploitation filmmaking'[2] but struggles to clarify what he means by this statement: 'a semi-forgotten desert paradise of raw cinematic experience ... a newly identified meta-subgenre, a remembered confluence of essentially unrelated phenomena defined by the circumstances in which they were originally viewed'.[3] A 'newly identified meta-subgenre'? If this were the case, then how could these films have (supposedly) escaped recognition for so long – especially given an apparent postmodern self-awareness that existed between text and viewer? And if this sort of reflexive understanding was to have existed, then how did these films ever cause any censorship problems in the first place?

In this book I have worked towards identifying exploitation cinema as a movement predicated around a similar stylistic approach to corporeal taboo. I have suggested that several key exploitation films, found in the three most commercially sustainable genres, exhibited a group style that influenced numerous copycat productions – and that this style is what we may see as the exploitation movement. Far from being defined solely by the circumstance of exhibition (that is, in theatres that one may choose to label as 'grindhouse', most likely in retrospect), this style moved towards a greater simulation of believable and gritty spectacle. It also did not last long: taboo was fatigued remarkably fast and audience disinterest became evident. Based around sensational acts of physical threat and corporeal exhibition, the exploitation style is aesthetically transgressive. Shock and salacity are motivating narrative factors. Contingent to the exploitation style is a heightened and gritty verisimilitude, both of spectacle and of surrounding: genuine locations, rundown urbanity, actual crowds, unknown actors, travelogue vérité and close-up depictions of sex/nudity or prolonged scenes of violence – all taking place in 'real time'. Handheld camera techniques bond all of the earliest key films in this study.

The exploitation film also has a consistent sense of *movement* – the exploitation lens follows the act of intercourse or brutal death until it is complete, documenting each display of sex or violence and leaving as little to the imagination as possible. The spectacle of time is also more protracted in these films. Sex often takes place in a permeable reproduction of undressing, intercourse and climax, and violent death unfolds in a mimesis of heightened detail. The exploitation film *shows* what the Hollywood film *hides*. Certainly, these films are reflexive – but they are reflexive of the voyeuristic transgression on display. For instance, exploitation films frequently place the viewer in a position of intrusion – watching other characters viewing, or participating in, on-screen 'group' acts of corporeality. Such stylistic consideration consequents a revelation of the forbidden: perhaps an understanding of the subversive nature inherent in watching these films in X-rated cinemas or bygone twenty-four-hour inner-city theatres/drive-ins with other people. The exploitation style was also motivated by a sense of chronological one-upmanship: as each film exhibited more 'daring' displays of sex and violence, the productions became increasingly more professional – or more 'cinematic', possibly as a reaction to the numerous low-budgeted 'B' film titles or big-budget Hollywood films (such as *Shaft* and *Last Tango in Paris*) that emerged in the wake of key successes.

Exploitation films are also evidently *of their time*. The race-rebellion of blaxploitation, the critical and commercial attention given to unsimulated sex films such as *Deep Throat, Behind the Green Door* and *The Devil in Miss Jones* and the vérité style horror of *Night of the Living Dead* and *The Last House on the Left* carried an impact that was attributable to their style: these films presented spectacles that audiences had never seen before. To attempt to recapture this innovation, with productions that evoke imagined grindhouse nostalgia, is pointless. The distribution practices (interlinked to provocative marketing), where word of mouth would carry a release from territory to territory, are no longer existent. The style is also doubtlessly unappealing to a new audience: the Hollywood remakes of *The Texas Chain Saw Massacre* (Marcus Nispel, 2003) and *The Last House on the Left* (Dennis Iliadis, 2009) indicate the difficulty of recapturing the look and feel of these older templates. In place of the original films' gritty documentary-style are 'safe' studio aesthetics, body-beautiful performers and impressive special effects. The sense of *danger* is absent. Wrote one critic of the 'new' *The Last House on the Left*: 'if one engages in such an endeavor to begin with, then filing away the harshest edges becomes counterproductive. What does it hope to preserve by averting its eyes from the worst moments? What part of this pill needs to be sugar-coated?'[4] The answer to these questions is that the 'new' *The Last House on the Left* wants to play to an audience that accepts the limitations of the 'R'-rated spectacle that the original transgressed. It is difficult to imagine that a mainstream viewership exists for grungy simulations of rape and torture that, in addition, question the voyeurism of these horrific acts. Less well known, but still worth briefly acknowledging, are remakes of *The Devil in Miss Jones* (Paul Thomas, 2005) and *The Opening of Misty Beethoven* (Veronica Hart, 2004). While made for video the bodies have changed alongside the spectacle. No longer is Miss Jones a middle-aged spinster with a body to suit, but rather a sex-bomb blonde with large obtrusive silicone implants. The same is true of the 'new' Misty Beethoven. The style of these films bears no similarity to what came before – and any attempt at realism is immediately curtailed by ridiculous casting decisions and the flashy but threadbare shot-on-digital video quality.

The exploitation films discussed in this book also belong to a period concurrent with the fall of censorship. Speaking about *The Outlaw* (Howard Hughes,

1943), Bazin argues that the 'real director'[5] was William M. Hays, America's chief censor: 'It was the censorship code that turned it into an erotic film.'[6] Without censorship guidelines to follow, exploitation films provided audiences with a screen assimilation of chaos and anarchy: evoking an atmosphere of unpredictability – the agitprop narrative of *Sweetback*, the collapse in human relations of *Night of the Living Dead* or the sexual damnation and unglamorous bodies of *The Devil in Miss Jones*. In Hollywood cinema there is a certain 'safety', a knowledge that the camera will refuse to present 'the money shot' or stage gruelling acts of violence that go 'beyond' the 'R-rating' necessitated by a major studio release. Exploitation cinema subverts these expectations by surpassing the boundaries of the comparatively 'safe', and expertly choreographed, Hollywood spectacle and de-glamorising acts of sex or violence with a minimalist, matter-of-fact, forthright presentation.

Drawing further upon the work of Bazin, I suggest that the exploitation films that were released after the collapse of the censorious Hay's Code provide some consolation to the question that the author once posited in regards to what screen 'realism' can, and indeed *should*, aspire to. Admitting his own contradictions – his opposition to 'evoking everything'[7] on the cinema screen while praising the 'air of documentary' and 'naturalness' of Italian neorealism[8] – Bazin mentioned the concept of showing real sex as oppositional to the artistry and fantasy of the filmed image. Bazin would not live to see such films as *Behind the Green Door* and *The Devil in Miss Jones* become commercial and critical successes but in these pages I have argued that the use of unsimulated sex be seen as a natural progression of exploitation cinema's assimilation of believable physical spectacles. The urbanity and violence of blaxploitation and the persuasive simulations of mortality in the exploitation-horror film caused controversy and outrage but serve a larger purpose when contextualised within the group style of a larger cinematic movement. These films were commercially salient because they provided an oppositional spectacle to Hollywood.

Bazin argues that 'cinema can say everything, but not show everything'.[9] He states, 'I ought to be able to look upon what takes place on the screen as a simple story, an evocation which never touches the level of reality.'[10] For an author whose work has been viewed as synonymous with an unshakable belief in cinema's ability to capture 'reality',[11] Bazin indicates a very vocal fear of what may happen without the censor to get in the way. Furthermore, while championing the neorealist approach to cinema, Bazin also predicts the eventuality of a filmmaking cycle with an actuality that is exhibited for more sensational conclusions. This cinema, this *style*, can be seen as exploitation. In his famous discussion of *The Outlaw*, Bazin mentions that were it not for censorship regulation the film might only be 'violent and realistic' (which he views critically) instead of 'erotic'.[12] Bazin also admits concern about the potential for the cinematic image to take on 'a documentary quality'.[13] The exploitation style indicates that cinema's potential to recreate images of horror or sex is considerable. With the fall of censorship, the obscenities that Bazin imagined possible are presented in full close-up. However, as I have argued, his belief that this anarchic documentation of sex and violence may result in something uncinematic – realism so gruelling or shocking that a 'simple story', or the 'art' of filmmaking, is disregarded – is incorrect. For a brief period, the exploitation film functioned as a movement of its own, with a style that challenged the 'safety' of antiquated presentations of visceral subject matter. The result, the films discussed in this book, are as *cinematic* – insofar as grounding and evolving a group style – as neorealism was in the 1940s.

In defining these films as part of a cinematic movement, I have stressed the importance of viewing each of the key titles as central to an expediency of generic intent. As Hollywood became adept at amalgamating exploitation elements into their major productions, underground filmmakers – having fatigued the surprise of race, sex and gruesome horror – began to copy the big studio releases. I have argued against an auteurist reading of the films themselves because the obligation to exploit specific generic spectacle maintains exploitation as a fastidiously commercial form. The auteur of the exploitation film is neither the director nor the producer but rather the market itself. This motivating factor is also what brought the form's downfall. The lone black detective of the Hollywood blockbuster *Shaft* became a fixture of the independently produced 'blaxploitation' films: *Truck Turner* (Jonathan Kaplan, 1974), *Sheba, Baby* (William Girdler, 1975), *Friday Foster* (Arthur Marks, 1975). These productions, both aesthetically and thematically, have little in common with the films that formed and distinguished the genre: *Sweet Sweetback's Baadasssss Song* and *Super Fly*.

Following the blockbuster success of *The Exorcist* and *Jaws*, the most prominent independent horror releases drew on the supernatural or 'nature run amok': *God Told Me To* (Larry Cohen, 1976), *Grizzly* (William Girdler, 1976), *Piranha* (Joe Dante, 1978). The follow-up to *Night of the Living Dead*, *Dawn of the Dead* (George Romero, 1978) is a polished two-hour epic with state-of-the-art special effects inspired by the gruesome excess of *The Exorcist*. The famous *Halloween* (John Carpenter, 1978) features Steadicam, professional actors and widescreen photography: *just like a Hollywood studio film*. *Halloween*'s story of teenage girls menaced by a masked killer aimed itself at a youth demographic and its success – which included numerous sequels – ensured that future horror productions catered to this lucrative market.

The merging of unsimulated sex with major Hollywood films never happened. Unlike blaxploitation and the exploitation-horror film, once audiences had seen graphic close-up presentations of fellatio, homosexuality, penetration and ejaculation there was little else for sexploitation to offer. The 'pornographic' film industry retreated to sex cinemas and then to videotape.

By the time a new generation of critics approached the nudity and simulations of *9½ Weeks*, a major studio picture with big name performers, it was
as if *The Devil in Miss Jones* had never been one of the highest grossing
films of the 1970s. Surprisingly, given the popularity of the hardcore form a
decade earlier, one critic even found the simulated (tame) sex of *9½ Weeks*
'loathsome'.[14] As with new labels such as 'paracinema' or the popular use of
'grindhouse' as a signifier to an 'outsider' sense of place and time that is now
mostly imagined and romanticised, we are perhaps too quick to forget the
reception that earlier texts had and the fact that exploitation once attracted
a large audience.

Schaefer stops short of arguing that 'exploitation' – as a style or method
of production and release – existed after the demise of the classical period.
I have maintained otherwise. There are elements of the classical form that
are appropriated into the key films singled out by this book. The concept of
'this really happened' – either a 'true story' genesis or a 'square up' in which
there is an explicit moral basis (or 'excuse') for the on-screen sensationalism
– remained common. If the classical form 'at least recognised that desire
was fundamentally sexual' then the films of this book go to great lengths to
demonstrate what their predecessors could only hint at. The 'exploitation' in
question evolved from a tease to the unveiling of increasingly more graphic
spectacles of sex and violence. As censorship collapsed, exploitation filmmakers could adapt the commercially salient presentation of 'taboo' images into
linear narratives. *Lorna* does not need a narrator to tell audiences about the
dangers of extramarital affairs: the film itself needs no excuse for either its
story or the presentation of nudity. Likewise, *Night of the Living Dead* and
Sweet Sweetback candidly display images that a decade previously would have
been unthinkable. The use of the close-up, to define the excess of the spectacle,
is evidenced in both the classical and the post-classical exploitation film. As
with the classical form, the condemning of the very taboo being exploited was
also frequent in key exploitation films: even in explicit sex productions, as
evidenced by *The Devil in Miss Jones*.

Exploitation cinema was not the utopia of fun, frivolous, escapist imagery
promoted by *Grindhouse* or that Sconce imagines: 'that moment when the
narrative logic and diegetic illusions of cheap exploitation cinema disintegrate
into a brutally blissful encounter with profilmic failure'.[15] While many technically inept films may have followed the key productions, such as the poorly
made *I Spit on Your Grave*, the motivating exploitation style identified here
was interlinked by a convincing thread of apprehension and even malevolence.
The more 'fun' spectacles of *Vixen* and *The Opening of Misty Beethoven* still
question the challenges that a sexually liberated female may face in a society
built upon patriarchal dominance. Further, the outrage caused by the 'diegetic
illusions' of the blaxploitation or exploitation-horror films suggest that the

impact of this style was far more skilful, studied and deliberate than (as Sconce seems to indicate) accidental.

This book opted to begin at the point where Schaefer finished his own exhaustive work on the classical exploitation form. The intention of this approach was to show that influential features that have previously been identified either as unique aberrations in otherwise generic and repetitive trends (as seen by Wood's Freudian approach to the exploitation-horror film), or simply homogenised under unhelpful and far-reaching terminology, frequently display greater intertextuality with comparable 'marginal' trends. As Weiner mentions: 'The early pioneers of exploitation cinema are really the fathers of the modern independent film.'[16] In order to understand and identify this transition – from the classical exploitation feature that typically dealt with drugs, nudity and sex to the later titles of the 1960s and 1970s – this study has provided a historical basis to the rise and fall of the exploitation film. Independent cinema today, in its *ethos* of 'doing it yourself',[17] relates back to the exploitation movement – but the channels available to exhibit *any* new feature film, made outside of the studio system, is thinner than it has ever been. It is the trend adopted by *Super Fly* – which was purchased for distribution by Warner Bros. following the success of *Sweet Sweetback's Baadasssss Song* – that continues to inspire makeshift filmmakers today. The most notable independent successes of recent years – *Clerks* (Kevin Smith, 1994), *The Blair Witch Project* (Eduardo Sánchez and Daniel Myrick, 1999) and *Open Water* (Chris Kentis, 2003) – were all purchased, marketed and distributed by a leading Hollywood label. Without this support, it is difficult to imagine any of them achieving the financial returns that *Behind the Green Door* or *The Last House on the Left* once occurred via state-by-state theatrical bookings. Only *The Room* (Tommy Wiseau, 2003) perhaps takes us back to the power of word of mouth and limited bookings, although its entrance to the pop-culture lexicon took years to achieve and it was no immediate sensation.

While numerous American (and international) films were, and still are, inspired by the key productions identified in this study, the exploitation style emanated and evolved from a small group of influential releases.[18] This 'imitative' appropriation of familiar aesthetic and thematic traits is not uncommon to any cinematic movement. It is probable that exploitation maintained so many copycat releases because of the easily mimicked *spectacle* of each genre. Sex, violent death and urbanity, presented in actual locations and with non-actors, are easier to reproduce than, for instance, the technically proficient special effects of *The Exorcist* or *Star Wars*. The success of *Snuff* is a testament to how the exploitation spectacle, if not the style, could be used to the benefit of aspiring filmmakers.

In addition, Hollywood was also quick to imitate the exploitation *spectacle* but not the *style*. The marketing of *Shaft*, *The Exorcist* and *Last Tango in Paris* draw upon audience awareness of the salacious thrills that the exploitation film delivers but provide them in a more 'acceptable' form. These films borrowed key tropes from their sources but diluted the gritty verisimilitude, transgressive imagery and inconclusive thematic elements in order to broaden the audience appeal. The sex and violence of the Hollywood variants remains comparatively hidden or presented within a deliberate unreality of studio wizardry and lavish production values. The influence of Hollywood cinema on the movement's style is considerable (that is, many of the blaxploitation films following *Shaft* presented a James Bond-style 'hero'). Fresh innovation was also problematic: the exploitation style is based upon the idea that people will pay money to be shocked. However, the explicit display of sex, violence and race relations was fatigued after only a few innovative films – and blockbuster returns petered out fast. By the beginning of the 1980s, for instance, unsimulated sex productions were made predominantly for video and shot on tape. The opportunity to repeat the critical and commercial success of *The Devil in Miss Jones* was now impossible because the distribution channels for sexploitation had concluded; adult theatres had closed as audiences watched sex films at home. The success of *The Devil in Miss Jones*, with its middle-aged heroine, however, indicates that using the sex spectacle for reasons other than just providing masturbatory relief could have – maybe even should have – evolved further.

A group style should also not be confused with a group manifesto. Exploitation films frequently borrowed from one another, as regards both style and spectacle, but it would be incorrect to make a case for a united auteurist-led attempt to create a distinct movement based upon a desire to *change* the Hollywood style of filmmaking. Exploitation cinema gained commercial friction from its inimitable ability to provide something that mainstream films could not. The movement's key films were thus dependent – however coincidentally – on a congregation of independence, minimal resources and innovation, especially as regards capturing their respective epoch by a transgressive presentation of contemporary taboo. Seen today, some of the stylistic facets of exploitation are so widespread in contemporaneous cinema that we take them for granted. The veracity and variety of spectacle – sex, *death* and *urban violence* – as well as the presence of interracial coupling, multiracial heroes, the inconclusive nature of identifiably generic films, the forthright depiction of the erogenous feminine and the decision to *show* – rather than to *tease* – 'shocking' imagery indicate the lineage of exploitation cinema far more than *Grindhouse* or any similar sound-alike 'homage'. This factor is probably why the recent remakes of key exploitation films have been unable to capture the zeitgeist of their own era.

As evidenced by *Grindhouse*, today the *idea* of exploitation – *abrasive, subversive* and *transgressive* – has been abridged by Hollywood's most successful filmmakers. The style may not be evidenced but what exploitation has come to *represent* continues to be, without any hint of irony, exploited by the major American film studios. The term is now so frequently related – the blockbuster action production *Machete* (Robert Rodriguez, 2010) – reviewed as a 'gleefully excessive pastiche of an exploitation film', for instance[19] – that it seems to represent nothing outside of what any specific author wants it to mean. The protracted spectacle of exploitation cinema, the low-rent gritty visuals of unprofessional actors, frequently unglamorous faces and bodies and themes of cynicism, displeasure, individualism and sexual repression are certainly not explored by the so-called 'pastiches' of the form released to multiplex audiences today.

Of course, this book has focused on the American exploitation film. However, every country has seen its own emergence of marginal cinema, including the creation of similar genres as those discussed here and during similarly turbulent socio-political and censorious periods. To give just one fascinating example: the Spanish horror film, during the reign of Francisco Franco, produced texts of extraordinary sexual repression and cruelty. Film titles such as *Gritos en la Noche* (The Awful Dr Orloff) (Jess Franco, 1962), *La Noche del terror ciego* (Tombs of the Blind Dead) (Amando De Ossorio, 1972) and *La semana del asesino* (Cannibal Man) (Eloy de la Iglesia, 1973) warrant a study of their own rather than a blanketing under confusing titles such as 'Eurotrash'.[20] Perhaps greater stylistic identification between key Spanish (and other European) horror films will indicate that such productions as those mentioned warrant more than just occasional scrutiny as part of a paracinematic trash/'excessive' or just 'weird' and inept umbrella label.

In sum, then, the key films in the American exploitation movement present a style that transgresses any contemporary comparison: examples of a cinema that is raw, gritty, shocking and even upsetting. In closing this study, therefore, it is easy to understand why this cinema has lasted for decades and will probably last for decades more. These films engage with spectacles that confound and disorient. While many will argue with my own conclusions, it is my hope that exploitation may be viewed as a style in forthcoming studies – a style that inspired filmmaking for decades afterwards. As we go into the 1980s, certainly, a further study is required – a discussion of how this exploitation style found itself caught between the 'quick fix' of the VHS market and the more commercial (but safe) ambitions of Hollywood studios. If these words assist in encouraging others to identify a movement or consistency within further examples of marginal and hitherto loosely defined/identified cinema then *The Style of Sleaze* will surely have achieved a worthwhile step in the close scrutiny and evaluation of marginal moviemaking.

NOTES

1. Nashawaty, C, 'Bloodbath and Beyond' (30 March 2007), www.ew.com/ew/article/0,,20015706,00.html, last accessed 20 August 2017.
2. Atkinson, M, 'Givers of the Viscera', *Sight and Sound* (vol. 19. 7, June 2007, BFI, London), p. 19.
3. Ibid.
4. Vaux, R, '*The Last House on the Left*: Something Cut Out in Transition' (13 March 2009), http://www.mania.com/last-house-left_article_113664.html, last accessed 12 September 2012.
5. Bazin, A, *What is Cinema? Vol 1* (University of California Press, Los Angeles, 1967), p. 167.
6. Ibid.
7. Bazin, A, *What Is Cinema? Vol 2* (University of California Press, Los Angeles, 2005 [1971]), p. 175.
8. Ibid., p. 32.
9. Ibid., p. 174.
10. Ibid.
11. See the discussion in Carroll, N, 'Power of Movies', *The Moving Image* (vol. 114. 4, autumn 1985, University of Minnesota Press, Minnesota) for evidence of how Bazin has generally been viewed as a commentator of supposed cinematic 'realism'. In fact, Bazin's comments on the need for film to remain part of a larger artistic illusion complicates such a conclusion.
12. Bazin, A, *What Is Cinema? Vol 2* (University of California Press, Los Angeles, 2005 [1971]), p. 174.
13. Ibid.
14. Briggs, J, *Profoundly Erotic: Sexy Movies that Changed History* (Plexus Publishing, London, 2005), p. 286.
15. Sconce, J (ed.), *Sleaze Artists* (Duke University Press, Durham, NC and London, 2007), p. 9.
16. Weiner, Robert G, 'The Prince of Exploitation Dwain Esper'. In Cline, J and Weiner, R, *From the Arthouse to the Grindhouse: Highbrow and Lowbrow Transgression in Cinema's First Century* (Scarecrow Press, London, 2010), p. 41.
17. For instance, *Clerks* (Kevin Smith, 1995) and *The Blair Witch Project* (Eduardo Sanchez and Daniel Myrick, 1999).
18. I have, for all intents and purposes, avoided Canada in this study – which means that there has been no discussion of early David Cronenberg, whose work shares a similar style to his American contemporaries, or the Cinepix shocker *Ilsa, She Wolf of the SS* (Don Edmonds, 1975). *Ilsa, She Wolf of the SS*, which was produced by Canadians but filmed in California with an American director and star, can trace its lineage back to *The Damned* (Luchino Visconti, 1969). Kerner mentions that *Ilsa* be seen as an exploitation film because it has little to offer *but* a carnival of sex and violence – although the author is careful to still imbed this cheap and nasty lunacy with some social consideration by insisting that it offers 'a picture of male anxiety in the 1970s'. Kerner, A, *Torture Porn in the Wake of 9/11: Horror, Exploitation, and the Cinema of Sensation* (Rutgers University Press, New Brunswick, NJ, 2015), p. 62. I do think *Ilsa*'s interesting mix of pastness (Nazi atrocities) with present (retrospection and possibly perverse interest in war crimes – spoken about in a Chinese-whispers sort of way and fed to the My Lai generation) deserves further consideration. Is it *exploitation*? Insofar as being shamefully cynical about the general public's willingness to glare at concentration-camp horrors – yes, *of course*, it most surely is. But, nationality aside, does it

belong to the exploitation *movement* set out and defined in this book? Of that, I am less confident. As with the mondo cycle, the short-lived Nazisploitation film has threads and influences that exist outside of American exploitation cinema and the spectacle of *Ilsa* is dressed up in reconstructed sets and period costuming. Indeed, I am tempted to see the foremost identity of *Ilsa* as being that of a (certainly exploitative) B-action film more than even a down-and-dirty horror movie: right down to its 'bombs away' adventure *Boy's Own*-style ending in which the Allies liberate the on-screen concentration camp amidst gunfire and patronage.

19. Floyd, N, '*Machete* Review', *Time Out* (23 November 2010), http://www.timeout. com/london/film/machete, last accessed 20 August 2017.
20. Mathijs, E and Mendik, X (eds), *Alternative Europe: Eurotrash and Exploitation Cinema since 1945* (Wallflower Press, London, 2004), p. 9.

SELECT BIBLIOGRAPHY

BOOKS

Allen, R, and Gomery, D, *Film History: Theory and Practice* (McGraw-Hill, New York, 1985)

Anger, K, *Hollywood Babylon* (Arrow Books, San Francisco, 1986 [1959])

Baxter, P, *Rhodesia: Last Outpost of the British Empire* (Galago Books, Cape Town, 2010)

Bazin, A, *What is Cinema? Vol 1* (University of California Press, Los Angeles, 1967)

Bazin, A, *What Is Cinema? Vol 2* (University of California Press, Los Angeles, 2005 [1971])

Bazin, A, '*Umberto D*: A Great Work'. In Bazin, A and Cardullo, B (eds), *André Bazin and Neorealism* (Continuum, New York, 2011), pp. 111–16

Betrock, A, *The I Was a Teenage Juvenile Delinquent Rock'N'Roll Horror Beach Party Movie Book: A Complete Guide to the Teen Exploitation Film, 1954–1969* (St Martin's Press, London, 1986)

Betz, M, 'Art Exploitation Underground'. In Jancovich, M, Reboll, A, Stringer, J and Willis, A, *Defining Cult Movies: The Cultural Politics of Oppositional Taste* (Manchester University Press, Manchester, 2003), pp. 202–22

Black, J, 'Real(ist) Horror: From Execution Videos to *Snuff* Films'. In Mendik, Xavier and Schneider, Steven Jay (eds), *Underground USA: Filmmaking beyond the Hollywood Canon* (Wallflower Press, New York, 2002), pp. 63–75

Bordwell, D, *Poetics of Cinema* (Routledge, New York, 2007)

Bordwell, D and Thompson, J, *Film History: An Introduction* (McGraw-Hill, New York, 1994)

Bordwell, D and Thompson, K, *Minding Movies, Observations on the Art, Craft and Business of Filmmaking* (The University of Chicago Press, Chicago, 2011)

Bordwell, D, Staiger, J and Thompson, K, *The Classical Hollywood Cinema* (Routledge, London, 1991 [1985])

Briggs, J, *Profoundly Disturbing* (Plexus Publishing, London, 2003)

Briggs, J, *Profoundly Erotic: Sexy Movies that Changed History* (Plexus Publishing, London, 2005)

Brottman, M, *Offensive Films* (Vanderbilt University Press, Nashville, 2005 [1997])

Cardullo, B, 'What is Neorealism?' In Bazin, A and Cardullo, B (eds), *André Bazin and Neorealism* (Continuum, New York, 2011), pp. 18–29

Carter, D, 'It's Only a Movie? Reality as Transgression in Exploitation Cinema'. In Cline, J and Weiner, R, *From the Arthouse to the Grindhouse: Highbrow and Lowbrow Transgression in Cinema's First Century* (Scarecrow Press, Blue Ridge Summit, 2010), pp. 297–317

Chaffin-Quiray, G, 'The Underground Trio of Melvin Van Peebles'. In Mendik, X and Schneider, S, *Underground U.S.A. Filmmaking beyond the Hollywood Canon* (Wallflower Press, New York, 2002)

Church, D, *Grindhouse Nostalgia: Memory, Home Video and Exploitation Film Fandom* (Edinburgh University Press, Edinburgh, 2016)

Church, D, *Disposable Passions: Vintage Pornography and the Material Legacies of Adult Cinema (Global Exploitation Cinemas)* (Bloomsbury Academic, London, 2016)

Clover, C, *Men, Women and Chainsaws: Gender in the Modern Horror Film* (BFI, London, 1996 [1992])

Cowie, P, *Revolution, The Explosion of World Cinema in the 60s* (Faber and Faber, London, 2004)

Crane, J, 'A Lust for Life: The Cult Films of Russ Meyer'. In Harper, G and Mendik, X (eds) *Unruly Pleasures: The Cult Film and its Critics* (FAB Press, London, 2000), pp. 87–101

Crane, J, 'Come On-A My House: The Inescapable Legacy of Wes Craven's *The Last House on the Left*'. In Mendik, X (ed.) *Shocking Cinema of the Seventies* (Noir Publishing, London, 2002)

Creed, B, *Phallic Panic* (Melbourne University Publishing, Melbourne, 2005)

Dancyger, K and Rush, J, *Alternative Screenwriting* (Focal Press, London, 2013)

Daniels, S, *Masterpieces*, Revised edition (Heinemann, London, 1984)

Doherty, T, *Teenagers and Teenpics: The Juvenilization of American Movies in the 1950's* (Temple University Press, Philadelphia, 2002)

Douglas, M, *Implicit Meanings* (Routledge, New York, 2002,)

Dunn, S, *Baad Bitches and Sassy Supermamas: Black Power Action Films* (University of Illinois Press, Chicago, 2008)

Egan, K, *Trash or Treasure: Censorship and the Changing Meanings of the Video Nasties* (Manchester University Press, Manchester, 2008)

Feaster, F, and Wood, B, *Forbidden Fruit: The Golden Age of Exploitation Film* (Midnight Marquee Publishing, Baltimore, 1999)

Fisher, A, ' Go West, Brother: The Politics of Landscape in the Blaxpoitation Western'. In Fisher, A and Walker, J (eds), *Grindhouse (Global Exploitation Cinemas)* (Bloomsbury Academic, London, 2016)

Fisher, A and Walker, J (eds), *Grindhouse (Global Exploitation Cinemas)* (Bloomsbury Academic, London, 2016)

Foucault, M, *The Will to Knowledge* (Penguin Books, London, 1998 [1976])

Freeland, C, *The Naked and the Undead: Evil and the Appeal of Horror* (Westview Press, Boulder, 2002)

Freud, S, *The Ego and the Id* (W.W. Norton & Company, New York, 1989 [1960])

Gorfinkel, E, 'Radley Metzger's "Elegant Arousal": Taste, Aesthetic Distinction, and Sexploitation'. In Mendik, X and Schneider, S, *Underground U.S.A. Filmmaking beyond the Hollywood Canon* (Wallflower Press, New York, 2002)

Guerrero, E, *Framing Blackness: The African American Image in Film* (Temple University Press, Philadelphia, 1993)
Hames, P, *The Czechoslovak New Wave* (Columbia University Press, New York, 2005)
Hallam, J and Marshment, M, *Realism and Popular Cinema* (Manchester University Press, Manchester, 2000)
Hoberman, J, *The Dream Life, Movies, Media, and the Mythology of the Sixties* (The New Press, New York, 2003)
Howard, J, *Blaxploitation Cinema: The Essential Reference Guide* (FAB Press, London, 2008)
Jancovich, M, *Rational Fears: American Horror in the 1950s* (Manchester University Press, Manchester, 1996)
Jaworzyn, S (ed.), *Shock Xpress: The Essential Guide to Exploitation Cinema, Vol. 1* (Titan Books, London, 1991)
Jaworzyn, S, *The Texas Chain Saw Massacre Companion* (Titan Books, London, 2003)
Jeffords, S, *Hard Bodies: Hollywood Masculinity in the Reagan Era* (Rutgers University Press, New Brunswick, NJ, 1994)
Kerekes, D and Slater, D, *Killing for Culture* (Creation Books, London, 1995)
Kerekes, D and Slater, D, *See No Evil: Banned Films and Video Controversy* (Critical Vision, Manchester, 2001)
Kerner, A, *Torture Porn in the Wake of 9/11: Horror, Exploitation, and the Cinema of Sensation* (Rutgers University Press, New Brunswick, NJ, 2015)
Kleinhans, C, 'Porn and Documentary: Narrating the Alibi'. In Sconce, J, *Sleaze Artists* (Duke University Press, Durham, NC and London, 2007), pp. 96–121
Koch, G, 'The Body's Shadow Realm'. In Gibson, P and Gibson, R (eds), *Dirty Looks: Women, Pornography, Power* (BFI, London, 1993), pp. 25–45
Koven, M, *Blaxploitation Films* (Kamera Books, London, 2010)
Kracauer, S, *From Caligari to Hitler* (Princeton University Press, Princeton, 1974 [1947])
Kracauer, S, *Theory of Film: The Redemption of Physical Reality* (Princeton University Press, Princeton, 1997 [1960])
Lewis, J, *Hollywood v. Hardcore* (New York University Press, New York and London, 2000)
Lisanti, T, *Drive-in Dream Girls: A Galaxy of B-movie Starlets of the Sixties* (McFarland Publishing, Jefferson, 2003)
Lowenstein, A, *Shocking Representations* (Columbia University Press, New York, 2005)
Luckett, M, 'Sexploitation as Feminine Territory'. In Jancovich, M, Reboll, A, Stringer, J and Willis, A (eds), *Defining Cult Movies: The Cultural Politics of Oppositional Taste* (Manchester University Press, Manchester, 2003), pp. 142–56
McDonough, J, *Big Bosoms and Square Jaws* (Vintage, New York, 2006)
McDonough, M, *Broken Mirrors, Broken Minds* (The Guernsey Press, Guernsey, 2001)
McNeill, L and Osborne, J, *The Other Hollywood: An Uncensored Oral History of the Porn Film Industry* (HarperCollins, New York, 2004)
McRoy, J, 'Parts is Parts'. In Conrich, I (ed.), *Horror Zone* (I. B. Tauris, London, 2010), pp. 191–206
Maltby, R, and Craven, I, *Hollywood Cinema* (Blackwell, Oxford, 1995)
Marx, K and Engels, F, *The Communist Manifesto* (Penguin Classics, London, 2002 [1888])
Mathijs, E and Mendik, X (eds), *Alternative Europe: Eurotrash and Exploitation Cinema since 1945* (Wallflower Press, London, 2004)
Miller, C. 'Exploring Cinema's Sordid Side: The Films of Sonney and Friedman'. In

Cline, J and Weiner, R (eds), *From the Arthouse to the Grindhouse* (Scarecrow Press, Blue Ridge Summit, 2010), pp. 75–85

Milligan, S, *Conservative Politics, 'Porno Chic' and Snuff* (Headpress, London, 2014)

Muller, E and Faris, D, *Grindhouse: The Forbidden World of 'Adults Only' Cinema* (St Martin's Press, New York, 1996)

Newman, K, *Nightmare Movies* (Bloomsbury, London, 1988)

Reid, J., *Hollywood 'B' Movies: A Treasury of Spills, Chills & Thrills* (LuLu Press, Morrisville, 2005)

Robb, B, *Screams and Nightmares: The Films of Wes Craven* (Overlook Press, New York, 2000)

Romer, J, 'A Bloody New Wave in the United States'. In Silver, A and Ursini, J (eds), *The Horror Film Reader* (Limelight Editions, New York, 2004), pp. 63–6.

Sanders, E, *The Family* (Thunder's Mouth Press, New York, 2002 [1971])

Schaefer, E, *'Bold! Daring! Shocking! True!' A History of Exploitation Films, 1919–1959* (Duke University Press, Durham, NC and London, 1999)

Sconce, J, '"Trashing" the Academy: Taste, Excess and an Emerging Politics of Cinematic Style'. In Mathijs, E and Mendik, X (eds), *The Cult Film Reader* (Open University Press, London, 2007), pp. 100–19

Sieving, C, *Soul Searching* (Wesleyan University Press, Middletown, 2011)

Sims, Y, *Women of Blaxploitation: How the Black Action Film Heroine Changed American Popular Culture* (McFarland Publishing, Jefferson, 2006)

Spelvin, G, *The Devil Made Me Do It* (Little Red Hen Books, Los Angeles, 2008)

Staiger, J, 'Hybrid or Inbred'. In Grant, B (ed.) *Film Genre Reader III* (University of Texas Press, Austin, 2004), pp. 185–99

Szulkin, D, The Last House on the Left: *The Making of a Cult Classic* (FAB Press, London, 1997)

Ward, G, 'Grinding out the Grind House: Exploitation, Myth and Memory'. In Fisher, A and Walker, J (eds), *Grindhouse (Global Exploitation Cinemas)* (Bloomsbury Academic, London, 2016), pp. 13–31

Watson, P, 'There's No Accounting for Taste'. In Cartmell, D, Hunter, I Q, Kaye, H and Whelehan, I (eds) *Trash Aesthetics: Popular Culture and its Audience* (Pluto Press, London and Chicago, 1997), pp. 66–84

Weiner, Robert G., 'The Prince of Exploitation Dwain Esper'. In Cline, J and Weiner, R, *From the Arthouse to the Grindhouse: Highbrow and Lowbrow Transgression in Cinema's First Century* (Scarecrow Press, London, 2010), pp. 41–57

Weitzer, R, *Sex for Sale: Prostitution, Pornography, and the Sex Industry* (Routledge, New York, 2010)

West, C, *Race Matters* (Vintage Books, New York, 2001 [1993])

Williams, L, *Hard Core: Power, Pleasure, and the 'Frenzy of the Visible'* (Pandora Press, London, 1990)

Williams, L, *Playing the Race Card: Melodramas of Black and White from Uncle Tom to O.J. Simpson* (Princeton University Press, Princeton, 2001)

Williams, L, *Screening Sex* (Duke University Press, Durham, NC, 2008)

Winston, B, *Claiming the Real: The Documentary Film Revisited* (BFI Publishing, London, 1995)

Wood, R, *From Vietnam to Reagan* (Columbia University Press, New York, 1986)

Wood, R, 'What Lies Beneath?' In Schneider, S (ed) *Horror Film and Psychoanalysis* (Cambridge University Press, Cambridge, 2004), pp. xi–xiii

Yearwood, G, *Black Film as a Signifying Practice: Cinema, Narration and the African-American Aesthetic Experience* (Africa World Press, Trenton, 2000)

Publications

Abadnato, G, 'Night of the Living Dead', Interview magazine (vo1. 4, 1969, New York)

Andrews, N, 'Shaft Review', Monthly Film Bulletin (vol. 39. 456, January 1972)

Blumenthal, R, 'Porno Chic', The New York Times (January 1973)

Carroll, N, 'The Cabinet of Dr. Kracauer', The Millennium Film Journal 2 (spring 1978, New York)

Carroll, N, 'Power of Movies', The Moving Image (vol. 114. 4, autumn 1985, University of Minnesota Press, Minnesota)

Champagne, J, 'A Foucauldian Reading of Hard Core', Boundary 2 (vol. 18. 2, summer 1991, Duke University Press, North Carolina)

Eshun, K, 'Escaping the Genre Ghetto', Sight and Sound (vol. 15. 6, June 2005, BFI, London)

Ferrante, T, 'Uncle George Remembers', The Bloody Best of Fangoria (vol. 7, 1988, Starlog Press, New York)

Glaessner, V, 'Coffy Review', Monthly Film Bulletin (vol. 41. 486, July 1974)

Hartmann, J, 'The Trope of Blaxploitation in Critical Responses to "Sweetback"', Film History (vol. 6. 3, autumn 1994, Indiana University Press, Bloomington)

Klemesrud, J, 'Maria Says her Tango is Not', The New York Times (4 February 1973)

McGillivray, D, 'The Story of Joanna Review', Monthly Film Bulletin (vol. 44. 522, 1977)

McGillivray, D, 'Vixen Review', Monthly Film Bulletin (vol. 4. 568, May 1981)

Morthland, J, 'Porno Films: An In-Depth Report', Take One magazine (vol. 4. 4, March–April 1973)

The New York Times, 'Film Pornography Flourishes Despite Court Ruling' (4 November 1973) – no author credited

O'Brian, Glenn, 'The Devil in Miss Jones', Interview magazine (vol. 33, 1973, New York)

Review of The Immoral Mr. Teas. In Variety magazine (27 January 1960, Variety Media, California) – no author credited

Review of Night of the Living Dead. (16 October 1968, Variety Media, California) – no author credited

Review of Lorna. In Variety magazine (vol. 11, 30 October 1968, Variety Media, California) – no author credited

Review of 'Deep Throat'. In Film Facts magazine (vol.15. 18, 1972 compendium, AFI, New York) – no author credited

Review of The Devil in Miss Jones. In Variety magazine (21 February 1973, Variety Media, California) – no author credited

Review of The Resurrection of Eve. In Variety magazine (17 October 1973, Variety Media, California) – no author credited

Review of The Devil and Mr. Jones. In Variety magazine (March 19th, 1975, Variety Media, California) - no author credited

Review of Autobiography of a Flea. In Variety magazine (9 February 1977, Variety Media, California) – no author credited

Sieving, C, 'Pam Grier as Star Text', Screening Noir (autumn/winter 2005, University of California, Santa Barbara)

Strick, P, 'Superfly Review', Monthly Film Bulletin (vol. 40. 469, February 1973)

Wiggins, B, 'You Talkin' Revolution, Sweetback: On Sweet Sweetback's Baadasssss Song and Revolutionary Filmmaking', Black Camera (vol. 4. 1, winter 2012, Indiana University Press, Bloomington)

Williams, L, 'Film Bodies: Gender, Genre, and Success', *Film Quarterly* (vol. 44. 4, summer 1991, University of California Press, Los Angeles)

Wolf, W, '*The Last House on the Left* Review', reprinted in *Film Facts* magazine, (vol. 15. 24, 1972)

WEBSITES

BBFC information on *Blood Feast*. Available At http://bbfc.co.uk/search/releases/blood%2Bfeast

Canby, V, '*Memories within Miss Aggie* Review', *The New York Times* (23 June 1974), http://movies.nytimes.com/movie/review?res=9E0DE4DA113BE53ABC4B51DFB06 6838F669EDE

Clark, J, '10 Noteworthy Exploitation Films' (n.d.), http://entertainment.howstuff-works.com/10-noteworthy-exploitation-films.htm#page=0https://en.wikipedia.org/wiki/Exploitation_film

Cumbrow, R, 'After Sunset' (15 August 2011), http://parallax-view.org/2011/08/15/after-sunset/

Cohen, J, 'Top Ten Death Proof Exploitation Films: The Films that Wouldn't Die' (13 March 2008), http://www.rottentomatoes.com/m/death_proof/news/1715158/top-ten-death-proof-exploitation-films-the-films-that-wouldnt-die/

'Elvis Presley Filmography', http://en.wikipedia.org/wiki/Elvis_Presley_filmography

Floyd, N, '*Machete* Review', *Time Out* (23 November 2010), http://www.timeout.com/london/film/machete

Graham-Harrison, E, 'Black Man is Washed Whiter in China's Racist Detergent Advert' (28 May 2016), https://www.theguardian.com/world/2016/may/28/china-racist-detergent-advert-outrage

Nashawaty, C, 'Bloodbath and Beyond' (30 March 2007), www.ew.com/ew/article/0,,20015706,00.html

O'Reilly, Bill, 'The Devil Behind *The Devil in Miss Jones*' (26 August 1974),– originally available at http://thephoenix.com/Boston/news/107158-devil-behind-the-devil-in-miss-jones/?page=1#TOPCONTENT – page offline, referenced at: http://boingboing.net/2010/08/26/bill-oreilly-reviews.html, last accessed 20 August 2017.

Robinson, C, 'Blaxploitation and the Misrepresentation of Liberation', *Race & Class* (vol. 40. 1, 1998), http://journals.sagepub.com/doi/pdf/10.1177/030639689804000101, accessed 8 August 2017

Vaux, R, '*The Last House on the Left*: Something Cut Out in Transition' (13 March 2009), http://www.mania.com/last-house-left_article_113664.html

INTERVIEWS BY AUTHOR (AND AVAILABILITY)

'Grier, P, Interview' by Waddell, C, Conducted by phone, 6 November 2012. Available on Arrow Video *Foxy Brown* Blu-ray (2012) as part of booklet 'The Foxiest Femme' (Calum Waddell, 2013)

'Wes Craven: The Last Word on *Last House*', by Waddell, Calum, http://totalscifion-line.com/interviews/3601-wes-craven-the-last-word-on-last-house [no longer available]

INDEX

Willis, Bruce, 185
Winston, Brian, 53
Wood, Ed, 136
Wood, Robin, 27, 102–4, 106–7,
    115–16, 118–19, 121, 126–9,
    133–5, 191

Yearwood, Gladstone, 143, 146, 149–50,
    153, 159
Young Lady Chatterley, 6
Yuzna, Brian, 11n

Zedong, Mao, 128